"Mell, I don't want this to sound as if I'm sweepin' on your porch. I've had a mind to speak to you about this," then she lowered her voice and paused. Finally, in another breath she uttered the words, "Zola Porter."

Ozark's Seasons of the Heart

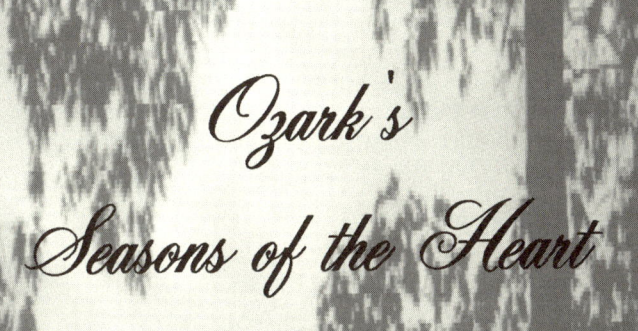

Marvin A. Matthews

ARC Press of Cane Hill
Cane Hill, Arkansas

© 1998 Marvin A. Matthews
All Rights Reserved

ISBN: 0-938041-34-7

No part of this book may be reproduced or transmitted in any form or by any means, electronic or mechanical, including photocopying, recording or by any informational storage or retreival system except by a reviewer who may quote brief passages in a review to be printed in a magazine or newspaper, without permission in writing from the publisher or author.

ARC Press of Cane Hill
13581 Tyree Mountain Road
P.O. Box 188
Cane Hill, Arkansas 72717
501-824-3821

Printed in the United States of America

Dedicated to Rosie, my loving wife. Without her encouragement and faithful help, this story would never have been written.

Acknowledgements — Special thanks to our son, "Wasaka" Mark B. Matthews for the illustrations. He may be contacted by mail to: WASAKA@BIGFOOT.COM.

Cover photos: Boston Mountains of the Arkansas Ozarks, taken by my late sister-in-law, Barbara Ward Bone.

To the reader . . .

The characters herein are composites of real people who lived in northwest Arkansas during the great depression.

Do not try to separate the facts from the fiction in this book — consider one necessary for the other in order for it to merge into an enjoyable piece of historical fiction.

MAM
wasakamm@juno.com

Contents

I	Time of the Trillium	9
II	Wild Flowers of Clear Creek	26
III	Then Came the Roses	43
IV	The Garden of Peculiar Souls	60
V	The Thistle	76
VI	Coming to the Arbor	97
VII	The Rose around the Briar	115
VIII	White unto Harvest	135
IX	The Missing Moss	154
X	The Money Tree	162
XI	The Pawpaw Harvest	192
XII	White Lilies	219
XIII	Autumn Leaves	243
XIV	Bouquets	261
XV	From Trillium to Orchids	278

I

Time of the Trillium

IT was the season of the trillium and deep in the Ozarks, it was first, a season of the heart. The cold dark days of winter were now behind. Moderation daily let in sunbeams, casting away a touch of languor, which for so long, clung to the body like a winter woolen shirt. The passing of the late winter days let in more than a beam of light! As the lilies of the field appeared, hope was renewed. A rejuvenation of spirit sprang from what had been discouraging moments.

Day by day the canopy of naked trees opened still further as the spring buds pushed the final dead leaves from the branches. This gave the notion that the old Farmers' Almanac must be consulted yet again. It was spring. The plausibility could not be denied. Still, the early days of spring in 1936 were unusually cool. Year after year spring came with various and often suspicious moods. In like a lamb, out like a lion; dark as the crucifixion, or bright as a bead of light from above.

Verification from one, still deeper in the forest, had revealed more accurately the sought after truth. His day had been February second, and his name, Old Patmus — the ground hog.

However, that was another story. Daniel was the one at hand. Glancing into the fireplace, Mell felt the warmth of the vanishing tongues of fire still dancing along the banked logs. Here and there a blue curl of smoke rose up the chimney while amber coals of fire grew dimmer along the hearth. Mell gave a tender glance at the child; he had fallen asleep. Smiling, the reader closed the worn pages of Egermeier's *Bible Story Book*, knowing there would be another day for the conclusion of Daniel and Obie's favorite men, Shadrach, Meshach and Abednego.

The father carried the young child to a nearby cot, unfolded a comforter taken from a stack of quilts nearby and gently tucked his son in for the night. Returning to his chair by the fire, Mell sat in the quietness of the room for several minutes gazing at the smoldering logs. The fire had diminished to a mere backlog secured by a primitive andiron and the excessive accumulation of ashes. The room gradually took on more darkness as the kerosene lamp also grew dim from need of fuel and a clean globe. Casting a shadow against the wall as he rose, Mell turned down the light and walked out into the night.

Carnie heard the old Model-T start up where it was parked under the chinquapin tree, then more clearly heard it sputter again as it made its way to the top of the ridge. As Carnie stepped out of the kitchen onto the long porch that led to the living room, Martha called after her, "Was that Dad's car I heard?"

"Yes," the grandmother replied, knowing Mell was alone on his way home to Briarcliff Cottage having arranged for little Obie and Martha to spend the night with her at Hurst Manor.

Then Martha, having finished the dishes, joined her grandmother and together they walked to the living room. As they said good night, Martha tiptoed over to where her brother was sleeping, patted his head, then went directly to the guest room always kept ready for such a visit.

Night broke into the twilight of morning. A penetrating chill had settled into Rivendell Valley and with it, heavy fog.

Patches of frost gave a silver cast to the vegetation and looking down upon the dells one had reason to wonder if this, after all, would be the last killing frost of the season. Mell hoped it would be. He had not found fault with winter but was anxiously waiting for spring to bring new life into the land. He watched for buds to appear in the orchards. Just as the daffodils had brought color to Briarcliff, he knew the uniqueness of the pawpaw blossoms would bring more than color; they would again bring hope for a new season and a rewarding harvest.

Somewhere under this cover of fog the mooing of a cow could be heard. Close at hand a rooster gave a hearty herald of the coming day. It was a cool breezy day, but then it was April. The weather could, and often did, change without warning and faster than a wrap could be found to afford comfort. Now that the silence of the dawn was broken, Mell heard other sounds around his home. Briarcliff Cottage and Rivendell Valley were never silent for long. He stirred, then rose to meet the day.

From the wood box near the hearth, Mell took up a few dry and tender shavings and placed them near the charred backlog. Adding a few dead-brown sticks, he lit a match. Then mumbling to himself, he said, "In two shakes of a lamb's tail this April chill will be gone from this room and by the time I get back from the chores there will be hot water for coffee."

The dull flames quickly became a cozy fire and the pervading scent of cedar filled the room. It was still well before sunrise as Mell donned a light coat, took up the milk pail, and set out to do the chores. The gray dawn revealed interesting cloud formations that appeared to be out of focus, thin and broken. This was hopefully a good omen of what the day would be.

Up on Norwood Prairie, Hurst Manor reflected the rays of the sun's ageless patterns, fused between light and dark. These sky lanes, for Carnie, promised the approaching day would be serene and beautiful.

Watching the sunrise and the drifting clouds, Obie put his hands up to the window, amused at the cloud patterns, wondering if they would bring snow, rain or just go away. Martha was more concerned with the things at hand and oblivious to such details as fleeting patterns that seemingly intermingled with heavenly bodies. For such things, she had no time.

While this day's activities had been planned well in advance, Martha, in keeping with her personality, had from time to time wavered in her thinking. Considering that she knew it was expected of her to go along on the afternoon trek, helped her to be willing to go. This, in the eyes of others at least, was the only acceptable thing to do. Yet, she felt this decision was not really hers and she felt no better for having made it. Wistfully looking into the sudsy water, a tear fell from her cheek as she continued doing the breakfast dishes.

It wasn't as if she did not like to go along on these trips; she did. Many were the times she had sat somewhere along a trail, listening to the rippling water of a creek and talking with her mother. Today that intimacy would be missing and the ardent desire to be a part of the family outing had vanished. Work, she understood; tramping through the woods, bundled up in cumbersome clothing, she did not. Precisely as the weather effected her grandmother's rheumatism, so might it move Martha to change her mind. It had done so before.

Though the dishes were now washed, dried, and put away, there was yet a great deal of housework she wanted to do for her grandmother. For Martha, it was easier to keep her mind on these chores, than daydreaming of finding a certain elusive trillium. As far as she could tell it was no different from any other wild flower. So far as Martha was concerned, all posies were uncommonly pretty. They were all Wake-Robins. Grandmother had tried to explain that the three petals and three sepals of the trillium reminded her of the trinity — the Father, the Son, and the Holy Ghost. Martha had understood enough to know that this annual trek had been special to her grandmother as it had been to her mother.

As the hours went by, Martha kept busy with the work she loved to do: dusting this, polishing that and sorting the clothes in preparation for the laundry. In the warmth of the late morning, she dashed down the steps, following a trail into the woods just beyond the spacious yard, in a search of another kind — that of finding wood. Martha knew this would not take long. She hoped to be able to gather enough wood for tomorrow's washing and return to the house before her father came up the lane. She had taken longer than planned, and had not heard him arrive, but spotted the horse and buggy under the chinquapin tree, just outside the yard.

Carnie had set a place for her son-in-law at the end of the table and little Obie sat near him. Both were finished eating when Martha entered the kitchen. She poured her father a cup of coffee and sat down by Obie. Looking sternly into his face she asked, "What's that on your sleeve, Obie?"

Rising from the bench, she proceeded to find a wash cloth and rub at the spot. "Hold still, Obie, I've got to get this off," said Martha, but Obie was not troubled by the little dirt Martha tried to remove.

"It can wait 'til wash day," said Obie.

The grandmother picked up the empty plates and Mell rose from the table saying how good the coffee tasted. "I want to repair a halter before we leave," Mell said as he took a final sip, placed the cup on the table and left the room.

Martha helped her grandmother put away the food, and partially clean the kitchen, then somewhat begrudgingly left the rest for later. Gathering their wraps, they hurried for the buggy, not wanting to try Mell's patience.

An air of excitement filled their hearts as one of the farm's work horses, old Dobbin, pulled away from the hitching post. April's bright blue sky was spread as paint on a canvas. Fluffy white clouds filled in a boundless sea of periwinkle blue. A southerly breeze gave an irregular sway to the branches that grew out over the lane. This to and fro movement brought a challenge for the squirrels jumping from limb to limb. Their antic plays caught the attention of Martha who smiled, watching their dazzling acrobatic jumps until they were no longer in sight. Then she spoke to her grandmother, who turned, looked up into the trees and smiled. The old lady sensed the importance of the outing, and in her heart was thankful that she, too, was a part of it.

The short drive to the main road was quickly covered. Dobbin picked up speed, taking the party through apple orchards still bare from the winter. Suddenly the sharp eyes of Martha caught sight of a large flock of geese flying due north for the summer. Their distinct V-shape went directly overhead and their honk, honk brought laughter to Martha as she tried to count them and watch as they disappeared from sight.

The party spoke little as they were drawn along, until Martha was startled by a big bump as they left the main road for Briarcliff Cottage. Ruts in the lane still held water from the recent shower and mud splashed up on the buggy causing Martha to give a fearful look of concern. "Dad's clean buggy is going to be a mess, just look at this mud," whispered

Martha to her grandmother. The horse's hoofs and the steel wheels of the buggy passed over the many flint stones, giving new cause for Martha to be troubled.

Approaching Briarcliff cottage the lane widened as most of the stones there had been removed. Carnie had not been to Mell's place for some time and noticed several changes about. Having no fenced yard, chickens fed on the grassy lawn and sat on the steps to the house. A sagging clothesline still held several pair of trousers and a few slightly dingy shirts. The cottage still looked drab and obviously in need, as a bachelor's place might. She did not speak. Sitting with her hands in her lap she looked on down the road.

It was Obie who broke the silence, "See my dogs, Grandma." Then he pointed toward the two blue tick hounds tied to a post at the end of the yard. "Didn't I tell you they were getting big." He kept his eyes on the barking dogs until the road turned and they were out of sight.

Mell slapped the lines to Dobbin's back and they moved on through the forest of bare oaks and green pines. Sarvis berry bushes growing along the ridges and deep in the valleys displayed their lacy white flowers. This remarkably reflected the fleecy white clouds that could be seen in patches above. The forest floor held a bit of yellow here and there as the buttercups grew out from under the old dead leaves. Color rose too as a covey of quail, flushed from a thicket, found cover in the heavy underbrush.

On down the narrow trail they wound their way until coming out onto a large clearing and an overlook of the ridges far beyond. Here the family stopped. Obie quickly jumped out to help his dad tie Dobbin to a tree. Martha helped her grandmother out of the buggy.

The huge flat sandstone on which they now stood, covered hundreds of square feet and with little exception, was flat as a table and bare. To one side of this massive rock a gentle slope led down to another smaller boulder and from there natural steps led on down into the valley. They were at the top of a ridge with a southern exposure, pleasantly warm and free from wind. Mell and Obie walked to a safe distance from the edge and viewed the valley below. High above the river this overlook gave an impressive view of Rivendell Valley.

"Obie, some folks call this Lover's Leap, but I prefer to think more positive and simply call it Grand View," said the father.

"I call it Table Rock, because that's what it is," Obie replied. He had been taught to show respect for such a place and had been here before with his father. Martha had been here also, but never got near the edge! Grandmother, too, kept her distance and shuddered to see little Obie moving about so freely.

After only a short time at the viewpoint, Martha and her grandmother followed the little used trail that led to the next level. It was to this second overlook that they came to enjoy the safety of the incredible view. From here the trail downward was relatively safe, and Obie had already disappeared from view. As always, he was excited to again be exploring the canyon.

Mell stood alone for some time, then sat at the base of an old pine looking at the distant range of the blue mountains beyond. An indefinable peace seemed to pervade the whole earth and all was a wash of color of another day. His recollection took him back to a time of his life that had been difficult and thorny. Seemingly he had sunk deeper with each despair but to rise again more determined to master his life and move on. With success he had managed his life this past year and had taken on a hardness of steel. Yet his unselfishness and tempered manner revealed his gentleness as a father and provider.

Obie's absence had been long enough for Martha and her grandmother to become concerned. With that in mind they little by little ventured down the trail he had taken, calling his name. Martha saw his footprints in the moist sand and heard the resounding echo, "Obie . . . Obie . . . Obie." There was no response.

Carnie's thoughts were as usual, and she spoke them before she thought. "Why doesn't Mell keep that child close at hand? Land sakes, he's going to get hurt!"

Then came a cry from Martha. "What's the matter, child?" asked the grandmother, seeing blood on Martha's arm.

"I got caught by a bramble. I'm not going a step further!" cried Martha.

"Oh, yes, you are! We're looking for your brother!"

Again the echoes sounded across the valley. "Obie . . . Obie . . . Obie! Where is that kid?" asked Martha.

"What's the commotion?" Mell asked as he came down the trail meeting the concerned Martha and her grandmother.

From the other direction Obie emerged, wanting to know, "What's the problem?"

"It is," replied Mell, "that we should begin our search for the trillium."

They made their way down the side of the hill. Mell led them to where the paths were lined with flowers, and all merging trails from the prairie seemed to take on the beauty of spring. As these trails found their way through the great forest, all of them ended either on the lower slopes along the waterways or on a high rocky bluff. These were the paths, though unknown but to a few, which offered the first glimpse of the changing season.

Dells, filled with splendor, were the habitats of the floral patterns. Each in its own hue, brought about a special and always different impression. Those who strolled under this canopy of forest, searching only for what lay at their feet, found again a closeness to Mother Earth. Found too, in their memories, were the treks of other times and the blessings that were brought afresh from just a brush with the trillium that lined the paths.

Both Grandmother and Martha carried a vase and all looked intently for the elusive painted trillium. The April carpet of wild flowers consisted of a variety of color, and for that matter a vastness of shapes and sizes. Many species were decked out in full splendor and yet the bareness of others foretold of a later outing.

Under the sprawling branches where sunlight filtered through, wide beds of tiny bluets grew and bloomed in perfusion. Bordering the massive boulders and outcroppings of sandstone, grew the many varieties of violets dressed in their purple-blue and violet hues. High up in the massive rock formation, growing out of a cliff, the bright faces of the laurel, rhododendron and azalea made their appearance for a new season. And everywhere there was the sweet music of birds. It was impossible to make one's way through the forest without walking on something that gave beauty. Obie liked the tangy taste of the sorrel and he always knew just where it was to be found. For grandma, it was also impossible not to find something to pick, pluck or dig. It all savored the appetite or accentuated the vase in natural beauty.

Grandma kept her eyes open for senna, from which she made tea. Mell's favorite tea was always the one he was enjoying at the moment; although in spring, sassafras was his special cup of tea. Carnie tried to keep plenty on hand for an aromatic drink. Martha didn't really care for any of them.

As the group strolled down the gentle sloping hills, each added to the collection they would be taking home. Mell and Obie had gone on ahead, searching for the elusive morels, the choice specie of the mushroom world. These honeycombed conical fungi were highly prized, but not to be gathered by just anyone, and the family knew it. Mell gathered, Carnie prepared the gourmet dish, and all enjoyed the fruits of nature. They had gathered a small flour sack full when Martha and Carnie caught up with them.

No one had yet found the painted trillium, although continuing down the hillside toward the bottom of the hollow, many kinds abounded and were lush in their beauty. The dell became wider and the little creek that flowed down from the top of the mountain cut its way near the center. Near the bottom of the valley another spring gushed out from under a limestone boulder, clean, pure and cold. Here the trillium grew in profusion sharing the space with the Mayapple. Expectancy grew and each flower got a personal inspection. The troop worked hard, if the painted trillium was there, it would be found.

"Look what I have," shouted Martha.

All hands ran to her side before they realized it was not the desired flower. Holding up a chunk of rock Martha asked, "Can I take it home? It is a shell fossil."

"It's a perfect example, Martha; do take it and add it to our collection." As he spoke, Mell took the stone from his daughter and placed it in a sack he had slung over his shoulder.

The search continued; Carnie hoped it might soon end for she was getting tired and weary and found it necessary to tighten up the shawl about her shoulders. Passing a large flat rock, she yielded to the temptation of affording herself a rest. For a few moments she caught her breath, then raising both arms she almost lost her balance. She was staring straight into the face of the one-in-a-million.

"Law me! Come here, did you ever see such a thing?" she exclaimed, waving her arms to include all. "In all my born days I've never seen a flower head held in such an upright position. It's sturdy and tall. The leaves have variegated patterns of dark and light green. Look, Mell, those center markings on the petals, all a scarlet red. And here, only the center vein of each petal has the marking extending the full length. What a color! Can you beat that!"

As the children congratulated their grandmother and hugged her neck, Mell cautioned them to be careful not to damage the prize specimen. "I'll place a marker here and come back after it in the fall," said Mell. That drew a favorable response from Carnie. Although presently having a fine collection of these lilies, this specie was not in her collection. She immediately set a high value on it and would prepare a special place for it.

"I'm getting cold, Dad, could we go home?" asked Martha. She was more than cold; her patience was gone from having been out in the hills so long. Her mind was now on preparing the supper meal for she knew they were all hungry.

Climbing back to the top of the ridge, their footsteps were more deliberate and slower than they had been on the downward trek. Martha stopped with her grandmother and rested every few steps on the steepest part of the climb. By the time they returned to the buggy, all except Obie were winded and tired. "I've had enough climbing to do me for a long time, how about you, Grandmother?" asked Martha as she seated herself in the buggy.

"My land yes, I'll be so sore I can't get out of bed in the morning. But then the family has enjoyed a well spent day, and we have achieved our goal in many ways. It was worth it, every bit of the trouble," said the old lady of Hurst Manor, looking over at the vases filled with their choice collections of flowers. Then nodding her head toward Mell and Obie sitting near him, she continued, "This is part of the makings of a family. We must keep close together, Martha."

Quickly came the reply, "Not all the family Grandmother, Clem is not with us, but I wish he was. When do you think we'll see him again?"

Carnie leaned over and softly spoke in her ear, "I don't know, my child. He's a fine young man, and I know he has the right to be out on his own, but I too worry about him." Then Carnie patted the girls hand, "I wish he wasn't out there in that oil field, but in time he'll be back." She knew the course of Clem's leaving home had been thorny and did not want to pursue the subject further here.

"Make sure the vases are secure, Martha, I think we are about ready to move."

Mell tapped Dobbin with the ends of the reins. The mare responded with a neigh and seemed willing to take them back to Norwood Prairie.

Direct sunlight had disappeared and in the west only rays of various shades reflected the warmth that had made the perfect day down in Rivendell Valley.

Again they crossed and crisscrossed the paths that have been there for generations. In a more progressive tomorrow, Mell knew they would most certainly be joined by a new and wider byway. Hopefully it would be able to take the travelers of that day further than they now were able to go and to places yet unseen. But for today the narrow trails had brought them again into nature's paths and to their sought-for lilies.

The time of the trillium was not an overnight extravaganza. Nature awakes this lovely member of the lily family, which is called "Wake-Robin." Carnie with her love for flowers knew this was the day of the trillium and along these trails and low in the meadows were nature's showcases. She remarked, "Martha, we only have to watch as all nature bursts forth from the cold earth and finds new growth. It gives us hope and expectation. Spring doesn't come overnight, it's a season. I'm glad it's here."

Retrieving his sweater from under the seat of the carriage, Mell placed it around the shoulders of the slender stripling snuggled close to his side. "There, my boy," said he, and tapped him on the head. "Is that better?"

The movement of the carriage and the lateness of the hour caused heads to nod, and eyes became heavy. The "little man," as Obie was sometimes referred to, was asleep. Martha and her grandmother had settled into a conversation of how they could, quite quickly, put a bite together before Mell returned home to Briarcliff.

As the buggy pulled up to the spot from which it left several hours before, Carnie straightened up and looked in Mell's direction. "Well, I declare, it's been some kind of a day. I reckon you'll stay for supper? Martha and I will hurry right in and fetch it on the table as soon as we can. I know you're starving."

Martha was the first to get out of the buggy. Then helping her grandmother down, they hurried to the side porch and into the kitchen. Carnie lit the old oil lamp and set it on the table.

Then she gathered a handful of shavings and quickly had a fire in the stove and coffee ready to perk. Martha set the table, softened the bread and placed the pan of leftover stew on the cap to simmer.

Mell and Obie took in the flowers the ladies had brought back from Beaver Creek. They built a gentle fire in the fireplace, and its light now brightened the room. Taking his corn cob pipe down from the mantle, Mell packed it tight and lit up, puffing it into a glow, patiently waiting for dinner.

Following the meal Obie curled up on the cot and went to sleep. Mell returned to his favorite stuffed chair. Alone with his thoughts, he pushed back from the faint flames and listened to them whisper. Back there under the big pine, high on the plateau, he had not been restrained in his thoughts. Out there, the breeze that swept through the trees, also lured the mind. Tonight it was first the light, then a spark, that ushered dreamy thoughts to the soul and unleashed a chord.

These seasons that brought revival healed the heart. They purged the past that so easily caused unnecessary pain and fanned away the flames that would have otherwise been kept.

Enough of the past remained, and always would, to fill that portion of his aching heart where memories were now deliberate, and inexhaustible. He had begun to pick up the pieces, face the world and again search for life.

Reflections from the soft firelight caught the deep color of Mell's face. While the years had been spent in hard work, they were kind to him. His hair had taken on a sheen that brought out the gray along the temples. Lines in his high forehead were like those of a much younger man. His muscular build gave evidence of hard work that so commonly went with the hills men. He was proud of the great strength in his hands, proud of his stature, and so were those who looked at him.

None of this spelled gentleness in the past, as he now wished it had. True, he had been a gentle man, a loving husband, a good father, but all these fell short of what could have been. Yet there were meaningful times. Indeed, looking back in retrospect, Mell knew he had nothing of which to be ashamed. In fact, he reasoned correctly, he had not done so badly.

Health had been for him, a positive force, where sickness had taken its toll on Thalia. Both had dealt with extremes. He still held a positive attitude. Physically, Thalia's life had been up and down, pain and sorrow, sweet and bitter, tears of joy and tears assailed with brine. She had been to him all a man could hope for. Her kind and loving spirit gave him strength and kept him going through the hard times of his life. She had been more than his wife and the mother of his children, there had never been another woman in his life.

An almost angelic figure came plainly into view whenever Mell fell into these restless moments. The visions were as if he and Thalia were still walking the romantic trails that, in the course of time, wove their lives into a bliss of oneness. His vision of the old mailbox was still sharp — the false bottom, where he hid letters to Thalia. There he also found her replies.

Neither was he able to forget the contention between the two houses. While they lived as neighbors only a mile apart, they were separated by a gulf, most surely by clan.

Fate, too, had played a role in Mell's life and brought back memories in times like these. Through the years Hampton Moss had learned to trust his son-in-law and the respect had been mutual. Upon his death bed, Hampton asked Mell to promise that he would care for Carnie. Provisions for Carnie's care were not sufficient and Mell understood. He gladly picked up that obligation, but in so doing, he had limited himself in what he might do and where he might go.

Burdened with the three children to care for and raise by himself, Mell had an ever-pressing concern. Under this situation Mell lived from day to day. These were difficult days, but not bleak. There were more questions than doubt. But above all, there was always love. The question was, how could he relate that to the children in a more positive way? He knew the farm, and could relate to it. His concern could not be questioned as it related to the family, but three young children, what could be done!

Amber coals of fire again lay upon a hearth, losing their brightness and spreading as cold ashes in the lateness of the hour. Mell stepped to the kitchen and said good night, then walked out into the cold loneliness of night. Soon he and Dobbin were on their way home to Briarcliff Cottage. A full moon shed light on Dobbin's path as she clipped along at a fast gait with loose reins, leaving Mell to his thoughts.

II

Wild Flowers of Clear Creek

DARK clouds were gathering over the mountains as Mell pulled up under the big pine. He recognized the signs of the gathering storm and preferred to wait it out under the safety of the overhanging bluffs.

At this cave that now sheltered him, Mell had, on various occasions stopped before. From time to time many pleasant memories had been formed. These were edged in his heart and were still refreshing. Today, the threatening wind that came thrashing through the boughs of the pines, gave yet another motive for being shielded under the broad overhang at the mouth of a massive cave.

Mell, dismounting, led his pony under the shelf of the rock and tethered her to a stone column rising up from the floor. He slapped her on the hip with his broad hand to reassure her of safety against the storm. "Rest a spell, Lena, you'll be safe and dry here."

He took the slicker from the saddle and put it on as he walked the few yards to the big grove of old oaks and the monarch pine. Standing for a few moments, he looked out over the valley below, veiled in a mist and brightened occasionally by streaks of lightning that seemed to be moving toward his Rock of Ages.

His nostrils filled with the fresh mountain air and he breathed in the unmistakable smell of fresh falling rain. The stimulating ride up the mountain, the view, the pungent scent of the pine, gave cause for deep breathing. It allowed time to fix his eyes on the distant mountains and enjoy the misty valleys that flanked the sides of the promenade. The vastness that swept beyond left the viewer in awe. This, where he sat, was his. And there to his back were the trees: huge majestic oaks, tall and sturdy hickory, while further down in the lower valleys grew the mighty walnut. These for him had been the means of many provisions and cash in his pocket. They too had provided him with his favorite kernel and his favorite gun stock that proudly hung on his bedroom wall. The mountain was always the provider.

Heavy rain poured down after shattering thunder claps came closer. The valleys became completely obscure. Gusty wind turned violent, tearing and thrashing into the forest with full vengeance. From the outset, Mell had watched the storm gather, huddled against the mighty tree. It was obvious now that a more protective shelter was needed, he would seek the one he could share with Lena.

Nature's unleashed fury always drew extravagant patterns, and harsh forms reaching the zenith of awesome power. Volleys of rumbling thunder now moved closer, bringing bolts of deadly lightning. This was followed by squalls of water, driven against the buttes, thrashing leaves and breaking limbs. The storm had hit with all its fury; little could be seen save the onslaught that bellowed on and on.

He found the horse restive and pawing the earth, showing her spirit against the relentless storm. Lena was sensitive and found little comfort from the protection of the overhanging rock. Mell understood the safety here and would wait out the thunderstorm along the lee side of the bluff.

By now it was obvious that today's plans for inspecting the root cellar must me aborted. Another time would do just as well and in all probability it wasn't necessary. Sassafras roots, properly handled in their dormant stage needed little attention. He and Lena had not been out on the trail for weeks, he would simply change course. Instead of backtracking he would take the trail through Hog Valley and Clear Creek. Yet he wondered aloud, "When would it blow over? But don't worry, little girl," said he. "We have nothing but time." He stood there awhile then patted her on the neck and set about gathering up some dry wood that had been left at the mouth of the cave. Several branches of dry cedar were added to the charred logs left by campers. Lighting a match, Mell watched the faint flame quickly flare up with the crackling so characteristic of dry cedar. Soon the spicy smell of cedar spread throughout the mouth of the cave-like recess. Then his attention was drawn to an old downed treetop just beyond the cover of the overhang. Tugging with a limb for a moment rewarded him with a sizeable gain. Now he knew, he, too, would be able to leave more wood than he would burn.

Having removed his raincoat he stood close to the fire and dried his face on his shirt. Removing his hat he placed it near the heat, and sat down. The storm gave no sign of abating. Yet now relaxed, neither man nor beast was troubled by the indomitable tide now thrust against them.

Echoes of defying thunder rumbled across the great plateau. Lurid skies continued to grip the face of darkness and strut it across the stage as being moved about by an unnatural force.

Mell had scarcely filled his pipe with Bull Durham when in a wreath of blinding light he fell to the floor of the cave from the force of a nearby lightning strike. Miraculously neither he nor Lena were directly hit. Lena pawed the air with her front feet as she might have done among a herd of wild stallions. A look through her wild glassy eyes told her the rider was safe, then nudging him with her nose she waited for the response.

Shaken and stunned, he opened his eyes in time to see a giant oak come slamming toward the ground. Before he regained his hearing, the limbs split and broken lay in a tangled clutter about the mouth of his shelter.

His ears still rang with the sound of a muted burst while spots before his eyes told of the shock from which he had awakened. In the frontage now stood what had been one of the many grand characters of the forest. It had stood through many and diverse periods of extremes, yet it could take no more. The huge trunk, slashed and jagged from the bolt of lightning, was now only an ugly scar standing bare against the darkened sky.

How many other such strikes would there be across the great northwest? By now he realized, with certainty, the forecast of a thunderstorm had been totally inaccurate. Indeed, conditions were right for a tornado! Mell wondered if such had not skirted the area, leaving other destruction in its wake.

Pondering still further, Mell took a visual fix of the valley below, of the ridges in his view and at the water now pouring off the ledge from above him. He could only guess at the volume of water swirling in the river below. Surmising it to be considerable, he again gave thought to what some of the damages might be. "Lena," he said, in a strong tone, "we're going to be held up here for some time." He arose, puffing on the pipe and stroked the mare's mane. "Damages there will be, to what extent is the question."

He still felt shaky from the force that struck so close, knocked him off his feet. Regaining his composure, he placed a few more pieces of firewood into position, returned to the bench of stone, and again sat down.

"Mr. Marshall," spoke Mell to himself, "you'll have one snarled sassafras patch and it will be bound in a sea of mud!" With the recent digging, he reasoned, the soft earth would surely erode away, causing massive furrows of exposed roots. The good news was that all the commercial diggings had been laid by and had time to heal, therefore the loss would be moderate.

Unorthodox in his farming, Mell was always followed by shadows of doubt; men who questioned his work and who had few answers of their own. Some of these were good men of the prairie who harvested acres of wheat. Others sold fields of tomatoes and beans to the Allen's cannery and in good years, did well.

But it wasn't the manner of the men to openly criticize or condemn. So Mell kept some of his thought, often produced in times like these, to himself. Yet he knew, for he had, from time to time, worked for some of them. Farming on Norwood Prairie was quite different from hill farming, nor was it as promising as river bottom land. Ozark farming was as varied as the hills. One method worked in certain areas while other area needs were quite different. Mell's farming was neither the prairie nor river bottom but gentle sloping hills.

Mell had become restless, rose from the bench and walked closer about the fire. "One thing is as sure as shooting," spoke he. "We're innovating. Now all we need is a little time and a lot of luck."

While most of the thunder and lightning had gone around, gentle rain was tapering off. He put on his slicker and hat and hurried over to the edge of the bluff. The river was rising; there had been heavy rains upstream. Still darkened skies to the north foretold of more rain in that area.

This time, Mell remained for only a brief spell, returning to the shelter and the warmth of the scant fire and bright bed of coals. Little could be done but wait.

Patient at the beginning, Mell's concern was beginning to show. Standing by his horse, he looked her in the face but did not speak. All eyes, however, seemed to cast further doubt on the weather and Mell knew his departure from the hill must be forthcoming and, no doubt, in the rain.

So it was, he had waited, for what seemed to be, the last moment. Though in that quickness of time the sky became, for the moment, relatively light and the heavens seemed to have run out of water. Only a steady sprinkle kept falling, giving the impression that it, too, might cease.

Lena headed down the slope, out to the trail that led to Clear Creek. Her direction was sure and she needed little rein from the rider. They both were glad to be on their way home.

Following the hogback that wound its way lower and lower, the old wagon road trail was of little use in the last few years. Brush having grown up along the sides, swished against the rider and horse as they hurried along. Under the mighty oaks, cedars, and beech, like a needle with a long thread, they wound in and out through the trees.

Lena trotted on, still following the now swollen stream. Her pace became slower and her hoofs splashed up the thick muddy water of which the rider kept watch with a wary eye. The plan, to look in on the sassafras diggin' of the last few weeks, had been thwarted by the passing deluge. Yet logic told Mell, from what he had seen today, that in all likelihood, the hillside would wash away. The deep furrows had not had time to heal, or settle, consequently wasteful erosion would inevitably occur. Fortunately, most of the disturbed earth had been packed by previous gentle rains, and the February diggin' had settled.

Still unsettled in his mind was the concern for how severely the storm may have hit across the upper slopes and upon the prairie. Warm southern breezes and the rain of the past several days had given new life to the forest floor. Bright yellow, woolly yarn-like blossoms of the hazelnut thicket brightened up the drab banks of the stream which the trail now followed.

In a clearing with a high rolling bank Lena's attention was drawn to a small field of clover, she came to a stop. As best she could with bits in her mouth, she tried to bite off a few leaves and moved on. Mell appreciated the view and saw still more for which to be thankful. The sun rays had penetrated through enough to cast rays of light at the crest of the ridge and down the southern slope. Confederate violets grew in such an array of beauty they could have filled a greenhouse, they too, welcomed the bit of late afternoon sun.

Not only was this a true sign of spring, it had given assurances that the harsh storm was over. The rumbling had ceased. Streaks of flashing light through the sky had moved out of sight. Only the running water remained from the storm. In its wake the storm had left great puddles of water in the low flat trail. While over the boulders, strewn along the stream, swirling white water brought debris that hurried on down to a wider stream. Now splashing through ankle-deep water, Lena, stopping abruptly, had no trouble in catching Mell's attention. They were at the brink of a washout, while just beyond, another hit of lightning had brought down a large tree. This completely covered the trail and obscured much of the turbulent water swirling through its branches.

Dismounting, Mell took the reins from around the mare's neck, leading her back the way they came for a few yards.

Then through a gap in the bluff that rose above Clear Creek, they followed a rocky incline only a short distance to the top. The detour, while offering an alternate course, brought the narrow valley into better view and that froze Mell dead in his tracks.

What had been an enchanted valley yesterday had suddenly been reduced to little more than a landlocked lake today. The chagrin facts alarmed Mell — stress could be seen across his ruddy forehead.

The flooded river had overflowed its banks, cutting a channel through a narrow low portion of its weaker side. A large flow of the river now followed an old bed that had once been the main stream. It cut into Clear Creek and soon poured out into all the lower fields of Hog Valley. The few acres of cultivated farmland were now totally inundated, and there was no stopping the surging water that had destroyed this portion of the placid creek.

Straining for a view of the first farmhouse downstream, Mell quickly saw the predicament which he faced. The McGreggor farm was fully visible. Water had undercut Clear Creek, and was inching closer and closer to their island home. It was still safe; that is, it had not been damaged and apparently they were in no life threatening situation. Being on an upward slope and at the very crest, the house was still high and dry.

Because the lay of the land was typically Ozark hill country, flat here, a knoll there, rocks jetting up over the flat valley, there was a chain of bobbing earth not yet swallowed by the muddy water. This chain paralleled those along the ridge, and in normal times their beauty set the stage for a postcard picture of Hog Valley. There was nothing pretty today. Fog had begun to filter in, giving it a drab and dismal appearance. Yet it was to this farm, at the beginning of the chain that Mell drew his attention, and toward that end, hit the trail.

Hurrying from his vantage point high up on the craggy ridge, Mell led Lena down the back side of the hump, being a less arduous descent. Down the lane, along the water's edge, they moved in and out of the trees, splashing through shallow standing water, skirting the deeper places, and avoiding the unknown.

Without delay Mell again mounted the saddle and followed a little used farm lane that led to the house still above the water. Lena, taking the slap of the rein, moved unhesitatingly into the still cold water, fording it quickly, pulling up in front of the McGreggor home.

"Hello, is anybody home?" He waited for an answer, but none came. Again he sounded out, louder, and pounded on the wall with his boot. Still there was no evidence that the couple was home. Springing from Lena's back he climbed the steps of the porch and gave a hard puzzling knock. Still no answer. He tried the door, it was unlocked. Pushing it ajar he called again. As before, no one answered. Grasping the knob he slammed the door shut and hustled to Lena's side and mounted.

Lena again went splashing through the water, fording the lane and following the wagon tracks along the foothills that quickly took her and the rider to the next farmhouse downstream.

Following the worn country lane, the horse and rider were again well above the waters of the flooded valley, making good time toward the next farm. It was known to be on lower ground, and Mell shuddered to think just what the situation might be. There was little time to ponder that thought for hardly had they rounded the next bend when they found the lane closed by fallen branches and high water.

As before, Lena took to the higher ground along the cedar, edging her way down the narrow valley. Suddenly, Mell tightened up on the reins and Lena stopped. This house, too, was totally surrounded by the rushing water. A barn and other outbuildings on a bench above the house were still above the water line.

An uneasy eerie feeling gnawed at Mell's innards. The dimness about the house, the gray nebulous sky which still threatened, all these spawned a doleful sound like the ringing of a knell.

Perhaps the gibberish sounds he now heard were nothing more than a haunting hope against hope. Still the indiscernible clamor told him these sounds were physical. Positioning the reins around the pommel, Mell listened. Then came a mournful cry from someone and the ominous crash that followed.

Standing in front of what had been, before the shattering fall of glass, a large picture window, a child now framed the jagged debris. Without moving, the boy eyed the rider on the horse and hoped for help, while the rider eyed the figure in the window and sought to be helpful. Neither spoke although each took immediate action!

Lena waded up the lane, stopping under a tree in the yard near the house. There she was secured. Mell eased out of the saddle and rushed through the water, meeting the lad on the little porch way. The Porter child recognized the visitor and bellowed out, "Mr. Marshall, can you help us?"

Moments later the boy's mother came to the door of the porch, peaked, wet and near exhaustion. Her first reaction, typically that of a woman in such a plight, was to cry. He could take that no better than most other men, and out of pity he took her arm, guided her inside, and then spoke. "Are you all safe?"

"What's happening, Mr. Marshall? Where's this water coming from? Oh dear, what will I do? I'm losing everything!"

Mell looked Miss Porter in the eye, still hoping for an answer to his question. "First things first, now is everyone safe?"

"Yes, we are all well, but wet and cold. Billy here is helping me to move things, trying to keep them above the water line."

Showing signs of further stress, she spoke to her son, "Tell Bud to come here; what's taking him so long?"

Giving a piercing look at his mother, Billy turned as if speaking to Mell. "He ain't come back yet from the hog pen; he's movin' old Satan out so's he won't get drown'ded."

Nervously clasping her hands, Miss Porter again asked the question, "What, oh what, am I to do?" Then she waited for an answer from the man about whom she knew so little. Though painfully she realized he knew more about her.

"I think," said Mell, "you must prepare to evacuate immediately!"

"You mean leave the house, leave my things?" Then in a sorrowful tone she looked at Mell. "I don't have a way to go no place, and if'n I did, I don't have no place to go to."

"It's not a question of leaving," Mell replied. "It's essential, and the sooner the better! The river has cut out of its bank, joined Clear Creek, and another break could be eminent. If it does it's, Katy bar the door! Gather what clothing you and the children will need for tonight, and take shelter in the barn! It will be safe there. Billy and I will go see about Bud." Then speaking to the frightened child, Mell called back as he headed for the barn, "Billy, come with me." Both hurried out to locate Bud. "Where did you see him last?" asked Mell.

"Here at the gate, Mr. Marshall, Bud was chasing old Satan." Mell began to call Bud's name aloud, then hurried to the barn and searched there, still no one.

"Go help your mother, Billy. Take what you must for the night and get to the barn! I'm going down stream looking for Bud."

He saw the child into the house, got on the horse, and turned, following the edge of the flowing water. He knew the area, it was rough and tedious but he must search! Calling and waiting, Mell heard no response. Finally, after covering a considerable distance, there was little left to do but to go back. It was regrettable and he hesitated to think of returning empty handed. He thought of little Obie, and said a prayer. Lena, secured in a stall at the barn, fed on the fresh hay while Mell took the inevitable news to the distraught mother. They had not yet moved to the barn, and Mell wondered why.

"Zola, we haven't found him yet, but he may be up the draw. I'll check that out, but first let's all get to higher ground. We're only an accident waiting to happen standing here!"

With a resolved look and tears in her eyes, she pointed for Billy to pick up a prepared bed roll. Carrying a satchel strung across her shoulder, she spoke to Mell, "You can bring the box of food." Then taking one final look, she blew out the flickering kerosene lamp. Holding it tight, she carried it with her as they left the untidy room.

Mell knew the barn had a large, probably empty, grain bin. He took them there. "This will at least afford you a dry place to spend the night, and it will be safe, the water will not rise this high. I'm going to give another search for Bud before it gets dark."

Mell, back in the saddle, again returned to the rising stream, searching its banks for the young lad who had disappeared.

In her corner of the barn, Zola had become willing to bear the burden of wait and see. The clean, dry grain bin gave some note of comfort. "Billy, Mell seems to think Bud's all right. I reckon it won't do no good to sit and brood. Why don't you go to the house and get the little table in the bedroom, and my jewelry box, too? It's all I've got left of Mother's. And Billy, be quick and don't poke along!"

While Bud's disappearance was certain, Zola held little else in her heart that was. All her loneliness and confusion welded together her aching heart, filling her eyes with a dullness and the look of torture. She was now alone with her thoughts and they troubled her. There were times when she wished things were different, such as the rare occasion when she went to church, or in the bad times of need, such as tonight. Uncertainly, she waited restlessly for Billy's quick return. Shivering, cold and hungry she waited on, and would still be waiting until Mell returned bringing Bud.

Her conscience, while certainly no road map to rightness, did from time to time, function. At those times she swore to turn over a new leaf. Those thoughts were like the leaves of autumn, they were soon lost to the wind! It troubled her deeply to know folks called the children ragamuffins, urchins. Then talking to herself, she said, "And God only knows what else!"

It was taking the child longer than Zola thought it should, and she wondered aloud, "Did I act foolish to send him back to the house?" When he did return, he bounced into the compartment holding the items she had sent for and a surprise, stuffed into a drawer of the night stand. Then reaching in he took a handful of flowers and gave them to his mother. "Here are the Easter Lilies we picked this afternoon, I hope they make you happy."

"Oh, Billy, you brought the bouquet of narcissus!" Then holding the flowers, she kissed her son on the cheek. "There's a saying hereabouts that white narcissus brings good luck."

"If that's so," said Billy, "We'll have a lot of good luck 'cause there's bunches of 'em around the old house."

Unfolding drama, stark and turgid, filled the late hours with an epic tale of heroism. The hill man was dogged to work upon his mulish expectation, which he kept from the start, that he'd find the boy!

He knew Zola was not exactly a Sunday School teacher. She needed help, and so did the children, and he could give that. He well knew how they were sometimes treated, the names they were given to downgrade their morality, as "woods colts." Moreover, he saw through some of their plight and knew them to be good kids that needed a chance. Of the woods they truly were, but they were the real wild flowers of Clear Creek.

Bud had worked, off and on, in the orchards and was a better farm hand than Clem had been. His natural abilities flourished in the horticulture field, and he could bud and graft with precision. In spite of the family difficulty, he was never down and out from the verbal onslaught that troubled his mother or for that matter her sister, Nellie. Bud's help made life easier for all the family except for Nellie who was no longer with them. His help was essential for his mother, and she knew his worth.

Nellie, sick and frail much of the time, had gone to live with her aunt in the city. There receiving proper care, she improved. She was a fine young lady, though that had been discredited by some. Clem had taken a shine for her in his senior year, and for a time they were very close. This closeness became their downfall, as rumors abounded and innuendos were shot like hot arrows. Bud never discussed their affairs with anyone, though he always spoke highly of Clem.

Mell had no idea what might have happened to Bud, but worked on the theory that he must of been, for some reason, swept downstream. He was quiet capable of taking care of himself. A robust young man of seventeen, Bud had proven himself in many ways. During the past year Bud had worked for Mell, at times, always performing beyond expectation. Clem too, had noticed the lad's character and talent and had spoken to his dad about it. With tenacity undaunted by the circumstances of the moment, Mell searched on.

The lateness of the hour foretold the dimness would soon turn to darkness. Time was running out. Carefully he hurried Lena along, calling for Bud, without an answer. Small debris continued floating downstream, some collecting on a log jam at a bend in Clear Creek, now a river. Carefully Mell fixed his eyes on the accumulation of rubble heaped up along the bank and extending out into the water. Again he saw nothing. Continuing to call his name, he had moved on when faintly he thought he heard a voice. "Bud, is that you?" Unmistakenly he now heard Bud's call, coming from the back side of the log jam. Quickly, Mell dismounted and climbed out on the logs to find Bud with one leg below the water, fighting to free himself from the entanglement that bound him.

Seeing a figure approach, Bud called out loudly, "Over here." Then recognizing Mell as he came closer, Bud called again, "My leg is caught between some logs, I can't get it free."

"Stay calm, Bud, I'll get you out soon. Are you in pain?"

"It hurts," said Bud, "but I'm not in pain, I think my ankle is broken."

The anguish on the lad's face spoke more than words and he anxiously watched Mell, search for a prize pole that might free him. Finding one to his liking, Mell carefully forced the pole between the logs holding Bud in place. He knew moving the logs could create a hazard. Looking at Bud, Mell began to apply his weight to the pole. "We must be careful not to upset the balance of the logs. Be ready and when I pry, act quickly, freeing yourself if possible."

The moments were filled with anxiety, Bud somberly watched Mell's force against the pole. Pain gripped his ankle, he pulled but could not get free. Again and again Mell forced the pole down farther against the logs. Suddenly Bud pulled free! With no further movement of the log jam, the wet and exhausted lad sat, gritting his teeth against the pain, waiting for Mell to help him to further safety.

Now, Mell could see a few cuts about the boy's head, neck and one arm, but it was the ankle that he drew his attention. "Besides having lost some skin, your leg doesn't seem to be bad hurt, perhaps bruised." Then further examining the ankle he smiled, "I don't believe it's broken, Bud. Let's see if we can get off this jumbled stack of wood."

"I'm sure lucky you came along, Mell. I would have been here to the end I'm afraid." Then reaching the bank they both sat, resting their exhausted bodies. "I kept hoping the log jam would break up, without taking me with it. I don't mind telling you, I thought I was going to go down!"

"Well you made it, in fine shape I'd say, considering everything."

"Yes," said Bud, "But I went over and under, then found myself pinned between the logs, sitting there helplessly. I can tell you I was scared, that's for sure." Then rising and with help, he hobbled to where Lena was waiting. "Are the folks alright, Mister Marshall?" Then softly said. "I sure got myself in a mess. I don't have any idea as to where old Satan might be. I was chasing him near the water, when my foot slipped on the wet muddy grass and the current washed me down. I was able to grab onto a log and rode that for a ways then it rolled and I fell off into the water again. It was some trip, I'll tell you what!"

"Let's see if we can get you back home and into some warm dry clothes," said Mell, climbing into the saddle and helping Bud get settled behind him.

For Mell the ride back was anticlimactic. His broad shoulders drooped from the strain. The big powerful hill man, drained of physical strength leaned forward in the saddle. The ordeal had passed. The riders rode on through the early night, "Hold on tight, Bud," said Mell. "I'm taking you home!"

III

Then Came the Roses

IN a bold and vivid contrast, the colors of spring burst forth as an avalanche, cascading down upon the ancient hills, called the Ozarks.

This spectacle of nature stages her unveiling exhibit week after week. One specie of the floral domain comes to a grand finale. Then its beauty is diffused in lacy fallen patterns beneath its branches. Other species promenade into full array. At last, they all, one by one, have taken the season's stage of spring's pageantry. From the ecru-hued tones of the apple blossom, to the bright and domineering ox-blood of the rose, they tint the hills and cast a tone upon the lives of the hills people.

Creatures of all kinds, attracted by a diversity of reasons, gather or look upon the flowering branches and deem them a necessity. The cardinal finds a nesting place. The bees dance in their hives and swish to a newly opened flower in search of nectar and honey. Carnie opens her windows and breathes in her favored fragrance, that of the lilacs.

Over the freshly cleaned mantle in the living room sits an antique vase, artistically arranged with lilacs, ruffled from the breeze that comes in from the open window. This is distinctively Carnie's Hurst Manor.

In the guest bedroom another bunch of flowers, dogwoods, have been placed in an old copper kettle. These fresh bouquets are not overbearing, they bring in a bit of charm from her garden and add a cheerful freshness to the rooms.

Carnie's "White House," as some called it, had just recently been built and there were none about that equaled its beauty. A long porch led from the living room to the kitchen with banisters along its full length. A similar porch was on the back side of the house with a walk from it that went to the well. Shrubs and flower beds were neatly arranged along the walk, accenting the home in the splendor of the season. The kitchen windows looked out upon a well-kept lawn with a winding path, much like an old English garden with trellis and vines.

It was to this home that the evangelist would be coming soon for meals during the revival. It was a busy time on the farm, plowing and planting, grubbing and orchard work. The pawpaw orchards had to be sprayed, and it was time for the last picking of the strawberries. Now they must find time for the services and of course the visitation, and someone to entertain the preacher. Widow Moss left much of this up to Mell. She knew the thoughts of most of the local men, regarding traveling preachers. Openly, she spoke Mell's words from last year. "Aw, you have to take care of them like sheep in poor health." She kept that thought in the secrets of her soul, and hoped she wouldn't hear it again.

From her position at the edge of the forest, Martha tossed another armful of carefully chosen dry wood over the fence. Then stooping, she crawled under the barbed wire and stood up.

In the distance she heard a noise which seemed to be coming from the direction of the lane and supposed it to be someone riding up in a wagon. "Land sakes, who would be comin' up here on wash day?" Then listening more closely she said aloud, "Now that I hear it better I reckon it ain't a wagon after all. It's one of them Tin Lizzies."

She pushed aside her extremely long dark hair which tumbled carelessly down her back. Standing there for a moment, Martha pondered her course of action. Then toying with her apron, she broke and ran the few yards to the porch of the house and hurried on into the kitchen to warn her grandmother of the approaching caller.

Interruptions such as this, greatly altered the organization Martha had outlined for today. Her plans were set in cement and cured ahead of time. She didn't take to strangers and was unforgiving when they barged in unexpectedly. Not so for the older lady, it could be a chance to learn of the happenings about, and she did look presentable. She had heard the racket, being out near the open wash kettle, and was all ears when Martha came running up and spoke.

"Grandma, who do you suspect it could be? Do we know anybody with one of those fancy cars? I know there's some in the community, but they surely wouldn't be coming here!"

Carnie looked concerned, then tapped the girl on the shoulder. "Martha, that's the very sound that Gypsy car had when they all came drivin' up yesterday. I hope we're shed of that bunch, but you can't never tell."

By now the vehicle had topped the ridge and was approaching the house. It was an older Model T and had been constructed with an enclosed frame box on the pickup bed. The inside of the peddler's wagon, lined with shelves, provided rows of displayed merchandise. From these the country folk could choose items of special interest or the simple necessities of the day.

Stopping his automobile at the yard gate, the peddler straightened his little bow-tie, slicked back his hair and wiped the dust from his shoes. In his manner of fast talk, and confidential delivery, he greeted the ladies with a tip of the hat and a smile as big as all outdoors. Without wasting any time the peddler swung open the back doors of the compartment and proudly stepped back. "Mrs. Moss, you're looking well, and you, Martha, how's your father and all?"

Martha, without looking at the man, gave an evasive reply, "Well, thank you." Her bright blue eyes shifted from one article to another as she stood close to her grandmother. Tilting her head, she spotted an article on the top shelf and pointed it out to her grandmother. Neither spoke.

"I have your number 30 white thread, Mrs. Moss, and a good assortment of other dress making materials." He watched the expressions on their faces then said, "There's ribbons, bows and the like and as you can see, bolts of yardage."

Nervously, the young girl moistened her dry lips and softly spoke. "What's them things up yonder?" She said, pointing to a pair of scissors, to the delight of the peddler.

He stepped up into the compartment and handed the item to Martha. "Ah, young lady, you sure do have an eye for knowing the latest! These are pinking shears, sells like hot cakes; that's the last one I have." Curiosity held Martha in a spell and the salesman lost no time in taking advantage of his latest possibility.

"Your neighbor, Mrs. McGreggor bought a pair, though I reckon not as expensive as these," said the peddler. "Mrs. Moss," he continued, "These are rather expensive, I must say, but it's the quality of steel." Handing them to her along with a scrap of calico, "Try them on this," said he. While the ladies were busy looking over their new find, the old salesman placed a bolt of dress calico on the shelf for them to handle, and hopefully, want.

Demonstrating the scissors to Martha, Carnie handed the piece of rick-rack-like cut cloth to her granddaughter. The fascinated girl smiled and nodded her head decisively, "Shore does a pretty cut, what's them notches for?"

Mrs. Moss then fingered the cut edges of the material. "It helps in less fraying, and makes it easier to hem," said she.

"I'll tell you what I'll do," said the peddler. "See'n as how you always do a good business with me, I'll throw in the pinkin' sheers free for another big order." He knew the Watkins man had made his rounds recently, so didn't ask for an order of spices. Instead he showed them his muslin, lace, and sewing needles, the items in which she always showed interest. An expression of satisfaction showed in Martha's eyes when her grandmother picked up some yardage of gingham. "There's enough of this, my girl, to make a nice dress and wouldn't it be pretty?"

"Oh yes, Grandma. Do you think I could get it?"

"That's exactly what I'm goin' to do and I'll take that card of buttons," said Mrs. Moss. Martha's eyes gleamed with a sparkle and a smile came to her face expressing deep joy.

Chit-chat between the seller and the buyer wore on, sometimes neither party really cared to listen and was embarrassed to be found out when they were not. Such was the case when the salesman placed a large bag of sugar into the box of items which Mrs. Moss hade chosen.

"How's that?" said she. The man again, with detail, told of the troubles and woes along Clear Creek, and how the McGreggors were going to be forced to leave their home. How Miss Porter and her children were in dire need, living in that makeshift hovel right on the edge of the water. Then he went into detail how Ben Johnson's farm had been ruined by the flood.

"Yes, I heard something about that," replied Mrs. Moss. "It's a real pity . . . "

Then, somewhat interrupting, the man said, "Yes . . . yes so it 'tis . . . Mrs. Moss, do you still have some of that wild muscadine jelly left?"

"Yes, there's several small crocks and some in the quart jars. Would you like more?"

The peddler knew he had a ready market, at a good profit. "I'll take the crocks and perhaps a couple of quarts. That shore is good eat'n!"

"Martha, go and fetch up the jelly from the cellar, and don't drop it." While the peddler was tallying up the goods, Carnie was giving him "an invite" to the revival meetings. She touched upon the virtues of Brother Hallenbeck and his qualifications as far back as Anderson, Indiana. "He was ordained in the Spirit of the Living God, don't you know."

Carefully packing wadded newspapers around the jelly jars, Martha fitted the last one into place and closed the top of the box. Climbing out of the fruit cellar which was under the kitchen, she caught her breath, then hurried on to where she knew they would be waiting.

Approaching the couple, Martha overheard part of a conversation which seemed to be centered around the recent flooding in Clear Creek. She sat the box gently down and gave an ear to all that was being said. "Thank you, Martha," said the gentleman. " . . . and with all their woes they have to answer questions from those two government men from Little Rock. They say the survey will take weeks and it's not clear just what it's all about. Someone mentioned something about a dam across Hog Holler, backing up Clear Creek. Now, wouldn't that be something?"

"Law me, yes, what will they think of next? I hope the jelly is satisfactory."

The old man did more figuring, then handed her the statement, thanking her for her fine order. "I know you are going to thank me a thousand times for the scissors, and Martha, next time I come by I hope to see that pretty new dress of yours."

Sure, on wash day, thought Martha. Grandmother made no reply but watched as the old Model-T went out of sight at the top of the hill. "Oh, Grandmother, what a fine bunch of things you got!" Then Martha picked up the big sack of sugar. With the stock dip in the other hand she walked along with her grandmother, who carried the remaining load of newly purchased items. For some time the ladies occupied themselves with putting away the precious merchandise.

Martha scarcely could believe what she had seen. Her attention was drawn to the scissors and immediately she chose some salvaged remnants to try the unusual shape of the shears. Her excitement had clearly opened up a new field of interest, possibilities that before had been completely dormant now seemed to burst open with sharp curiosity. The grandmother understood the excitement with which Martha welcomed such a gadget. "Martha," said she, "as soon as we get our washing done we'll see what we can do with this new thing!"

Sunny meadows, swept by a gentle breeze moved the faces of countless wild flowers and gave a scent of freshness where Carnie worked. Again the laundry, laboriously drug on, for what today seemed forever.

Martha's new intoxication was not from the pollen of that carpet of color but rather a new infusion. Energy which had been sapped during the winter now like the bursting buds growing near the blackened kettle, brought new meaning to her life. Today there was a freshness in the morning air, sounds not heard yesterday were today bold as the chatter of the titmice. She felt the day was still as fresh as the call of the cardinal high in the maple tree. Her spirits were there, too, but with her feet still on the ground, she burst out singing one of her favorite gospel songs. Plunging her hands deep into the sudsy water of the tub of dirty clothes, she sang on.

Chores of the day continued for Martha until late afternoon, then she joined her grandmother in the garden among the herbs. Both smelled of onions, garlic, and leeks, an undesirable odor, but the task of thinning had been completed. For that matter Martha cared little for most of the garden and least of all, the allium family. "Grandma, these things always stink, burn my eyes or stain my clothes. How can you work with them so long?"

"Well, as you see, they aren't in the flower garden. They aren't anyone's favorite I reckon, they're just part of the overall farm and besides, your father loves them. We'll take some in for supper." Looking up at the sun which by now was low in the west, coloring a cloud-strewn sunset, she adjusted her bonnet. Placing her hands on her hips she smiled and smothered a groan, then stepped back from the row of chives she had finished. "It's enough for today. We have worked hard. We must hurry in and fix dinner. Mell will soon be in, and that poor child, he'll be a sight!"

Dinner was late because the men were late coming in from the field and little Obie was, as expected, quite a sight. He had spent the day in the dirt, up in the trees, and down on the creek. "Wash your face and hands, Obie, you can take a bath after dinner," said the grandmother, "and look at them clothes! What happened to the pocket?"

"I tore it."

"I can see that," replied the grandmother.

"You can patch it, can't you?"

"It's patch on top of patch already and another thread will hardly hold. But, yes, we'll do something, haf' to."

She finished setting the table and all began to tell the events of the day. Obie began by telling how he killed a rattlesnake. After they had settled down from his unpleasant description, Martha told of the peddler's visit and how she and Granny worked hard with the laundry and with the onions. Mrs. Moss mentioned that she needed more room in the garden. Then, looking at Mell, asked, "How is the washout work coming and how bad was the loss?"

"Could of been much worse, some of the rows of the last planting were lost. I still have enough roots in growing beds to put out several new rows this fall. The rains have really been good for the new growth. They sure are pretty, row after row of tender growth, even better than last year."

Following supper, Obie filled the number two tub with warm water near the kitchen stove and took his bath, then quickly went to bed. He knew tomorrow would be another working day and wanted to be ready when his dad left for the fields. Mell still had to do chores and the ladies worked in the kitchen, so it was much later when the rest of the family retired.

Moonlight shone through the cinnamon vines as Mell sat on the steps of the front porch. In the quietude of the late evening, he watched the bobbing about of the fireflies. The sky had every appearance of a special glow. The luminous band called the Milky Way stretched across the sky with its innumerable faint stars, so many light-years away. Yet from arms length came the sweet fragrance of the honeysuckle, laden to the brim with pastel colored blossoms touched with dew. In this pastoral setting Mell pondered over his labor and life of the day. Today's labor brought a promising future. The evening's view, out into the vast expanse brought back the memories of another time. The Ozarks were always full of "another time," full of hope, full of love. Love for so many ingredients that made life in the hills what it was, pure and simple.

How many were the nights that he and Thalia sat under the stars, under the flickering light of the fireflies such as these. Had she not often plucked a fragrant flower and held it close to her breast? Honeysuckles, often filled their room with a fragrance that spelled love. She always made life exciting. Out of the darkness she brought the dawn; out of the brambles she brought luscious fruit. From God she found a lasting faith, still showing in Mell, just as the stars shown in the vast canopy above.

Beneath this enchanting ecstasy of the evening, the man of the hills sat for a long time, alone. With his thoughts cloaked in the tenderness of the past, surrounded with the present, he possessed a fascination for the good life among the folks of these hills. He knew the land of his birth and chose to remain here, for home it would always be.

He had seen the other side of the mountain and he had been to the back side of the world. From those places he sent Thalia postcards: from Paris, pictures of the "Arc de Triumph," where he marched. There were also pictures of Notre Dame, the Louvre, and many from the Botanical Gardens and in particular the herbarium. In Ireland he walked along the heather, while in the English countryside he slept under thatched roofs. Postcards of these, too, were added to Thalia's keepsakes. Then when he was "home" again there were pictures of New York, the mountains of Tennessee and Kentucky, and even a postcard of the Ozarks.

He had seen the beauty, and he had seen the scars of war. Now he held an even greater passion for home, the little hills, his Ozarks. His fascination for the hills was now an obsession and so were his plans. The status quo must change. It was a new world; he wanted to see a new and productive state. He wanted the land of opportunity to take on new meaning, and he was seeing results.

Soft shadows danced in the moonlight as the gentle breezes of May swept across the face of the man who sat on the steps of Hurst Manor. Across the prairie field, deep in a thicket, came the arresting call from a Whippoorwill. Obie often explained that the name uttered over and over, was the bird saying, "Whip poor Will, whip poor Will, whip poor Will." But tonight Obie did not hear the bird call, nor had he heard his grandmother walk down the long porch and sit on the steps by his father. The young lad had gone to sleep. Martha, too, missed the dialogue from the front steps as both parties scanned the skies and spoke with carefully chosen words.

Thinking of how best to approach the subject, the old woman searched with all her presence of mind, before opening the conversation she now chose. She spoke in a soft low tone, though her voice was crisp and clear as the night. Unlike the stage before them, however, the pain in her heart gave her a sick and gnawing feeling as if she were stepping out of bounds. She was losing sight of all the loveliness, being torn by her conflicting emotions.

"Mell, I don't want this to sound as if I'm sweepin' on your porch. I've had a mind to speak to you about this," then she lowered her voice and paused. Finally, in another breath she uttered the words, "Zola Porter."

Silence replaced the gentle call of the whippoorwill, and shadows veiled the expressions that shot across Mell's face. Carnie knew the darkness hid far more than his face. It was a shroud, wrapped around his heart. She knew, also, that she was on thin ice, but it had to be broken, and a woman's intuition told her this was the time.

A silhouette advanced along the wall as Mell leaned forward. For a season, Carnie gave thought to the possibility that he was leaving; then he cleared his throat in a controlled tone and sat, silently. "Well, Grandma, I'm goin' to tell you. There's just a lot of talk. Everyone, it seems, wants to put in his two-cents worth."

"Gossip, you say?"

"And idle talk. But while they are talking about me they're letting someone else rest!"

In her uneasiness, Carnie sat wringing her hands in a stew, not wanting to further offend. At the same time she was hoping for more "enlightenment" from the man who really knew. Others only gave free scuttlebutt and dealt in mudslinging. But those were the ones she heard from; that had been her source of information.

Shifting from her position, Carnie spoke again. "Well, as I said before, I don't want to seem to be meddling in your affairs, but Martha is quite concerned, don't you know."

"I know quite well, of Martha's, uh, problem. Yes, indeed, I'm aware of her thoughts, concerning Zola, she's expressed them often enough!"

"Perhaps she is busying herself with what's not her business, but she simply dislikes the woman!"

Head bowed, his body slumped in despair, Mell rose and this time his soft voice breaking, focused on the cinnamon vine. Taking a deep, unsteady breath, he stepped back and spoke, "She hasn't gotten over losing her mother!"

"Well, that's so." Carnie rose from her seated position and faced Mell, then moving down the porch, added, "Let me fix you a cup of coffee."

Slowly they found their way around the large oak table, Mell sitting at his usual place, at the end. Unvoiced silence loomed between them like a heavy mist as each waited for the other to speak. Carnie saw a frown set upon his features and moved away, stirring about the stove making his coffee.

"Martha still believes in the old fairy tale of the wicked stepmother! No one is ever going to even begin to take her mother's place, if she can help it. As far as I know, no one is contemplating such an attempt! Zola hasn't proposed to me."

There was a trace of humor in his voice and Carnie too found a spark of joy and gave a sigh of relief as she poured his coffee. Mell held the cup to his lips, then paused, set it down on the saucer, and smiled. "There's another verse to that song, but I'll sing it later."

Neither pursued the awkward conversation any further, yet they both reckoned within themselves that it must be dealt with more fully, somewhere down the road.

The firm set of his jaw, the intense brown eyes, his muscular and broad shoulders were never unnoticed by any of the ladies of Norwood. Neither had his strong frame been passed by tonight. Carnie admired his strength and vitality which were that of a much younger man. His hard working days, and nights, had always given him an admirable standing from Carnie. She was thankful for his support to her, for the way he managed the farm, and she was thankful for his loyalty since the passing of Hampton.

They were both alone: he, at the well drawing water for the stock; she, standing at the stove finishing the dishes. Both were in a world of thoughts all of their own. Neither dwelt on the negative, and tonight Carnie looked back with nostalgia, bathed in tender memory of her Hampton. His last request had been that Mell would care for Carnie. This, Mell had given his promise and had carried it out. Hurst Manor and the entourage, was now in his charge.

Carnie's days were often long and laborious also; today had been so. All sorts of preparations had at last been made. As she carried in the last of the pies from the screened shelf on the porch, the sweetness of the honeysuckle had its affect. It was another reminder for her early morning chore, that of gathering her most lovely blossoms. She would arrange them early for sprays and bouquets for the Decoration Day "doin's" at the cemetery.

Martha had everyone's clothes freshly ironed, and laid out. Their broaches and pins sparkled. As always for special gatherings, Carnie would wear her unique cameo Thalia had given her just a few years ago.

No sooner had the grand old lady of Hurst Manor lain down on her featherbed until she was in prayer. "I will both lay me down in peace, and sleep: for thou, Lord, only makes me dwell in safety." Then she drifted into restful slumber.

Dew Drops, as beads of pearls, clung to the foliage and flora. With the dawn, Hurst Manor and all the Ozarks, shimmered in the early morning light. These sun rays, beams of light, cast a faint hue of color and toned up the morning sky. Carnie, sensed their path in the sky and raised her hand in praise, "Thank you, Lord, I just know it's goin' to be a good day!"

Appropriate cans and jars had been filled with cold water, and again this year, she would carefully choose the flowers from her garden. And as she told Martha, "When the task shall have been completed, all the containers shall have been filled!"

From the cool and shaded veranda, Carnie placed the several containers in a circle around her and worked from a small bench in the center. Lard cans which had been especially decorated, would now bring together and hold, bouquets laced with love and beauty only Carnie could create. Her artistic ability, would no doubt, again be the talk of the day.

Each bough-pot was innovative and drew no lines of any other; they were original. Her first such creation was always in memory of Hampton. Her pale white hands held the rich deep burgundy blossoms of the peony. Small potatoes had been dipped in a flour and water paste and covered with poppy seed. These were now placed on a slender stem and woven into the arrangement with glossy ferns and the smoky gray-green branches of sage. The wire bail was covered with soft bark from a willow twig, and held a bow at one side. At the top and resting on the flowers, was a folded card, meant for no one to read. The tedious work continued, then Carnie paused. The spray was completed, placed on a rack and sprayed with a fine mist of cold water.

Immediately her attention was given to the creation of another. This one to be placed on Thalia's grave, and it, too, would be a singular labor of love. Carnie now stood in front of the bucket containing the old-fashioned lilacs. Their fragrance filled the air about them and brought to mind, the fine painting that for so many years hung above Thalia's bed. It was of a cluster of lilacs such as these, painted by the Frenchman Chaseaun deBouain. It was in like manner that Carnie aspired, in her design now at hand.

All the leaves had been stripped from the stems, and each placed in a frog, at the bottom of the bucket for proper spacing. Spikes of red cedar stood above the lilacs while Baby's Breath veiled them in a white mist. Cascading from the tip of the cedar to the floppy straw hat the bucket sat in, was the jaded foliage of the maidenhair ferns. Then for a special island of peace, Carnie placed a mound of forest moss, on which sat a small porcelain lamb.

Again the tall, thin, elegant and aging lady of Hurst Manor had achieved success. Gradually Carnie's little flower boutique had all but disappeared from around her. This quaint ornamentation graced the veranda where they sat among the Stars and Bars. They, too, would adorn the resting place for one who had fallen, and would furl in the breeze at Weddington.

Lost in her reflections and reminiscence of the past, Carnie pushed her stooped and aching shoulders against the wall and ran her fingers through her long gray hair. Although it was still before noon, the tranquil rest was as welcome as the spring day.

Early afternoon found them at the cemetery where folks were milling about, placing flowers on the graves and speaking in low conversations. Seeing Carnie near by, Mrs. McGreggor stepped to her side and spoke, "Guess we'll be leaving soon for California."

"Well, I had heard how you lost everything in the flood, but I didn't know you are leaving."

"Yeah, we're going to a place called Fresno, we heard they need fruit pickers. Dan thinks we can do better there. Me and the two boys will be able to work as well. We just can't do no good here."

Carnie put her arm around her neighbor, "We'll miss you, Mary and I sure hate to hear how you lost all your belongings, just seems that things are going from bad to worse."

"Yeah, I know. We have all had our losses. I do have my family, however, and thank God for that. Are the flowers for Hampton? Lord knows he was a godly man. We all miss him Carnie." Then she placed her arm around her weeping friend.

"Sometimes I think I can't go on, but then one has to. Mell has been a heap of help. Without him and the children I don't know what I would have done." Holding the wreath she had arranged for Hampton, she said, "I must go, Mary, I hope we can see you before you leave."

Parting, Carnie joined the others and they followed her to Hampton's grave. Placing the flowers carefully, they waiting until she was ready to leave. A short distance away another granite grave marker was reverently approached, that of Thalia's. It was quickly noticed by all that again, someone had been there first. Again, a spray of red roses had been placed across the mound of earth. No one spoke. Kneeling, Carnie placed one hand on the headstone and with the other put a handkerchief to her eyes. On the opposite side, Mell too, knelt, placing the arrangement against the stone. The children knelt by their father. Finally, Martha looked intently at the roses, sobbing, she rose and joined her grandmother. In time the family departed, much like the one who had brought the roses and left unseen.

IV

The Garden of Peculiar Souls

SHIMMERING waves of heat swirled across the withering sea of grass on Norwood Prairie. An early summer had, without fair warning, brought an omen that not only could be seen, but felt.

The men set under their newly constructed brush arbor, sweltering in the heat. While there was speculation as to whose idea it was for the timing of this year's revival, no one could recall. The hills men, all exhausted, felt the fatigue and showed weariness from this labor of love. The task, thought of as a mission by some, was an annual charge from the circuit rider. He realized not all the workmen in the community felt it necessary, nor did all feel obligated to so much as lift a hand. Yet there were these men before him, faithful to the cause, who knew they were not prevailed upon. They had chosen again this year to join the adventure that was in the spirit of kinship. While the arbor did little to protect against the heat, it did provide shade and would, if prayer was answered, repel the rain.

Sid was one of the men who labored most. It had been he who cut the large posts that held the heavy load of leaves. This was their shade and would be for the extent of the revival. The men annually exhibited their arbor for the scrutiny of those who took special notice of such things.

It was not coincidental that Sid and his right-hand men were muscular and lean; it had been a necessity. Grit, too, played the game in each tired and weary soul. Sore muscles, drooped shoulders and tired feet brought life-weary lines upon the brow of each man. The saved and the unsaved, Sid being the latter. Nevertheless, unvarnished Sid held a special pride in his heart for Norwood and all his neighbors secretly shared a piece of it, as well.

A member of the school board, Sid had helped formulate a forward policy in education. With a little arm twisting, he had handpicked his men for the job that for too long had not been well done. He had once said, "I've hitched the right horses to the team, and they moved the community." It had not been with the speed of light, nor from sheer yearning for change. Rather it was, the times, catapulting this part of the Ozarks into a generation on the move.

Arkansas' new governor had done as much for the road system. Politics in Little Rock were changing. A new breed of men was emerging and Sid longed to lead. There was plenty of room for expansion, or as the slogan said, this was the land of opportunity. The hills men saw the handwriting on the wall and at last moved with the times.

The church, too, saw the dawning of a new day and plans were underway for a new worship center, considered by some to be extravagant. The steeple would rise high into the sky, the basement dug well into the earth, and a baptistery would be the likes of which many folks had never seen. Nevertheless there was unity, and this they had kept from the founding date back in early statehood.

Shifting from an old idea to a new way often brought pain, but the burden was shared by the community. As men had done here, they dug, cut, built and invited. Results were expected.

Perspiration rolled down Sid's cheek, his movements were stiff and awkward as he moved from his seat on the bench and stood before the group.

Squaring his shoulders he spoke. "It's been lingering on the edge of my mind . . . ." Then he paused, reaching for his pack of Bull Durham. The quietness was more than a hush. They waited for the quiet man to speak, seldom had he been so bold. The breeze, too, no longer touched the leaves, causing a shortness in one's breath. Patiently the men waited for Sid's disclosure, finally he moved to the center of the arbor and continued to speak.

"I took a notion, boys, to run for office. Now hear me out!" said he, holding up both arms. But it was no use, the quietness had been broken. Inquisitive minds were pricked as if stinging quills of sharpness had been thrust into them from a porcupine!

"Your times not up already?" asked one.

Before Sid had time to answer, another of the men spoke. "Kind of reminds me of the old farmer that was outstanding in his field, maybe you're in the wrong field."

Everyone laughed and slapped their hands against their legs. Another of the group who had just finished drinking from an old tin cup set the bucket of cool water down and added to the conversation. "I reckon it's hot enough to slip hair off a hog; I expect some of the heat went through your hat!"

Again everyone chuckled and waited for the point he had tried to make about running for office.

Ben Davis, who seldom joined this prestigious group of arbor builders, and who less frequently joined any of them in church, gave a twisted smile toward the allegation relating to the heat. "One can almost smell the sulfur and it's close enough to get singed! Or does this preacher rant and rave about hell fire and brimstone?"

There was a stillness, then Mell spoke as he stood and wiped his brow with an old and previously used handkerchief. "Well, it's not good for the crops either, unless there is a change in the weather soon my pawpaws are likely to get blister spots. Other farmers have already suffered."

He was interrupted by a vehicle stirring up a cloud of dust as it turned from the main road onto the church grounds. It was the parson who drove under the shade of the old oak. Momentarily he waited for the dust to settle, gathered up his Bible and some papers then stepped down onto the running board of the old car.

Dressed in a seersucker suit and carrying a light straw hat, Pastor Wright sauntered from the oasis of green, with his eyes set upon the arbor. He was visibly seeing what he had seen with his heart last night as he then knelt and prayed. He felt the bond among the men and saw, with clarity, the results. Praise was short coming. Reaching the shade of the arbor, the pastor raised his free arm and exclaimed, "Praise the Lord!"

Placing the Bible on a bench and the hat to one side, he stepped up to the men and started shaking hands. Most of the men were known to him, with the exception of Sid and a new man visiting in the community, whom Mell introduced as Buck Jones.

Pastor Wright spoke a few words to each man commenting on their fine work in bringing the arbor to completion and inviting each to the services. "Men, the sweat poured from you as you labored on this arbor under the hot summer sun. You have strained muscles in putting up the heavy framework which now securely holds the fresh smelling leaves. Tomorrow they may well repel the rain. Our Lord often dramatized how the seeds would grow on good soil. This is that good soil, and like a flourishing field, we'll see a productive harvest!"

Without a sermon, he wanted them to see that their lives too, would, through God's Gracious Spirit, be fruitful. He knew their character, basically, and their conversation. He wanted to encourage them, knowing that simply hearing about the Word, was not enough. A Godly response had been what he had prayed for, and he expected to see it happen under the arbor. He had made that a matter of prayer and he believed the scriptural truth, "To every thing there is a season." The minister was claiming that season for souls in this revival.

Some of the men were milling about, obviously waiting to leave, when Brother Wright spoke again. "I wonder if we might not have a word of prayer before you leave, asking His blessings upon the work that has been done here.

"Gentlemen, I love to study the character of men, talk eye to eye, and learn what brings each man to an absolute personality that's his alone. Many of your lives were utterly transformed by the Word of God. He's still in the same business today, and I believe He has a definite work to do among us here on Norwood Prairie. So come to as many of the services as possible. The evangelist, Brother Hallenbeck is a fine speaker and a true man of God. I know you'll be blessed!"

With that having been said, he paused, lowered his head and asked a blessing upon them. "In the name of the Father, the Son, and the Holy Ghost, Amen." The activities at the arbor momentarily came to a close.

Meanwhile, the hustle and bustle at Hurst Manor had reached a feverish pitch. Both Martha and the tired herb lady planned to leave no stone unturned in preparation for the revival. They were not only setting the house in order, but the garden and grounds as well.

Martha was consumed, body and soul, with the laundry, undaunted by hard work and the searing summer heat that droned on and on. The table linen and lace curtains occupied her entire day. Bent on perfection, her keen sensitivity caused the savoir-faire young lady to know in her heart they were well done. That was reward enough — save for the admiration of the ladies of Norwood.

While Martha felt the heat of the flat iron, her grandmother endured the heat from above. The better part of her day had been spent gathering herbs, working in the drying shed and selecting fresh table vegetables for the next few days.

Around her were these prime species of the horticulture world, selected from the good soil, the garden. Here they were kept in large glass jars or tied in neat bunches, secured to the wall. Canisters and freshly cleaned lard cans also contained choice and rare herbs that had grown up from around her feet. These generic species now gave a feeling of fulfillment to the old lady's heart. They gave her a proper image of herself as she affixed a label to the botanical ledger and capped another page of her life with success.

Lengthening shadows fell across the room and the dim light hastened Carnie to leave the undone work for another day. Carefully stepping down from the cabin, she closed the door behind her and paused for a moment, enjoying the fragrance of the honeysuckle blossoms which seemed to fill the air with a lingering aroma.

The western sky, still holding a late evening exhibition of color, gave an unfrequented view of exceptional cloud silhouettes. Strangely formed streaks of hues dazzled the eyes, while beams from the last rays of the sun gave the horizon the appearance of an eruption, such as Armageddon.

Aunt Carnie paused a few precious moments longer, lingering in the beauty of an Ozark summer. She now drew this quiet season to her heart and, with nostalgia of the past, thought of lovely memories of other times.

Her obsession with the seasons since coming to the hills as a child, had nourished and restored her tired body time and again. This evening, too, she took to heart the moment in time, and pressing her long gray hair back from her face, she felt the presence of God's love and recognized He had truly filled her life with blessings!

From overhead, high in the maple tree, came the song of a cardinal. More joined until their repeated trill quashed the serenity of what had been a melody. Rising, she realized the shadows had totally replaced the light. Laboriously she climbed the steps leading to the porch and her kitchen.

Lamplight in the room bordered the outer darkness at the windows. Realizing the lateness of the evening, Martha hastened to ask her grandmother what had kept her out so long. Secretly she wondered at the value of such time away from the housework, and her conjectures were, by no means, all silent!

Dishes from the evening meal had been put away. Ironing hung from the window rod, telling of another chore completed. Heat from the wood stove still brought discomfort to the room causing both ladies to seek relief on the steps of the front porch. There so often, in the heat of summer, a refreshing change of pace could be found. So it was that here too, many heartrending discussions not only took place, but had a forever lasting effect upon many folk. Here the custom was to speak one's piece, the pretentious ways of thinking were veneered away for what they were worth — a facade. In getting to the facts, Mell would often say, "This is where the rubber meets the road." The sentiment expressed by Aunt Carnie often would be, "Don't beat around the bush." Martha well knew these expressions. Neither did she mince words, but got to the point straightway often blunt and coarse.

An unsteady breeze ruffled the leaves of the honeysuckle vines, sweeping over each latent blossom. The early evening dew carried the spicy aroma as a miniature bouquet, awakening their sensitivity.

A low crescent moon rose above the densely oak covered ridge that sloped downward from Hurst Manor. Performing on nature's stage, the soft orange glow filtered through the tops of the trees, while the sparkle of the stars reached down to earth. In the quietness, the ladies sat enjoying the exhibit of the summer's evening. Across this backdrop of artistry came the fireflies, gliding about as if they were propelled on a cushion of air.

"Did you ever see such an evening, Grandma? Just look at all them fireflies, whirlin' and swooshin' about topsy turvy. Sure is a fracas. But they are pretty, turning their lights on and off."

"A heap of them out tonight all right." And pointing with her extended arm, the granny spoke again, "There, did you see the lightning? There's another flash, far off in the distance."

"Oh, Granny, I love to sit here on the porch and pass the time of evening, just chit-chat, you and me watchin' the sky."

"We've done our chores for today my girl and tomorrow we'll more than likely do more than we did today. Yes, a little reflection is good for a body."

"This is about all the world that Mother saw. She never got out to Tennessee or Kentucky, did she?" quizzed the child.

"Your father was looking for work back there, and, for a time, worked in a smelter. Your mother stayed to home here. He did take the family with him when he went to the oil field in Ponca City. But my dear, she saw more of the world than most folks who travel. She loved it all, all she could see. And land sakes I haven't been anywhere a'tall, myself. But I can read."

Martha, shifting her seating position on the concrete steps, spoke again. "I read where some folks from Arkansas went to places I ain't ever heard of, just to see the world I reckon."

"I read that article, too," said Granny. "Some time back I read of a feller telling how he saw a world in a grain of sand. Don't know as if I could do that, seems the longer I run my eyes over the stuff the more it looks like plain sand."

"Our world is small, Granny. We just sit right here in these poor and tortured hills. Don't know where the balance of the world is a'tall."

"Oh, no, child, the hills are not dark and dreadful any more than the night is black and ugly. I've thought of them," then she paused a moment or so. Staring down toward the pastoral valley, now cloaked in illumination from the heavenly sphere above, she continued reminiscing, "I've thought of them these many years as, well, the everlasting hills of home!"

"They don't amount to that much, do they, Granny? My teacher once told me there was no such place as this. That the Ozark Mountains were merely a figment of my imagination. She said we live on a 'plateau,' which goes to show she ain't done much climbin' about."

"Wherever the place of abode might be, whether it's deep in the hills or high on the desert, a cottage or a castle, honey, that's home! And child as far as I'm concerned our home is definitely in the hills. Matters not what name they go by, it's still home. No, I can't say we've seen much of the world, but you will. You will; be patient my girl. Find happiness here and you'll take it with you wherever you go!"

"I ain't planning on going nowhere, Granny, I'm staying right here. Goin' to help you and the boys like Mama wanted me to do."

"I never allowed for much plannin' neither, my old Pappy did all of that — that is in shaping our course to Arkansas. My, what method and means we had to use in those days! Then in later years Hampton made all the decisions, well at least some of them. Now, Mell does most what he wants, and I just have to keep still, got nothing to do anything with. Hampton and I got by pretty good, but then, after his passing," she paused with a faraway look that brought a tear walling down her cheek. "I still miss him terribly."

The moon rose higher and brighter until overshadowing clouds cast a blurring veil brightened only by distressing claps of lightning. Both sat motionless for a time, catching sight of a moment of solace as nature continued to uncover her pageantry in another season on stage. The gentle breeze became a refreshing delight, ushering in the smell of rain as the storm approached. Still they sat, unruffled and reluctant to be persuaded to move indoors, preferring to see the tempest rather than hearing it from the inside. Besides this, there was yet another obvious reason for their endurance on the front steps. Neither soul had yet breathed a whisper which could, if only spoken, unburden their troubled hearts!

Unlike plenty of others, these ladies, the young and the old, paused, in times like this, waited for their kindred thoughts to come up side by side just like they sat. In time this had been achieved, who knew how. It would suffice to know that it happened.

Finally, the wise old matriarch, perceiving the moment had arrived, spoke. "I've been thinking of Clem."

As if she had not heard, Martha sat in a hushed silence. Then she knew the ice had been broken, and she would not be afraid to speak. The grandmother spoke again, still in a solemn tone. "I reckon it's the weather and our loneliness."

"I reckon it's a heap more than that!" replied the girl. Tender emotions from the heart built up within her, and as she so easily could, she shed a few tender tears. The old grandmother, of whom it could be said, had been hardened by her many years of seeing life lived, understood with less emotion.

In so many ways the wintry past still dealt a chilly blow and the present depressed state of affairs virtually held a lock that bound Martha with a gnawing remorse. Natural feelings that touched the very soul, sifted the chaff from the grain and helped sort out the facts of life. Her "experience," as she called it, living with the Lord, overshadowed all adversity. This love affair with Him gave her motivation and sustained her drive to the point that many called it fanaticism. "Peculiar," was the term she used. And firing back at the ones she called heathen she hoped they would someday understand.

The grandmother, in her usual dignified posture, so graceful for her years, heard a tear-smothered voice whisper beside her. Again she heard the fragile and shaking voice probe further. "Granny, are you listening? Did you hear what I said? Do you really think Clem will be coming soon — for the revival?"

"I think," said she, "we'll just have to wait a mite longer for that answer."

"He could."

"If he wants to, yes."

Perhaps it was simply her own uneasiness that kept her from the certainty she so desperately needed at this time. Carrying her thoughts back over the several months, Martha realized there would be no answer for the moment. Only with time would they know for certain, of the effectual chord he still might have for them.

"Mell acted in a rash manner. He ought not to have done that, he should have given the boy more room," said the woman. Then she paused and did some thinking to herself.

Martha understood her brother very well and reasoned that he had done no wrong. She too, knew her father had been too strict. Then looking at her grandmother, she spoke again. "Clem has a mind of his own, too. It's in his blood to be headstrong. I guess that's why they say, he's just like his dad."

"In some ways, contrary in others. Mell expects too much out of the chap, expects him to be steady and mature beyond his years. I think I know him better than his father, but I'd dare not let your dad know that. He expects Clem to be a chip off the old block. Well, he ain't."

"He tired of the farm, didn't he, Granny!"

The gathering storm, edging closer with the clashing of thunder, drowned their voices and silhouetted their frames in flashing light. When she could be heard again, the wise old lady returned to their discussion, "No, I wouldn't say he did. He's just not a farm boy. He's cut out for other work, and Mell, like it or not, must swallow some pride and help that boy."

"Well, Granny, Clem does have a good job."

"For now, yes, but I don't like it a'tall the way he's out of school. He ought to be up at the university. He's got a good head on his shoulders. He ought to make something of himself! If he has a fault, that's 'hit. He oughtn't to be satisfied to stick around and be another apple-knocker! That money won't last till it's gone, then what?"

"You don't mean to point the finger of blame at him do you, Granny?"

"Land sakes, child, that chap is as pure as the driven snow, but the world's changing. We hill folks are goin' a change or we'll be left out in the cold!"

"He may get left out in the cold, but Granny, I wish he was only an apple-knocker. But he's an oil man, Granny. He brings in Black Gold."

"Land sakes, child, I never forget that. I worry about him in my sleep! I don't know why Mell allowed that boy to be drug off over there in the first place."

"We all worry about him, Granny, but you know he wasn't drug. He insisted that he was old enough to make decisions on his own, and so he did. Dad could have stopped him, but I think he was glad to see him go. I know Clem was mad and thinking he was a man and wanted to leave home. But still and all, I pray for him every day. Oh, I hate that awful job! I despise that awful smell, that everlastin' muck. What do they do with all that awful stuff anyway?"

"Well, I can tell you that George Fetterly sells it. I know that much. He says there's enough down in the earth to last forever!"

"George Fetterly also sells bad eggs. He makes money just sittin' there on that three legged stool. If he'd work and earn a livin' there wouldn't be a need for the stuff."

Granny, pointing out into the direction of the off and on flashing light, remarked again, "Well, I can tell you that there's nothing we can do about it but as you say, pray."

"And that we will do!" said the girl.

Although the piercing burst broke the silence around them, the ladies bowed their heads, closing out their physical senses to the dark and sinister world. In this manner of calling upon the Divine Being, each lay hold to what they knew to be the Light of the World. Transformed in this fashion, they met the Master in a crystal clean and holy scene, unswerving on account of His Divine presence.

Invariably Martha chose to be first in prayer time. Her passion in waiting for prayer was held by a short fuse and an explosive spark. "Almighty God, we beseech Thee for Thy mercy of the hour. Grant unto us the wisdom of knowing how to pray. Strengthen our faith and make us believe in and be aware of answered prayer! Oh, righteous Father . . . ."

Unaware of the tempest, now moved as directed by the Omnipotent and Merciful God, Martha continued to implore His divine providence upon His children. The blackness of night lost its color. A serene peace fell around the kneeling ladies as the storm in life ebbed away.

Driving winds brought remnants of rolling clouds swiftly passing over the face of the moon. Hanging like a giant orange ball, the celestial body appeared to give off a hallowed light as it rose higher above the trees and out into the vastness of the sky.

In this soft glowing illuminate, the ladies, having finished their prayer time, rose. Martha took particular notice of the difficulty with which her grandmother had in standing. She also listened again to her recount the episode of her aging plight. The verbalizing of the old matron was soul-stirring and was spoken only in passing. Indeed it did not reflect her kind soul. The only lamentations she knew were from the Bible. Her aches and pains were walled within her troubled heart, unveiled only before the Lord.

"Martha, I'm so stiff my old joints will hardly bend. You'll have to help me inside. I'm just no good for nothin' anymore!" Then she chuckled and with a jovial grin, said, "Do you think we prayed too long?"

Devotedly Martha walked with her grandmother to the bannister of the porch. "There, Granny, rest and stretch your legs. Tomorrow you'll be like new. It's always good when two folks pray. Rheumatism may stiffen your joints, but it hasn't affected our hearts. I'm stiff, too, Granny. I think our trouble was that we sat a spell too long."

"Listen," said the grandmother as she turned her head back toward the direction of a sound coming from the woods. "Do you hear the whippoorwill?" She stopped, then spoke again. "Let's linger a bit before going in. The coolness of the evening is refreshing." The night bird lifted its voice in song repeatedly before moving on, perhaps to find its mate. "The call of the whippoorwill is another tonic for an old woman, my dear. We need them all."

"You're just like Mother was, Granny. Oh, I miss her so much." Both ladies felt a pang, a stabbing pain that went deep into their hearts. A moment of silence gripped their speech.

"She loved life, Martha. Through all her pain your mother still loved life. Yes, I suppose you could say she got it from me, Hampton always said so."

They stood, still leaning against the porch bannister until Martha spoke words of going in and moved toward the room. The old lady quietly followed. Although it was well past her bedtime, sleep had not filled her eyes. Then reaching above the mantle, she took down the Bible and sat near the light from the old oil lamp. Opening the familiar book, she placed it securely in her lap and read, Isaiah, chapter 40, verse 31. That reading began where she had finished reading yesterday.

> "But they that wait upon the Lord shall renew
> their strength they shall mount up with wings
> as eagles; they shall run, and not be weary; and
> they shall walk, and not faint."

The straight-laced lady of life then took a faded and tattered bookmark, and as so often before, read again its lines.

> "God writes the gospel not in the Bible alone,
> but on trees, and flowers, and clouds and stars.
> It's heard from birds and bees and kittens and
> me."   — Anonymous

Drowsiness affected her hold on the paper gem and the Bible. Her tired eyes closed in refreshing peace. Somewhere between the bounds of reverie and reality, time, born like fog, meandered away. This tranquility was shattered with a roaring sound and glaring lights reflecting through the window glass. Into the sleeping face came the bright light that startled her from her sleep.

"What in the land of Goshen," exclaimed the old lady as she rose from her chair and ran to the doorway. In the bright moonlight she quickly recognized the overdue visitor who came to her door.

V

The Thistle

HURST Manor spread the word, The Prodigal Son had returned, coincidentally timed to the revival. He had been whisked away to Rivendell Valley without fanfare, and wrongfully so, in the sight of Mrs. Moss. Humbly, she spoke not of her empathy for the chap, knowing it best.

There would be other times and for all one knew, a sterling scene later. Martha, if she had had her druthers would have been content to remain with her grandmother. This, however, would offer an opportunity to speak to Clem and when those moments came, she would make the most of them. Those moments came sooner that she expected.

"Dad tells me you're spending more time at Granny's," said Clem. "Does that mean Dad spends more time alone?"

"Guess so, don't know who would be with him," Martha replied. Then looking up from her sewing on an old pair of Obie's pants she remarked. "Obie needs our attention, he gets better care staying with grandmother than he would have staying alone with daddy."

Looking down, Clem turned and spoke again. "Well before I left home I imagined Dad had an eye for Zola, though I know you hate to hear it, if it's true."

"It's true alright, I know that to be a fact. I think it's disgusting!"

"You'll have to admit, Zola is very pretty."

"No, I won't, and that has nothing to do with it. If you ever heard how the people talk you'd know what I mean."

"I've heard. Bud and I have talked, we're not naive."

"I don't like Bud either. I don't know why Dad has him working around the place sometimes."

"Martha, he's a good worker, that's why. You should be more charitable. He's a good guy."

"Nonetheless, I'll have nothing to do with the whole bunch."

"Don't you like Nellie? No, I guess you don't."

"I do not, not one bunch. I wish they would all move away, just go back where they came from."

"And where is that?"

"I have no idea; it makes no difference. They're not our type, anyway."

"Is that what Granny says?"

"No, I'm afraid not. But that's what I say."

The slamming of the back door closed the conversation abruptly. Martha left the room knowing she had said enough. Clem was thankful for the change of pace, allowing him to speak to his father. Perhaps speaking the right words might be good, but what were those words and who should speak?

It was Mell who spoke first with a kind and gentle voice. "Son, I want to take you out to the upper orchard in the morning and show you the work we've done there. It's all paying off, beginning to look as if we could hang a respectable sign above our gate, 'Marshall & Son Orchards.' It's not been easy for you either. We have worked hard, but finally things are falling into place." Then the father turned, facing his son and placed his hand on the young man's shoulder. "We'll talk more tomorrow." Smiling, he walked out the back door toward the car and drove away.

Days passed quickly. Delayed jobs were now finished. The premises were spruced up as if they were expecting John

Philip Sousa to step out of a band box. Clem sensed a change, yet he knew there had been, from the outset of his going away last fall, a degree of guilt. Now all set their hearts on healing the known hurt. Clem quickly understood their shenanigans for what they were and enjoyed then. He reasoned, perhaps he too had second thoughts and had grown up a bit. Feelings between him and his dad were improved, and things were going smooth around the farm. Yet he knew he had not changed that much. He still carried a chip on his shoulder knowing that someone, somewhere, would in time, knock it from his frame. There had been, in his time away from Briarcliff Cottage, upheavals in his life. He weathered each, as he had been taught. Absence from the family had helped him sift the wheat from the chaff and winnow with the wind the unpleasant. Now he was determined to further the effort, making his point known before returning to the oil fields.

This air of excitement spread throughout the valley. As one old-timer passing by reported, "They were skedaddling about like a bat out of Joplin!" The fervor, due to Clem's unexpected arrival, kept all hands in a dither. Neighbors did more passing by, giving more notice of what was happening, yet pretending to see nothing. The young oil-man's closeness again with those of Briarcliff had taken on a new and proper affection.

Today the brothers were busy in the city. Clem went to purchase items for the family and himself, in readiness for the revival. Little Obie would get what was given to him. He wanted a little car. He marveled at the many fascinating shops they passed. Many of them offering mouth-watering tidbits, just beyond his reach! In the window of Millsaps Grocery, Clem saw a large stalk of bananas hanging from the ceiling.

Entering the store, Clem asked, "Would you like a bunch of bananas, Obie?"

The child had never seen so many. "You mean the whole bunch?" His eyes just about popped out of his head.

"No, silly, just a bunch off the stalk, perhaps five or six."

"Yes, I could eat that many. How many do you want?" Before the answer came he spotted a Tootsie Toy. Tugging at Clem's sleeve, Obie pointed to the shiny red fire truck attached to the top of a box of oatmeal. That, too, Clem purchased for his sibling.

Following their shopping spree the boys sauntered on down to the barber shop where Clem went in for a haircut. Obie waited on the sidewalk watching the traffic go by. Curiosity overwhelmed the lad at seeing so many folks, old and young, straggling about. They were all carrying packages much like his. It reminded him of Christmas, but then he thought how hot it was. "It must be just a very special day," he said. Leaning against the wall, Obie placed the grocery bag aside, gently holding the fire truck in his hands.

Inside, Clem was the subject of investigation as the Marshalls were well-known. Many knew Mell by virtue of his veterinarian deeds as well as for his work with the orchards. Clem would have assessed such a checkup, had it been given in Ponca City, as someone pickin' his brain. Being a hill man, he understood the inquisitive men, knowing they meant nothing more than just barbershop talk. Following their little quiz, they were ready to inform Clem on many happenings here about. Concerning his friends, one name particularly stood out. He instantaneously felt a yearning to be with an old girlfriend again. With that uppermost on his mind, his step had a spring to it as he left the shop. "Let's be going Obie." They quickly moved along down Main Street, crossed Sager Creek and the Isle of Patmas.

"Where are we going now?" asked Obie.

"We are going to Fine's Mercantile, the big store at the end of the block."

"What are we going there for? Do you know somebody to talk to there, too?"

"We're going there for the reason to buy some things that I want and for things you need."

"What do you want?"

"I want something for each of us, then some things for Martha, dad and grandmother. Just things, you'll see."

"How come?" replied Obie, scampering along beside his brother, hard pressed to keep up.

"Well, Grandma is fussy about her dress. She wants us to look good for the revival. We're going to see that she does."

"Don't we look good now? I heard Billy Porter say Martha really looked good."

As they approached the mercantile, Obie stopped to more closely observe the beautiful red wagon filled with school supplies which sat among the window dressing.

"Come, Obie, let's see it from the inside." But as they did, Obie lagged behind and moped about as a fish out of water. On the other hand the young man with more experience moved about with assurance, as a broker at the bank. Then Obie stopped and gawked at the immense stairway to the balcony with its ornate wrought iron and gleaming oak. Huge columns reached to the high ceiling of the second floor. The wide, low steps of the stairway were covered with bright carpet. This matching carpet led to the mezzanine. "I sure hope no body falls on the way up. They could get killed," said Obie.

For a few moments the boys walked along together among the isles of clothing. "I didn't know there was this much clothes in the world!" the child remarked.

"It's quite impressive, isn't it?" said Clem, wondering to himself what Obie would think of a modern elevator.

"May I help you, young men?" came the greeting from a lady up in her years. Like their grandmother, the gray-haired saleswoman wore a bun tied up on the back of her head. Her long dark silken dress and friendly appearance went to their hearts, creating the likeness of a familiar family member.

"Oh, we're just looking at the stair steps. Where do they go to?" blurted out Obie.

"They are most sensational, aren't they? They extend to the second floor, would you like shinny up?"

"Oh, no, thank you. I don't want to do that. I'll stay right down here."

"Aren't you Mell's boy?" asked the lady, speaking to Clem. "I know your father well and how is Carnie?"

"They're fine Ma'am, just fine and busy, that's why we're here. We're having a revival and I want to purchase a few things. Could you help me?"

"Yes, indeed. What did you have in mind?"

"Well, first of all I want a pair of overalls for Dad, he likes the Bull Moose brand." They were shown to a counter where wearing apparel of many brands were stacked high. He would purchase one of these, knowing it would please his dad.

"Was there anything else?" asked the clerk.

"Well, yes, there was, but I've never done anything like this. You see, I want to get a dress, a Sunday dress for my sister."

"I believe I can help you. This way please." She led them to the ladies' department where she again offered them a large selection of garments of all sorts. When it came to a gift for his grandmother, Clem had decided to make it yardage. From the vast array of bolt material, he chose what he hoped would make her happy. The saleslady, understanding the awkwardness of the boyish shopper, did not wait to be asked, but recommended a number of notions. Lace, buttons, thread and other items which the lad would have never known were needed, were placed with the yardage. A smile indicated his pleasure in her services and he relaxed.

Tapping Obie on the shoulder, he continued, "Now, I'd like some shoes and socks for him." They were taken to the shoes where Obie tried on several pairs, so many in fact that he felt embarrassed at all the shoes around him. Finally that purchase, too, was final and an unavoidable smile crossed Obie's face.

Again the saleslady came to his rescue when Clem seemingly lost his voice and stood dead still in his tracks, his eyes riveted to the floor.

"Was there something else?" asked the clerk.

"Ah, yes, there is. I want a nice box of candy."

"We have a nice assortment of chocolates. You want it for a young lady, I assume?" In the confectionery department Clem was shown a vast array of sweets from which to choose. Some with fancy bows and ribbons, some imported from overseas, and as in all assortments, the cheap, unattractive boxes Clem could sort out for himself as undesirable. In this division of the emporium, Clem felt secure in his selection, choosing a rather expensive brand, one well known for its quality, and in like manner, price.

Young Marshall asked that each gift be wrapped, gladly shelling out the cold cash which came to a considerable amount. Leaving the store, the saleslady watched the boys with the same undivided attention she had devoted to them in her sales. Being a personal friend of Mrs. Moss, she well knew the pleasure and delight that each thoughtful gift would bring.

Once out on the street Clem started straight for City Hall, leaving Obie to wonder what business they had there. "That's where they keep the jail," said he. "And the big fire truck. Can we see it?"

"Only for a moment," replied Clem, "I want to go to the hospital."

Obie, hurrying along with his long-legged brother, trying to keep up, asked, "Is someone having a baby?"

"No, Obie, I'm just visiting a friend."

"Is your friend dying?"

"No, she is not dying. She's just ill, okay?"

To Obie at least, they seemed to be walking faster and faster toward that big brick three story building at the end of the block. The fire department occupied much of the first floor, while the city jail held the inmates on the third floor. Sandwiched in between was the hospital and the city library. A long and very wide staircase led to the second floor. Obie held tight to the railing, looking back about midway to see just how far he would fall, should he slip on the unfamiliar stairs. He feared winding up in the hospital himself! At the top of the stairs they saw the familiar hand pointing to the library and another pointing the opposite direction for the hospital.

At the information desk Clem was given directions to Nellie's room and told that Obie should wait at the desk. With the several packages around him, he waited, patiently at first, then just waited.

Clem quickly found his way to Nellie's room. It looked out over the beautiful Sager Creek, which meandered its way through the city. This was the room into which Clem quietly entered. He recognized her view today as muted and cold.

Step by step he crept closer to the motionless young lady lying passively among the white sheets. Softly his hand caressed hers and she opened her eyes and tightened her grip around his strong tanned arm. Neither spoke for a moment, then Clem broke the silence, "I only learned today that you were here. I hope you will allow me to stay a few minutes. We have so much to talk about."

Her soft ivory shoulders pressed against the pillow. Pulling against his arm, the petite and flower like girl sat up. Her smile found its way through the mask of uncertainty while Clem's tight expression relaxed into his familiar boyish smile. For another moment he stood at her bedside, awkwardly holding the box of candy. Then he placed it into her pale and frail hands. He remained silent, though his face spoke for him. It was the language they both understood. She saw an almost imperceptible note of pleading in his face and she flushed with color.

Theirs had been an interesting courtship, strangely woven with intricate threads easily tangled by thoughtless gossip. Often there were bonds with little binding. Pretty words and promises both had been spoken and broken. Young love building to a crescendo only to feel the pain of having been torn and mangled. Nellie had more than once remarked when their friendship fell apart, that their romance had been cast from an ill-fated mold. For the moment though, Clem was with her again. In the twinkle of their eyes, they held, for a little time, the enchantment lovers strive to keep. Looking into his smiling face, Nellie thought, if possible, God willing, this just may be the last of the ebbing tide.

Quickly came the response from Clem as he reached for her hand. Hesitantly he held her trembling palm, placing a lingering kiss upon her sweet soft-toned wrist. Still holding her, Clem tightened his grip and timidly whispered the three words Nellie longed most to hear.

This romantic moment of passion again touched a soft spot in their hearts, allowing Cupid to release the tenderness of young love. Nellie raised her head giving cause for her long soft curls to fall over her shoulder against his arm. Their eyes met and for a second she watched the play of emotions on his face, and smiled at the sparkle of love in his eyes. Nellie's appearance took on a glow of radiance quickly noticed by her young suitor. Softly, the roughness of his work-worn hand touched her long blond hair. He smiled and his features softened as she had known them before. His lips brushed against hers, bringing her gaunt face back to life and loveliness.

Reckoned in moments, neither was aware of time passing. Clem, still standing at her side, experienced a gamut of perplexing emotions. Nellie, lying on her hospital bed, was lost in her own reveries, feeling her heart swell with emotions she had thought long since dead. Gently breaking his hold, Nellie picked up the box of candy. Then hesitant to unwrap the gift, she placed her arm around his waist. Teasing her, he took both hands pulling the ribbon completely from around the box.

"There, shall I tear open the paper, also?"

"No, you'll tear it all up." Then pulling it aside she earnestly got at the task of unwrapping. The aroma of the sweet milk chocolate seemed to fill the room replacing the fragrance from the jasmine that drifted through the open window.

Nervously Clem approached the subject he so dreaded. He knew Nellie's color was not good. He further knew her recovery from the illness would be lengthy. What he did not know was just how sick she was! He knew her appetite had not suffered.

"How long will you be here, Nellie? How long will you be confined to a room like this?"

"Dr. Hughes said, if all goes well, I can go home soon. That's all I know. I am feeling better, and your visit," then looking into his face again, she smiled. "Well, it means so much. Will you come again?"

"You know I will, again and again and then when you're better I'll take you home."

Those words though optimistically spoken with love, stabbed at the heart of Nellie. Clem, too, felt her hurt. She placed the box of candy on the white sheets and placed her hands in his. "Life seems to get tangled like a ball of yarn, everything is being turned upside-down! I can't be sure of anything."

"Nellie, you can be sure of one thing; you and I have another chance. I came to you. I want you to get well and get out of here. We can do things like we used to do, go places we have dreamed about. We can have a life of our own. You can have all the candy you want."

Nellie did not find any comfort nor did she see any humor in his words. She prayed daily for guidance from above. In her heart she knew the time would come when things would be better.

"Walk with me to the window Clem, I want to clear my head. I want to see the beauty of life out there. I want to have time to think about us."

Placing her feet into her slippers, she shuffled across the room supported by Clem's strong arms. In her bright flower printed gown her paleness was even more noticeable than before.

"Are you alright?"

Her face seemed flushed and she was leaning against him and the window for support.

"I never felt better, and yes, you can take me home. Where is that Clem, where is my home?"

The idyllic setting was always a source of strength for Nellie. Here she watched a pair of swans gracefully moving freely about. She saw the rock of ages, the cleft in the rock, the nesting of a bird. She saw what she wanted to see. Deep in her heart she saw what she wanted in life and she saw herself freed from the walls, from her hideous illness and for the moment, from those who had not shown love or kindness to her.

"I don't have all the answers," exclaimed the young man. "In fact I don't have any answers at all. Trust me, Nellie. I will come up with some. When I come again I'll bring more than candy."

Nellie held his hand as she turned from the panoramic view and slowly walked back to her bed of confinement across the room. She wished this moment could last forever; then her tender feelings caught the vibrations of her lovers tightened hand. His expression stilled and grew serious. For a few moments neither spoke, they had broadened the bonds between them by simply being together.

"I must go now, but I'll see you again soon, and hopefully I'll have the answer for when you will be going home."

Like the silence of his arrival, he departed. His petite true love again lay convalescing among the sheets, and for the moment, in total bliss.

Obie had looked through all the magazines in the restricted area. He had taken in all the views from the windows and had found them all much less fascinating than what others might see from windows. Perturbed by the long wait for his brother's return, he sat pouting, waiting for an explanation which he doubted would ever be given. Even so, when Clem came down the corridor like greased lightning, Obie blurted out, "What kept you so long?"

"I'm sorry, Obie. We'll talk about it later. Help me gather up the packages and us get out of here."

As they made their way to the staircase, Obie began to shift his packages, freeing one hand for a death grip on the handrail. "This is more dangerous than climbing the mulberry tree," he told Clem as they descended the steps. "This is the longest bunch of stairs I've ever seen! Do you reckon many people fall?"

"No, I reckon not, most folks can do it better than they could climb trees. Grandma climbs them. Could you see her climbing a tree?"

"What about going up? How do the sick folks make it to the top?"

"I don't think they do, Obie."

"I bet they don't either. Nellie must of not been very sick or she wouldn't of made it either."

"Oh, she's sick all right, very sick; but I'm sure they have a freight elevator for patients."

"You mean they put all them people in with the freight to take them up."

"I mean, never mind, just watch your step."

As he put his feet on the main floor, Obie turned around to see the monstrous staircase which seemed to threaten him, even by his just looking up.

Back on the sidewalk they lost no time in making their way back to the car. As they passed the corner drugstore which was owned by their uncle, Clem recalled how his uncle would howl out in a strong voice, "I scream, you scream, we all scream for ice cream." Then Clem smiled at Obie and said, "It was more scream than cream, I can assure you that."

They again crossed Sager Creek, and Clem led the way into the Ben Franklin's ten cent store. Clem spent a nickel on a soda pop, and Obie spent the same amount on a package of spearmint gum.

Obie was fiddling with his sticks of gum when they passed Shorty's barber shop. Suddenly Obie stopped and turned around. Backing up a few steps, he picked up a brown paper sack. "What are you doing, Obie?" exclaimed Clem as he watched the lad open the sack and look in.

"I forgot my bananas and left them here while you were getting your haircut. They're all here." Clem smiled and gave the once-over through the barber shop window to see if they were being watched. They were not. Clem turned and hurried out of sight.

Near the car they had to pass a vacant lot where two men were laying in a ditch under some brush. Obie presumed them to be ill, and pointed them out to Clem. Since they had not stopped to offer help, Obie asked, "What are we going to do?"

"We're going to get into the car and forget we saw them. They're drunk."

"What do you mean?" asked Obie as he had never seen men in that condition.

"I mean they are drunk, drunk, boozehounds. A wino if you please, what Grandma calls a reprobate!"

"I bet she could do something with them."

"I have no doubt about that. She'd likely get a stick after them and then pray for their sin. Yes sirreebob, she would do that. She would do something."

Driving the winding gravel road, narrow and hilly, constantly kept Clem watchful and attentive. Obie, on the other hand, paid little concern. His mind was bent around the packages. He had never seen purchasing on such a grand scale! Nor had he ever seen all the members of the family get new clothing at the same time.

"I suppose you think we've gone from rags to riches," said Clem. "Do you remember the summer we spent with Grandma Marshall? Cousin Neb came to town and you didn't get to play because your clothes were being washed and you had to stay in bed. You were always tearing up your clothes. You'd catch them on the barbed wire fence or snag them in the trees. The dog would rip them apart, too. I guess it was like Grandma said, they were threadbare and patch upon top of patch."

"I wonder what she'll say when she sees all these and my new shoes."

"Can't rightly say, Obie, but it won't be long before we find out. We'll go there first, no doubt she'll think I've spent too much and Dad's verdict will probably be no less. They seem to say a penny spent is a penny wasted. It's not, all these things were needed. We should not have to live in rags! It doesn't matter who's spending the money; there's never enough to go around. Times are hard, Obie. We live on the edge of poverty; all of us in the hills do. It's a way of life. We can't and don't need to go on just being, well, as outsiders call us, hillbillies."

Miles went by, then Clem spoke again. "One thing I do know, is that we all must get more education. I know that isn't dad's view at the moment, but take my word, get all you can. Go on to college like I did. Without it Obie you'll be just like dad, unable to get a good paying job. Unable to have the things you'll want. Never able to go see the other side of the mountain. Too ignorant to find your way to California."

The young brother had carefully been scrutinizing his new shoes, but had heard every word and understood enough to realize there were differences of opinion. "Do I have to do all that? Besides, I don't want to go to the other side of the mountains."

"My point is, you will, you'll see. Do you want to raise pawpaws all your life? Do you like to pick apples for a living? Look how hard Dad has to work, from sunrise to sunset and he expects that of us. Is that what you want? Not me!"

"Me neither." Then with more enthusiasm he said, "I want to be an engineer and drive the trains from here to Kansas City. I want to watch the big wheels turn. And I want to pull the whistle."

"Then you do want to see the other side of the mountain. Things will get better, Obie. Dad could see it if he would. It's just luck I suppose, but Dad's woes are less this year. If the heat over the next few weeks doesn't burn the pawpaws, we'll have a good crop. Already Dad has more orders that he has ever had! Last spring orders for sassafras came in faster than Dad could fill them! Then last winter the hunting was good, more hides than the year before. Even if you had only a short memory, you could see improvements. Do you remember a couple of winters back walking through the snow with burlap wrapped around our shoes because the soles were worn off?"

"I won't forget that! I think I froze my toes. I don't like the snow, do you? Now I have two pairs of shoes."

"These things are good, Obie. You see, we Marshalls have something that many other folks don't — it's called spunk! We have drive and want to get somewhere. You don't see happy pappys in our family! Our uncles and cousins are not on the front porch swinging in a hammock. They're out with the thrashing machine stacking straw. Take Uncle Earl, he's working for Standard Oil. Uncle Zeb finished at the university, the first of our family to do so. He's got a good job out in California!"

"Yeah, how come we didn't move when Aunt Minnie and Uncle Joe took their kids and went out there?"

"Well, you see, they had to move. The government bought their place and it's going to be part of a big lake. They've already started to work on the dam. Dad said Joe told him while they had all that big money they would just pull up stakes and try their luck in California. Even with their money Uncle Joe pulled out in the middle of the night to keep from paying some bills. Anyway that's told on him, may not be true. Don't say anything in front of Grandma. She's hurt over it and embarrassed to death! Anyway, we didn't get any money and Dad wouldn't leave Arkansas come hell or high water!"

The brothers continued their conversation until they viewed the little narrow lane leading to Hurst Manor. A tumultuous storm front had just passed through the area. Billowing clouds had developed during the heat of the day and were now dissipating. Distant thunder continued to rumble and the sky began to clear and have an eerie color, common to the dog days of summer.

Heavy foliage of the chinquapin tree gave an umbrella effect against the gentle rain still falling. It was here that Martha waited for the boys once she saw them coming from the top of the knoll. Each had their series of events waiting to be told, and likely to be repeated again.

Martha had no difficulty in being heard first. She began to bring out the events of her day, most of which were trivial as far as they were concerned, being nothing more than her whimsical girl talk. Then she did make some sense about the revival and a stranger that was to arrive. For one thing no one on Norwood Prairie was ever more open or receptive to the cause than she. So the boys let her talk, on and on, until she got it off her mind. Finally Obie could stand it no longer. His blunt interruption shocked Martha to silence, for a time giving Obie his chance to speak. "Look, Martha. Guess what I have in this box." Then holding up the mercantile sack containing the shoes, he waited for her reply.

Her slender hands, unconsciously twisted together, were held about her breast. Still pausing with uncertainty she took Clem by the arm and looked directly into his face. A warning cloud settled on her features and a look of confusion crossed her face. "Never mind that now, Obie. Put it aside. I don't know what it means, Clem, but you got a letter from the box today from Spradley, Coker and Lowe, attorneys in Little Rock. What does all that mean?"

"Attorneys you say, well I suspect it means information about my injury," said Clem. And none of them could then know the difference!

Martha's fears surfacing over the letter from the attorney were laid to rest. Obie was unconcerned. Martha took her brother at face value and Clem just let it drop knowing he would deal with it later.

It had been a wonderful day in the Ozarks. The late August heat had moderated, light showers in the area gave promise of good things to come. Clem welcomed the breath of fresh air he found here. He also had given thanks with his grandmother that a very good harvest was about to begin in his dad's pawpaw orchards. They had prayed together for the revival and were awaiting Evangelist Hallenbeck's arrival.

Clem's thoughts raced from their shopping spree to his visit with Nellie. His spiritual thoughts took him into the revival soon to be held under the arbor. He waited for its start up and quietly held the notion to himself that Nellie, too, would attend and find help. Clem's strong ties with his God were woven through the years with lasting threads from his grandmother. The matron's spiritual leadership would continue and bring to bear precious fruit in the family of God.

Excitement overflowed from Clem's heart as he asked Martha to help with the packages that lay about the car. As he opened the door, Martha saw the gifts strewn about and gasped with disbelief.

Again Obie was not to be denied. "Here, Martha," said he. "I bet you'll be surprised at what's in this bag." He tossed the package to his sister then spoke again. "And that's not all. There's more, lots more, look at my shoes!"

"Land sakes, Obie." Then with a long straight face she seriously rolled her big eyes in the direction of Clem and asked, "Did you buy them shoes?"

"Yes, I did and here's another little package for you."

Martha could not believe her eyes when Clem handed her the fancy wrapped package. "Can I open them now?" she asked. With Clem's favorable response, Martha removed a beautiful box from the bag, and exclaimed, "Good land, is that a dress?" Dumbfoundedly, she fingered the material then spoke. "How in the world did you pick such a purty one?" Holding her new Sunday-Go-To-Meetin' Dress close against her, she quietly said, "I think it'll fit. Can I go try it on?"

Clem smiled. "If it doesn't fit, we'll exchange it for another one prettier that will."

"Oh, I must try it on." As she turned to go, she paused, returning the dress to its box and taking the small unopened package, she made a dash for the house.

The boys, taking the remaining packages inside, presented them to their grandmother.

"What on earth have you done, Clem, spent all that money?"

"I've had a wonderful day, Grandma, especially getting this one for you." Then he handed her the gift. The giving made him think of the joyous season of Christmas!

"Land sakes, boy, you've lost your reasoning. I'm too old for such as this."

"Go ahead, Grandma, open it up. I hope it's in time for the revival!"

"Law me," she exclaimed as yards of the soft material began to gently fall to the floor. She examined the tiny floral patterns. They were as she would have wanted, had she chosen it herself. Looking up to Clem somewhat apologetically, she wiped a tear from her eye. "But my, my, it's so expensive and times are so hard. I hate to see you use up all your money, Clem. Time will come when you'll need it so bad."

"Don't you worry about that, Grandma. I have a good job."

Martha rejoined them wearing her new frilly dress, less concerned of the cost than her grandmother had been. "I do declare if this ain't the purtiest dress a girl ever had. Won't I look nice at the revival?"

Clem was pleased all would look nice. He knew none of them ever possessed what most folks did, but now they could all be less concerned with that worry and more attuned to important things, theirs as well as his. The gospel truth was, that he could not extend his stay in the Ozarks long enough.

It was as he had often heard his father say, make hay while the sun shines, and there was a lot of haying to be done! When in the oil field he worked hard. When he was home he kept his nose clean and to the grindstone, yet enjoyed himself. When the revival was over he would be returning to Ponca City, and now he pondered a new twist, Nellie. "Grandma, I'm going to bring Nellie to the revival. What do you think about that?"

"Well, I'm afeared to do much thinking anymore but reckon if I did I'd think that's just the thing you ought to do! Oh, by the way, I almost forgot to tell you, there's a letter here for you from a lawyer company in Little Rock." Then she lowered her head and tears fell down her cheeks.

VI

Coming to the Arbor

REVEREND Hallenbeck had very carefully mulled over his plans for driving to the Ozarks. Beyond the spiritual aspects of the revival, there would be social and leisure time spent in the hills. From Norwood Prairie he could quickly travel with ease to the Boston Mountains. He was a man of God and no less a man of nature who loved to travel. He would see all the great plateau had to offer.

He called this time to the hills his mountaintop retreat and anticipated nothing less than going to Shangri-la. It would be a double-barreled exposure, the best of both worlds. He would be among old friends in the very old hills. He would be bringing the old gospel story, one he loved to tell and one he knew from experience, they loved to hear.

In the predawn hours the parson drove higher and higher, ever deeper into the hills. The breeze coming through the open window felt pleasantly refreshing and the pungent scent of the pines captivated his sense of smell.

At a roadside pullout he stopped. It was still before sunrise, brilliant chariot clouds drifted across the horizon while the deep valleys were veiled in blankets of fog. Looking ahead he saw higher mountain peaks, these were the great hills through which he must pass.

What could be seen were columns of curling smoke, drifting from cabins. Overhead an eagle soared gracefully to her nest perched among tight branches along the cliff's edge.

There were sermons here in the quiet restful niche. Regrettably they must wait for a more appropriate day. For now he wanted to move on. He was focusing on the valley far below and the unseen mountain lake. The downward side of the wooded peaks inspired the traveler to keep moving on. His intentions were to reach Hidden Valley in time for some good early morning fishing before pressing on to the Ozarks.

Heavy dewdrops glistened among the tall grasses, sparkling profusely like the polished diamonds of Murfreesboro. Whispering pines lined the roadway like sentinels guarding the way. The five or so miles of scenic drive from the summit passed quickly. With that range of mountains now behind him, ahead lay the idealistic Hidden Valley.

Gigantic walls of limestone formations jetting out from the back side of the mountain, framed the fountainhead of an emanating spring. This narrow gorge extending less than a mile, broadened out until it converged with a prairie, becoming flat and featureless. Halfway between these and tucked away among the groves of giant beech trees, loomed unforgettable Lake Lejeune.

Paradise. A fisherman's visualization of having arrived at the perfect place. This was one of those rare times in a man's life when all the necessary elements came into play at the precise moment. The time was right, and he was right at the time, for being there.

A sign by the highway department warned of "No maintenance beyond this point." Nevertheless, nature had provided a made-to-order parking lot without an attendant or fee. Cars, trucks and old jalopies were parked haphazardly about.

The clean crystal water, nippy even for trout, plunged over a small natural dam. Flowing gently on, the water formed a long narrow lake.

An early morning breeze ruffled treetops and brought down little droplets of dew which, when touched by the sun's rays, brought beams of light shimmering upward. A slight mist hovered over the water. The pastor, enjoying the invigorating time of day, listened to the murmuring among the needles of the pines. They were a welcoming voice. He stood there for a few moments, close to his mountain lake, eagerly looking down into the clear water. Deep down, near the bottom he could clearly see a big bass and his thoughts turned immediately to bringing him up. As he turned for the car and his gear, he saw, in a limited view, a large buck deer, standing somewhat camouflaged in the cattails of a nearby marsh.

The enormous buck stood still as a stone, looking dead away. But quickly he turned his head, eyeing this human figure closely. A smart old buck learns where to go and when to leave. The animal darted into the heavy brush and vanished from sight.

Jeremy Hallenbeck also did a disappearing act. He wanted to test the lake farther away from the regulars. He always found more to his liking beyond the thickets and overhanging rock. The water was deep, shaded, and seemed to be filled with a smorgasbord of aquatic foods. Among the food chain promoting growth, were the hellgrammites, leeches and salamanders. Also, small fish such as chubs and darters churned the water. Jeremy carefully hastened down the trail, yet cautiously for he knew the hazards of climbing over boulders that lay in the pathway. Underbrush and clinging vines constantly became entangled with his clothing and fishing gear. By the time he reached the chosen site, he and his gear appeared to be species of a horticultural collection. That did not matter. Instantly taking a minnow lure from the tackle box, he secured it to the line. Placing a light lead weight a few inches above the lure, he cast it far out into the lake.

As he began to work the line the minnow spun about, just under the ripples of the water. With experience and patience Jeremy reeled, then let the line drop. Again he would repeat the process until it came close to shore.

There were no strikes until his third cast. Then the lure gently fell at the trunk of a fallen tree. A strong hit from a trophy bass pulled the line into the lily pads and the pursuit was on!

The thick stems of the aquatic forest, in which the line had become tangled, suddenly became motionless. Jeremy felt the tug on the line and listened to the reel click, click, click as the fighter became free of the entanglement and darted for deeper water. Jeremy kept the line taut yet allowed enough pull on the line for the fight to continue. The fisherman knew he had a good size catch, and enjoyed the fight as a good part of fishing. He was in no hurry, allowing time and line to play its course.

When the rod began to show less of a curve, the angler reeled in the line closer and closer until a great splash troubled the still water. This was repeated again for the fight was not yet over. Then one final unyielding surge for freedom proved futile. Jeremy had his trophy, a large rainbow trout weighing in at seven pounds and four ounces.

Removing the lure, the fisherman spoke, "That's one minnow you didn't like the taste of old man. Let me take it away from your face." With a quick motion of the wrist the hook was removed and the lunker secured to a stringer.

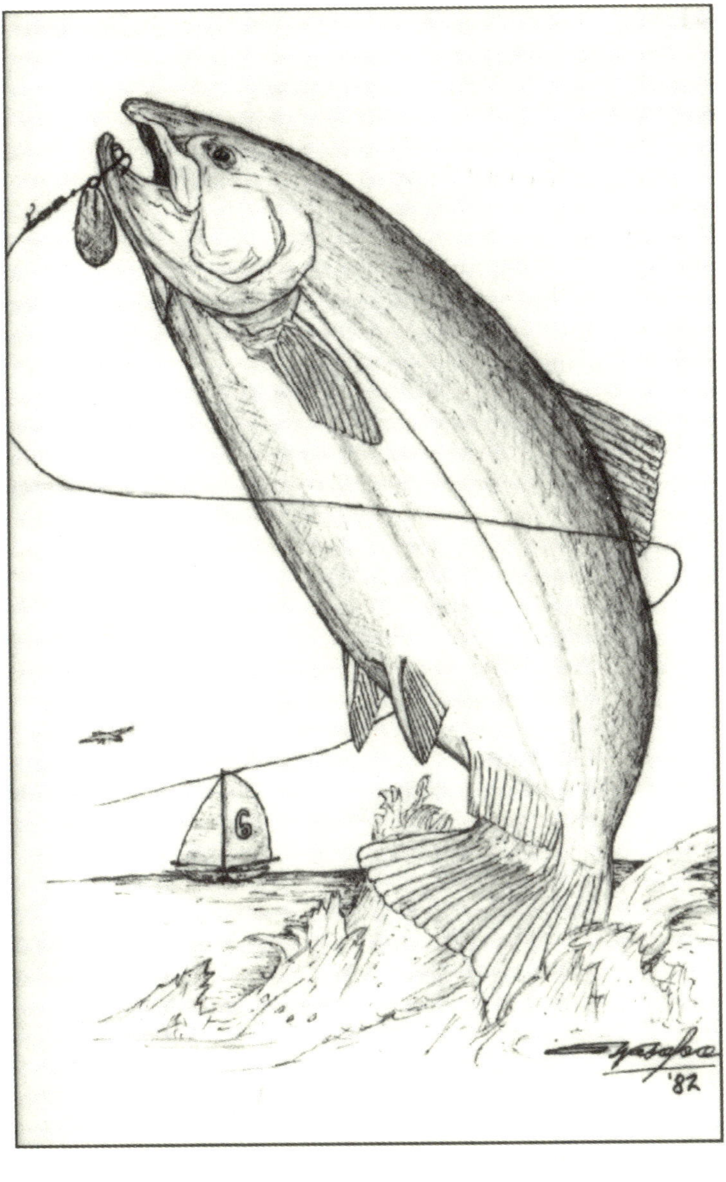

Lake Lejeune was more than a fisherman's paradise, it was a place of beauty. Formed with a small spit and on it Jeremy chose to make another cast.

Here he assured himself of another fine catch. It held another plus, also, the essence of serenity! Still water, like glass, reflected the morning rays of light. A perfect calm, a perfect time and place! There were movements occasionally when a frog hopped from a lily pad, making ripples in the sea of glass. Then, too, a fish thrashed up, starting other circles to move across the cold water.

With a change of menu, in went the hook. As it slowly sank, he felt play against the line and a burst of adrenaline brought him to full alertness. His sensitivity told him immediately that this was not in the same size bracket. But so what, let the less-than-hoped-for play. Jeremy would enjoy the action. After some length of time the rod moved, down went the line and the hook was set! Out of the water came the catch, a decent pan size bluegill. Jeremy held the fish firmly in his hand, then added him to the stringer. "Well, I'll have two at least when I stop for dinner," said he.

Now the old angler could be thankful for all his learning at the fishing hole. He was thankful for all the enjoyment found here. As the sun moved across the sky Jeremy knew he would be moving along up the mountain. Other sportsmen or just someone else looking for peace of mind would step where he now stood. He, too, would be anxious to take advantage of the wonderful opportunity Lake Lejeune provided.

There was yet time for the virtuous fisherman to afford the luxury of one more special touch of splendor. In doing so he used great caution in proceeding for the next cast. Choosing the right bait and placing the sinker strategically on the precise filament, were both of the utmost importance. Casting, too, was an artful piece of work. As he saw his canvas, from sky to sky, it was all laid out in perfect harmony. Streaks of light sun, played against the shadow of dancing leaves hanging above his head. Azure skies from the vault of heaven filled him with the closeness of God as having come afresh from a cathedral.

A coffee can containing crayfish, sat near the water and from that tin, Jeremy selected a nice big fat one, strong and active. Jeremy took the critter like a chicken after a June bug, "Buddy it's all over for you, no more backing away. You're a menu at the bottom of the lake." Spitting on the critter, the crustacean was then hurled to the depths pinching and probably still trying to back out.

Jeremy glanced up at the morning sun. Mere slivers of coral rays pushed back the low hanging mist that had been the screen between night and dawn. A water thrush flying low over the lake warbled at the intruder with the rod and reel. The aerial acrobatics of a pair of blue and green-winged teal rose from the lake. Circling they rose high into the sky. "Goodby my fine feathered friends and a happy flight if you're leavin' early for South America." The pigeon-sized ducks just gave several quacks, and moved on from their short stay on the picturesque body of water. They would quickly find another, being gregarious by nature. When fat and plump many of them would fly away from these Ozarks some never to return.

The great outdoors was indeed a challenge for Jeremy. Next to his spiritual fervency, the wonders of nature filled out his way of life. He was warm, and personable, strong yet gentle. His joy was part and parcel of harmony with his God, in whichever cathedral he might be found. Today he was found traveling through the lanes of the land, in nature's cathedral. Tomorrow he would be in the great hills of the

Ozarks, thus culminating his earthly and spiritual joys in the old brush arbor.

Overhead a pair of fox squirrels was chattering, romping and jumping from limb to limb. They had warmed themselves by the first rays of the sun, now a serving of acorns was on their menu.

These were the great woods, filled with adventure and grandeur. Enchanting lakes teaming with fish, lured those seeking diversion from the work-a-day world. Jeremy was enjoying his traveling time and the quietness of the near wilderness. Now his steps must take him back to the old fishing hole near the great gravelbar, where he had parked. Proudly carrying his take, he moved quickly along. The area was no longer quiet; sounds of a machine broke the stillness. An old pickup truck came bumping to a stop near him and a young man approached. Jeremy put down his bait-can, leaned the rod against a tree and spoke. "Good morning young man, I heard you coming back a ways, sounds as if your Tin Lizzie's got a rattle."

"Howdy. Nice mornin'. Catched any fish yet?"

"Well, yes, I have, praise the Lord." Then he pointing to the stringer, "A nice little catch, yes, indeed. Are you fishing this morning?"

"I'm going to cut me a pole and drop in a hook. Do you have any bailin' wire? I gotta tie up the old muffler if you have."

"I do happen to have some binder twine, do you suppose that would work?"

"Yeah, it will work. I don't recollect seeing you here before, where you from? That's a good piece of gear you got."

"I'm from down in the big valley, and no, I don't get to come up like I'd like to, but when I do, I fish. I'm on my way to the Ozarks, up around Fayetteville. Did you ever hear of the place?"

"Yeah, I know where it's at. What are you doin' up in the hills?"

"I'm a pastor, going there to hold a revival."

"You mean you're a preacher? Is that what you do?"

"You might say that. You see, young man we have it within our grasp to enrich the lives of our contemporaries by caring for them in a personal, meaningful, Christlike manner. I do my utmost to carry forth as He commands."

"Then I guess folks call you a 'do-gooder.' My papa would, but that wouldn't be any cause to hurt you. He's a drunkard."

"Son, I've been called pretty much everything, including the jargon of which you speak. It doesn't bother me. It's just part of the chaos and carnage that characterizes men without God."

"What teachin' do you hold to, Reverend. Sounds like you're a hard shell Baptist? Not that I have anything against them."

"I'm with the reformation movement known as the Church of God, ever heard of them?" Then he waited for an off the cuff remark. The young lad was still, perhaps troubled thoughts kept him from speaking.

"You all handle snakes then!"

"Lord, no, I'm deathly afraid of the devils! But you're right, there is a group who differs with us yet bear the name. You see, young man, we believe in a genuine experience of justification by faith in Jesus Christ, sanctification by the Holy Spirit, and holiness in our everyday living. We teach the thought, a united church for a divided world. That is, we aim for unity of faith and fellowship among believers. Allow me to get the binder twine and I'll help fix your car. Sounded like it's backfiring pretty bad too. Can't do any thing about that, but we sure can tie up the pieces."

The older man found the spool of heavy twine and placed it on the running board of the car. "Here, I want to give you a couple of magazines. They're from our movement headquarters in Anderson, Indiana." Then he handed the tall lanky boy the *Gospel Trumpet* magazines. "Take it and read it, young man, you'll see what the church is, and what it can do for your life! It's helped me! By the way, I'm Jeremy Hallenbeck. What might your name be?"

"Jed Farley. I live down the road a piece. My pa runs a sawmill and we hack a few ties for the railroad."

"Well, Jed, let's look at your trouble here." Then the pastor crawled under the car and began searching. "Oh, here it is. You've got a broken tail pipe, and a loose connection to the exhaust. Fetch me the twine. I can fix it up for a time, but you'll need to take care of it soon or this will break and worsen the problem. Is that your place back up the road a piece? I think I saw a small house in an isolated valley, perhaps smoke coming from a burner."

"That's it, that's where we live. Pa owns the whole valley."

"I'll tell you what, Jed, I'd like to stop and visit you and the family on my way back. I'm only going to be up there a few days and I'll have time to stop on my return. Tell the folks I'll stop. But for now let's get back to the fishing hole. I want to make another cast or two. Then I must hurry on."

It was a long quiet spell. Neither caught anything nor talked. Then as fishing goes, both anglers began to catch large bream. Time after time these scrappy little fighters were added to the stringers, the pastor giving the bulk of his to Jed.

Finally, time running its course, Jeremy knew it was time to put aside the rod and prepare for departure. Lifting the stringer from the water, Jeremy walked downstream a few paces and began the task of cleaning his fish. He had reason for being proud of his catch. They were the grand makings of his afternoon meal. He packed them well in the icy water of his food chest, then placed it back into the turtle hull of the car. "So long, Jed. I hope you catch the big ones and tell me all about it when we meet again. Remember to tell the family I'll be dropping by." Then they shook hands and the pastor waved goodby as he drove around the cane break and out of sight.

Reflections that lingered in his mind were of the young man, not of the placid lake or trappings of the worldly ways, including his. Rather, he thought of those preachers and teachers who would lead men to think that a Christian's life is trouble-free. Often had he heard it said, they surely have committed some sin for their plight to be in such a state.

"Nonsense!" he spoke aloud. The Farley family, thought he, may not be righteous, and if they are, like others, " . . . many are the afflictions . . ." Yes, he would indeed visit them on his return trip.

The Reverend pondered the thought of what the young Farley saw in him. Was it denominationalism? Was he a peculiar one? Had he represented the cause of Christ in a suitable fashion the young man could and would relate to?

The hours quickly passed. Rising hills were always followed by pastoral dells, nestled in the grandeur of green pastures and feeding cattle. Always the ranges beyond were edged in a misty blue, making the distance seem farther away.

From here one wondered if the road went on forever! But, no, he remembered being told, this road has never gone anywhere! It's the traveler who passes by seeing only that which he chooses.

The man of God who traveled these hills often, saw in them the works of God. He heard the pleasant sounds of His creation, and recognized all this as a sanctuary, a haven for weary souls. He had a vision of a place of worship nestled under the strong and mighty arching branches of the century old oaks. Music filled the valleys and echoed back to the mountain tops, each note pure and reviving. The wind that blew across the tree tops brought yet another majestic sound. It was the seasons which gave one the newness of change.

Spring brought music of hope, a symphonic orchestration of new life filled with faith. Summer held the notes that swayed the dog days of the season. Autumn, the season of color, held a myriad of splendor. Under a mantle of white, the hills sparkled like rhinestones, ushering in the season of winter. Each season played out its part in the sounds that moved the spirit. Jeremy heard each note and did more than dream of the day when he would see a church in this wildwood that truly reflected the image of the people who worshiped their God in such a natural setting.

Jeremy never forgot the standing invitation of the folks on the plateau. His acceptance would have been instantaneous to their calling had he made a personal decision. His desire to be a part of building up the Church was always like unto a consuming flame. Today there was still a spark. Undoubtedly, standing on the mountain top tomorrow, a new surge of thinking would again consume the man of God concerning his Ozark cathedral.

Shadows covered the roadway and great columns of dust swirled up behind the car as it continued to inch its way farther and farther toward the top of the mountain known as Petit Jean. Here Jeremy would camp for the night in what he often called "God's special gift to what later became Arkansas!"

While the wheels of his vehicle kicked up rock and more dust, Jeremy's mind was on the Word. He continued to drive on, yes, but his reflection was on God. "I will lift up mine eyes unto the hills, from whence cometh my help." And he seemed to see them all. One eye was looking Heavenward, the other kept on the terra firma. His memory turned the pages to the Old Testament and as easily as the Psalm had been recalled, so now was Deuteronomy 11:11.

> "But the land, whither ye go to possess it, is a land of hills and valleys, and drinketh water of the rain of heaven: A land which the Lord thy God careth for: the eyes of the Lord thy God are always upon it, from the beginning of the year even unto the end of the year."

Suddenly the weight of his foot on the accelerator pulled away, allowing the movement of the car to become slow. A rider with Jeremy always knew when he was either tired or in deep thought. It was always the same, less speed.

Bolts of lightning and earth shaking thunder returned his forward motion beyond what it had been; and caused his heart to skip a beat. He had neglected to notice the gathering storm presently descending upon him. In the space of a moment the dust had settled. Dark angry clouds gathered around him, forcing him to pull to the side of the road and wait out the storm. The fury, short in duration caused little delay. Water soon filled the low ditches as well as the chuckholes in the road.

Slowly, he continued on, anxiously watching for the sign, "Petit Jean's Viewpoint." Had it not been for the fact that he had been here before, he might have well become lost. The highway department had done next to nothing in welcoming the visitor to Petit Jean's mountain. Perhaps this was the reason he was the only visitor on the mountain. That within itself was of no concern. He would be among the finest company tomorrow. For the moment he must wait for the passing storm, then find, in some remotely dry corner of the canyon, kindling for starting a fire.

Natural hunger pains swept through his stomach like wild fire among the pines, gnawing away for his attention until decisive action was taken. Smoke billowing up around a pan of frying fish could no longer be delayed. A brief search quickly turned up the dry wood, where it was promptly placed about the wide flat rocks in the designated cooking area.

At the picnic table Jeremy arranged a few choice items he had brought for his evening meal. The fish, caught early in the morning, now went through careful inspection and passed. They had been kept very cold, and would now grace his table, a gourmet's delight truly fitting for a camper's prayer of thanksgiving.

Jeremy opened the attache case which lay on the corner of the table and removed his favorite Bible, a worn and well-marked King James which had been his father's. Wiping his hands on his trousers, he turned to the Word and for a few moments read in silence. When again he raised his eyes from the Book, skies had brightened, tranquil breezes stirred through the pine needles fabricating a soft gentle sound sweeping through the tops of the trees.

Before one could say Jack Robinson, flames fed by tender dry kindling swept up around smoking logs sending a woodsy scent drifting down the valley. Jeremy, the connoisseur, painstakingly watched the sizzling fish. The woodsy scent filled not only the valley downstream, but the cook's nostrils as well. He unconsciously moistened his lips as his taste buds became activated. Just a few seconds more and the tender morsel would be proof of the country's exquisite dining. He was ready. The man of God pushed back from the flame and the food, and bowed his head. "The heavens declare his righteousness, and all the people see his glory." Then he paused. Continuing with his prayer of thanksgiving he said, "And Lord, all my senses are acute for which I'm thankful. Now I ask that I may be blessed by these fish Thou has provided as I am now enjoying the aroma around the campfire in this mountain top experience. Amen."

Removing the green hickory rotisserie rod from its frame, the mountain cook carefully removed the smoked trout, placing it across his plate. Convinced cuisine cooking should be exotically prepared, Jeremy garnished the serving with a sprig of freshly taken watercress. Then with a tilt of the head he looked about and plucked a few leaves of the plentiful sheep sorrel for a special taste. "There," said he. "Was there ever such a spread on this table, and all to the glory of God?"

It had been a great dinner and a most wonderful day. From the top of the mountain where they long ago laid to rest the young French lady, Jeremy looked down on the beautiful Arkansas valley. It seemed as though he was standing on the top of the world, higher than Mount Everest. Actually he stood at the brink of the mountain, looking down into the chasm and the distant fields that spread out to the horizon. It gave him a dizzy feeling, then stepping back a pace he sat down and marveled at the view. Gradually, the hues of sunset turned the warm rays of color to that of pale blue and purple. Evening settled in along the canyons and long shadows seemed to march across the fields. It was time, too, for Jeremy to think of the night.

Finding a perfect group of old trees for shelter, Jeremy threw down his bedroll, content to spend the night among these snarled timbers that had been standing there for who knows how long. He marveled at the fossils embedded in the jagged columns rising from the valley floor and wondered how long it had been since creation, as in "the beginning." Sleep eluded him even after long prayers. Tossing about trying to find a more comfortable position he looked out into the darkening sky and the faint twinkling stars. He remembered the childhood prayer he had recited so often and spoke aloud the closing line:

> "If I should die before I wake,
> I pray thee Lord my soul to take."

It had been a long time since he had said those lines, indeed it had been a long time since he had enjoyed such a mountaintop experience. Sleep unexpectedly crept over Jeremy and colorful dreams filled his short season of night.

Rays of the rising sun flashed across the morning sky. The day brightened to full glow and fleecy clouds passed by almost within arms reach. Jeremy leaned against the limestone pillars and tightened a blanket about himself, fending off the sharp chilly wind that blew across the blunt end of the mountain.

The rarity of the moment dictated that he stand there a few more moments. This magnificent obsession could be an omen of another of God's perfect days. From his cleft of the rock, as it were, the pastor keenly watched a chipmunk play among the snarled and interwoven branches of an aged cedar. Somehow the tree had managed to withstand the force of the wind, and the lack of little moisture. He hoped the inquisitive little creature scurrying about the grotesque cedar would fare as well.

Cloaked in pockets of drifting fog, the lesser valleys which led away from the mountain, were hidden from view. The world seemed to be shut out and Jeremy alone seemed to be in possession of the land on which he stood. "Actually," said he, speaking to himself, "This is my Father's world, and I'm thankful to be able to trek across these parts again."

Being neither a loner nor a man without friends, the pastor nevertheless felt the closeness of his God. The vast expanse of the grand plateau was just that, an uplift, never depressing nor an empty void. Jeremy stood on the highlands with wonderment and praise, but he was not alone!

In this beauty that was as broad as one could see, the lone man viewing from the edge closed his heart and hands, closing everything away from his moment in prayer. It was a silent time, only the air current brushed against his face. Whispers echoed as the forces of nature continued to cut the canyon still wider and sharpen its edges. Erosion of time, too, met with force as Jeremy turned and slowly walked to the car.

Now it was on to the everlasting hills of the Ozarks, and in that direction he made his way down the mountain and out into a broad valley. A sea of grass waved before him, dotted with cattle. Here and there a farmhouse gave evidence of a prosperous family while at the same time an old rickety car passed telling another story, that of someone looking for still greener pastures. He knew they would find them, but wondered where!

Jeremy knew it was the best of times, and like the man writing so long ago, he, too, knew it was the worst of times! Mistral dust storms from the west choked the sky, while wailing winds incessantly raged for days. The burning and scorching of the dry and thirsty land outlasted many folk who were not heeled in. They traveled west, always west with little more of value than a prayer. Mattresses and old straw-filled ticks covered the top of cars while spare tires and utensils were often tied on the back. These were the good folks who had lost all. They had nothing more to give up.

Being a realist, Jeremy felt the heartache of these who fell through the cracks of society. Being a man of God, he also felt the plight of their worn, torn hearts. His dealing with it daily was more than this passing of the ways. It went beyond the bare and nugatory ditty, Go with God. His consciousness of life was God with us, and to that end he traveled on.

The weary travelers passed from his sight, as did the flat valley terrain. Pine trees now stood where grazing cattle only a few miles back dominated the landscape. Each winding turn of the road led farther upward into a forest of tall trees and floral fields of color. Suddenly, he knew he had made it to his beloved hills! A shot of adrenaline surged through his veins when before him he saw the sign, Welcome to the Ozark National Forest.

VII

The Rose around the Briar

WALKING through the pawpaw orchard Mell and Jeremy took careful stock of the fruit, some were ready for harvest. The summer heat which had given ample cause for apprehension only a few days ago, now faultlessly brought a sweet flavor and bouquet to the strange Ozark fruit. The slender branches curved downward from the weight of the ripening fruit as a bumper yield hung in Briarcliff Orchards.

"I haven't found a single ripened paw yet," said Mell, "which gives me time for the revival without interruption."

"Well, thank the Lord. Again we see that His timetable is calculated correctly."

Mell, reaching up, plucked a paw with uneven color. "This was my fear," he exclaimed, "blistered fruit, but the damage, if any, is negligible. I'll tell you, Jeremy, it looks more promising each day. Which reminds me, day after tomorrow I'm to go to the city and have dinner with the chamber of commerce. There I'll give a little speech, then do something like cut a ribbon. It's the first annual Pawpaw Festival. Can you beat that? How about going with me? It'll be the darnedest thing you've ever seen!"

"Yes, I expect it will. I've been to opossum pouts, frog jumps, watermelon festivals and other interesting festivals of the like. But I must say I've never had the occasion of being to anything associated with the pawpaw fruit. I dare say it's much like other festivals, isn't it?"

"I'm no authority on any of that stuff. As they say, it's a new wrinkle to me. I do know a good number of folks here about have been putting in a lot of time on the thing."

"It's wonderful, Mell, good publicity." The pastor then paused and picked a near ripened paw.

He held the small odd-shaped fruit in his hand. Then looking at Mell, the pastor reassuringly spoke of the virtues of a good man. "Like so many things in life, this paw is the ultimate fruit which God has in His plan for you. He truly wants to bless His people. Sometimes we are disappointed, there is no fruit. Or, what there is, may be sparse and of poor quality. Praise God, this year's harvest is evidence of His everlasting love. Proper conditions I'd say." Then the man gently kicked a few flint rocks with his boot, bending over he picked one up and held it in his other hand. "I'm reminded of the Song of Solomon where we're given a glance of God's view of His garden. There He calls us His chosen people, His bride, the Church, you and I, His garden. In those pure and poetic words He draws us a word picture, a garden filled with herbs and spices, flowers and fruit."

Tossing aside the flint rock, he cautiously put the paw into his shirt pocket. Taking a small Bible from another pocket, he opened it to the Song of Solomon. From chapter four verse fourteen, he read verbally until he had finished the passage.

> "Spikenard and saffron; calamus and cinnamon, with all trees of frankincense; myrrh and aloes, with all the chief spices:
>
> "A fountain of gardens, a well of living waters, and streams from Lebanon.

"Awake, O north wind; and come, thou south; blow upon my garden, that the spices thereof may flow out. Let my beloved come into his garden, and eat his pleasant fruits."

Then with a wave of the hand he spoke again, "Mell, you have taken this hilly, rocky land and turned it into a garden. Hard work and determination has brought you to the point where you can sing as Solomon did. You see, Mell, in the final analyses we are the total sum of all our own choices. You made those tough decisions as to who and what would be permitted to beat a path across your life."

Slowly, Jeremy moved on down between the rows of pawpaws. Mell followed, still giving the pastor time to speak again.

"I've been thinking, Mell. Isn't it about time you should find a beloved to share in your life and the children's? Someone who inspires, hears the sound of music such as you do. One who can enjoy the thundering waterfalls, and gentle streams. One who can hear the melodies of the wind blowing across the trees and grasslands. One to sit with, side by side and enjoy the fragrant blossoms in the season of spring. Mell, find a beloved to love and have compassion for. Find a wife whose music is hearing the laughter of the children and the respect of her husband's voice."

Jeremy closed the Old Testament and returned it to his pocket. "Our Lord's admonition was 'Seek ye first the Kingdom of God, and his righteousness; and all these things shall be added unto you.' Mell, someday, yes, someday someone, will walk through your garden of life. I hope you are planning that. Then the two of you can walk the pathways together, tend the orchards, care for the fruit and enjoy all the wonderful, Godly pleasures of life."

Mell was somewhat taken aback and momentarily reflected over the last few years of his life. He knew the most irresistible force upon the face of the earth was this love of which the pastor spoke. Love, the source of strength for men and women who would gladly serve and die for each other. It was this true and unselfish love he had known in Thalia. Though his love for her was emotionally difficult to express, it was enduring and eternal. There would never be another. Thalia was the only beloved he had ever known. The pain had lessened, yet no other name found lodging in his forever shattered heart.

The two men continued to walk the furrows neither speaking for several moments. Alone, in their anguish, neither knew how to speak. Both men still uncommunicative, did none-the-less, have the mind that they were up the creek without a paddle. They found themselves in an uncomfortable situation. Perhaps he had not dealt with it in the best manner, thought Jeremy. As men should do, they let the love of God fill their sorrowful hearts and His Spirit took ample care of their cries.

Finally, Mell could resist no longer. He frowned, though a brittle smile softened his face. Turning to his bachelor friend he said, half jokingly, "Jeremy, you're preaching to me about marriage?"

"Not preaching, just quoting scripture, 'And the Lord God said, it is not good that the man should be alone.' Has He directed you to Miss Right?"

"No, not yet, but I'm looking."

"That's what you said six months ago!"

"Yes, it's been that long and I'm still looking!"

With an almost hopeful glint in his eyes, Jeremy threw out another question. "Didn't I hear you were keeping company with Miss Porter?"

Mell's cheeks colored and he turned his eyes from the face of the evangelist.

Jeremy felt more secure in breaking the awkward silence as they sauntered down the orchard. His hope was that a conversation on the church would be just the positive change needed. "Changing the subject, Mell, what do you think of my sermon topic for tomorrow? I'm speaking on Rebirth, New life, and Recovery."

Mell smiled and began his reply, "You know my Papa used to say of bad lives and bad living, that it beats all hell. Sin to Moses, and sin to the world. Sounds to me your topic would surely cover all that sin. Yes, I'd say that was ready redemption."

The two men continued walking toward the end of the orchard. Rev. Hallenbeck thought of the importance of man's salvation. Mell thought of the spiritual awakening he hoped to see in the Norwood community. "Jeremy, I see it like this, it's true you have a hard work before you, but each one out there has his own responsibility. We'll work as if it all depends on us, and pray as if it all depends on Him. Remember even the prodigal son had to act. He arose and came to his father."

"Precisely! Through the foolishness of preaching, I feel many will come to receive Christ. A new chapter will be written here this week. I feel certain of that. Names will be added to the long list of those who walked with God. Those names of old, such as Able, Enoch, Noah, Abraham, will be joined by the Smiths and the Joneses here on Norwood Prairie. I believe it and thank God for it!"

Intermittent explosions suddenly shattered the silence around the men who now stood checked near the end of the orchard. Jeremy fixed his sharp gaze and tried to assess the disturbance in the lower valley.

"Oh, you'll have to get used to the death knell of that hollow. Its agonizing death is enough to tear out your hair. We call it the Big Bang. Those who are losing their farms and homes down there call it a steal by the government. Yes, it's a most unpopular adventure the government's taking on."

Long after the echoes ebbed away, columns of gray dust rose high into the crystal clear sky. The Ozark valley destined for change, could perhaps retain some of its respectable beauty. The useful dam holding back acres of water, could be seen, if properly viewed, as a sparkling gem rising out of the hardwood forest. The new lake would be surrounded by pedestal rock from an ancient sea. The new body of water would take its place in the community and only time would prove its worth.

Watching the big red sun cast a vermilion glow across the western sky, Jeremy was struck with awe! He could easily see, with vivid imagination, the future lake shimmering in a tincture mood of another sunset, another season.

Almost in reverence, Jeremy raised his hand, pointed to the picturesque view before him, then turning to Mell, he spoke. "I've seen the likes of this reflected out over the water as a tranquil sea of glass. I've seen the brightness aglow on the desert sand and watched the color of the mountain snow turn to hues of pink. But have I ever seen more splendor in a sunset than this Ozark spectacle now before us? I think not!"

At the edge of the pawpaw orchard, the men stood quietly for some time before moving on to Briarcliff Cottage. The afternoon had been well spent. Now evening silhouettes began to seal off the day.

Emanating from a cave under the house, a soothing flow of air cooled the cottage. For the time being Mell and Jeremy could relax and discuss a conglomeration of subjects close to their hearts. With the exchange of ideas and differences of opinion they sat well into the night. Finally, Mell realized it was time to retire and with a chuckle he slapped his hand against his leg, "I expect we've chewed that fat long enough."

Jeremy went straight to his quarters, knelt down by the side of the bed and prayed. As he was led by the spirit he petitioned the Lord for a spiritual harvest, praised Him for his many blessings, and remembered the low and lonely. Then he closed with the exhortation, "Bless the Lord, O my soul: and all that is within me, bless his holy name. Amen."

Rheumatism in a stiffened knee caused the pastor to flinch as he rose and stood by the window. Shifting his attention about the room, he was moved, becoming aware of the out-of-the-ordinary and remarkable room. It was as if an expression of the hills, scrupulously weighed and meticulously arranged, captivated the occupant altogether! The motif, perhaps best described as natural and raw, was done in good taste, and obviously by the hands of the Ozark man who indeed built the room from the ground up. It was his shangri-la!

Enchanted by the unique surroundings, the man of God felt at peace and relaxed in a cane bottom chair placed near a small table. As he studied the room more carefully, a prominent verse of scripture came to mind. In no time he had the makings for another sermon, paramount for his revival.

Hillside hideaways offering security and privacy are commonly found tucked under the canopy of the forest. This residence was no exception. What was unusual, was the manner of expression. Jeremy once again cast his eyes about the room, and as before, paused at the picture of Christ which hung above his bed. So dramatically framed, the unique sketch of the Lord truly reigned! It demanded more than a casual glance. The frame likewise, held a very special significance. Being a horse collar, it had previously cushioned the burden for the beast plowing furrows through the pawpaw orchards.

Tonight a man's burdens were lightened as he mentally plowed the fields of tomorrow's harvest. The flickering kerosene lamp cast faint shifting shadows across the bedroom only to fade away in the depth of night.

Seasons of prayer united the communities of Norwood Prairie and thereabouts, bringing the flock together in a call for "A United Church for a Divided World." Within this community of believers there were other factors at work as well.

One such dilemma, always present, was how to deal with the Hatfields and the McCoys. These disputes were not, nor could they be, kept hidden. At best, it could only be dealt with from time to time. This was again that season.

Delinquency of the spiritual nature brought causes of concern between brethren as well. One was unable or unwilling to understand the other. This too had to be redressed.

Business, everyone's business was the target aimed for by Mrs. Busybody! Many folks said she missed the target, or sinned, as it were. She saw it quite differently, just passing along information, not to go any further, you understand. She, too, was on the hearts who knelt in prayer just prior to the revival.

Doom and gloom, trial and tribulation gave a demoniac hold on those who were always negative. Nothing was white or black. Their cup, without exception, was always half empty!

These prayer concerns were truly a prerequisite for a great revival. As such, Rev. Jeremy Hallenbeck prayed.

Norwood Church again rang the bell, to summons the little congregation to worship. And, once again a rather large banner had been hung between two mighty oaks. The message, written with boldness, declared, HOLINESS UNTO THE LORD. Beneath it passed the men and women whose lives, with some variation, would be transformed.

Morning services found the faithful being blessed, the needy receiving help, and the Laodiceans in a quandary as to just what the phenomenon was all about. Throughout the day, individuals here and there commented about the morning service. Often their remarks could be measured by their position in the community. One such remark was made plain by an old-timer who was seldom seen, anywhere. "His sermon was as long as a well rope," remarked the old man. A young lady was heard telling her beau, "That preacher wasn't here the night they passed out the tune, I bet he couldn't carry it in a sack!"

The other side of the coin was heard also as two church fathers scrutinized the Reverend's message. Said one, "He sure knows how to talk turkey." Responding to the remarks the friend said, "Aye, he sure puts his cards on the table and his singing wasn't shabby either."

A more modest individual, speaking to her man over the dinner table guessed she was goin' to wait till the shoutin's over an' they gather up the singin' books, before she came to any conclusion. After all you can't judge the heat by one tongue of the fire.

Most everyone came to one conclusion, "We'll see what he can do tonight." They didn't have long to wait. Rev. Hallenbeck met with the spiritual life committee just before the evening service. He thanked them for their tireless effort and assured them of God's promises. Standing before them he smiled and inclined his head. "As the Father sent the Son into the world, so He sends us to serve our society. This is no soft life we live. But it is the restful way. It is the peaceful way. Indeed it is the best way, for after all it is His way!" Opening the Bible to Matthew 11:28 he read, "Come unto me, all ye that labor and are heavy laden, and I will give you rest."

As the services began the little party of believers rose from the slab benches and found their way toward the front of the arbor. Some brought quilts and blankets to cover the rock hard pews. Others braved the discomfort that might be prolonged.

Appropriate music flowed out from under the arbor bringing to life the quickening of God's word. As the song leader took his place a quietness fell across the gathering. Still, people filed in, taking what few seats were still empty. Among those finding their way to the back were Clem Marshall and Nellie Porter. Clem's father sat on the front pew with Mrs. Moss while Martha kept young Obie under control just behind them.

Most folks had no qualms with regard to craning their necks. Looking out of the corner of their eyes was also acceptable so long as they didn't turn their head sharply. Yet, knowing this would surely come about, they sat under the arbor unsure of what would happen next.

Nellie, frail and gaunt, also fixed her gaze on those around her. She saw no one except Mrs. Moss who had ever given her more than the time of day. She knew she could expect more than that. Nervously Nellie sat close to Clem and like a fish out of water, she felt a thirst to be elsewhere. But Clem had finally sweet-talked his dear friend into coming to the meeting with him. Now he, too, felt the tension over them and vaguely heard the liturgical sounds for which they came.

Martha observed her brother with Nellie as they entered the arbor. While her neck turned a shade of pink, it did not bend. She kept her vision straight ahead. It was no secret that she did not care for the girl, and she wouldn't try to hide it here tonight.

While father and son had, some time back, thrashed out their feelings, neither won. Consequently there were hurt feelings between them which would, from time to time become unleashed. There had been, however, virtually a cease and desist between them since Clem's return from the oil fields. This bonding was something the maternal grandmother prayed for daily.

Other eyes flashing about caught a glimpse of Buck Jones, a well-dressed man seated next to his wife and two children. Mell had made his acquaintance while touring the government project. As Chief Engineer, Mr. Jones was looking for a local man to help in the horticultural planning and future development of their undertaking. Mr. Jones, having heard of Mell's achievements and capabilities invited him to his office and gave him the grand tour. Impressed with what he saw and further information given on the project, Mell came to believe that after all, this was a good thing for the area. It had unquestionably stirred up the community like smoke in a beehive! Feelings ran high. Brother spoke against brother depending upon their relationship to the government's proposal.

Most of the citizens felt that the government was going too far in forcing relocation. Taking property, as they put it, that papa homesteaded. This was their roots. Their inability to eke out a living on the rocky hillsides changed few opinions. They were here and to this end they would remain!

Many of Mell's close friends had taken the egress path from their uprooted homes. Some had found a new life in faraway places. Others bemoaned the fact of defeat, only to resettle and live in discontent. If the government fared any better it certainly wasn't understood by the jaded feelings of the oppressed.

Day after day Mell lived with these inhibitions brought on by a changing society. Do this and do that. Take this and take that. Friends would say, "But Mell, you aren't losing your land to a lake." He fervently hoped that as he sat here night after night, he and all those with troubled hearts would find a quieting peace.

No doubt there were others who were hearing only part of what the evangelist was putting forth. Consequently, Mell was ashamed he had been unable to be completely attentive!

He stood with the others as the message came to a close and the many voices filled the night with a harmonious praise. Slowly, as always at a revival, the believers began to drift, one by one out from under the arbor. Obie broke loose from his sister's bounds to play with friends farther out in the church yard. Martha joined a small group of modest girls whose subject was songs for tomorrow night. Aunt Carnie politely listened to George Fetterly's retelling of his aches and pains. In turn he was courteous as she worked her way through the beds of leeks, garlic, and onions. Then of course their talk quickly focused on religion. On the other hand individual conversations could be heard which gave emphasis to another point of view.

Mell had worked his way from the arbor, intending to speak with a group of men standing under the trees. Quickly following behind him, Zola Porter breathed one word in a low, soft tone. "Mell." He recognized the tone of her voice and took the interception, coming to a standstill. They rarely spoke in public, yet Mell stood silent in a pensive mood undisturbed nor angered. Both were aware of the fact that various expressions and opinions would certainly follow them beyond this evening. Taking her arm, Mell tried to speak but his voice wavered as they strolled farther out into the parking lot under the darkness of night.

"I hope this isn't an inopportune time to speak to you, Mell, but I felt I must catch you before you got away."

"It's all right, Zola, they need to be doing something. Tomorrow they'll be as busy as a stumped-tailed cow in flytime. But what's on your mind?"

"More troubles, they seem to follow me like a shadow."

As they spoke, a respectable lady of the community could not resist the temptation to learn more from close up. Stepping out of her truck she hotfooted it directly across their path!

"Good evening, Zola and Mell." Then with a sheepish grin across her furrowed face, the unwanted stranger headed for the arbor.

"She's going to be late for the prayer time," declared Zola.

"She's going to be late for more than that, and you can bet she's not on her way to the mourners bench!" replied Mell. "But," said he, "back to your troubles, what are they?"

"I've got to move out of that shed-of-abode, and quick! It's the project men, they get closer and closer blading dirt and driving stakes. Right now there's a row of pickets up against the barn, looks like a fence. I know I was told to leave several days back, but to where, Mell?"

Pointing to the car he said, "Wait there, I'll be right back." Moving in opposite directions again, she only paused a moment, then reaching the car she quietly opened the door and sat, chagrined, flustered, and bothered.

In the light that came from the arbor she watched as Mell spoke to Clem. Their gyrations indicated a hurried conversation and indeed he did quickly turn, and leave. Rejoining Zola in the car Mell turned on the ignition and drove out onto the highway.

Neither spoke for several moments. Zola constrained by a woman's intuition. Mell's tight-lipped stillness shaded his private thoughts, protecting him in the way men understand.

Of the two, Zola at the moment was the stronger. Again her grasp of the situation came more easily and with strength, she was able to deal with it.

In a lamenting voice and with a rueful expression on her pale face, Zola spoke as tears welled up and ran down her cheeks. "Mell, as a woman I can be more forthright coming to a barbed point than can you as a man. It hurts just the same and I understand your hidden feelings, the inside of you that doesn't want to be known. Do you hear me?"

"I hear you."

"Mell, I yearn for a few moments to be with you. You're not as naive as not to know this, but I want you to hear it from me. I have no class, and you're the gentleman! I have not hounded you and you are not flirting with me, but I do ask that we make the most out of the moment. Do you hear me?"

"Yes, I hear you."

"I get so lonely for someone to talk to, I long to carry on a serious conversation with adults, unbound by the childish gibber so routine in my confines day after day. Do you know what I'm saying, Mell?"

"Yes, I think I do."

"Do you know the hurt and humiliation of having been too cheap? Of course you don't!" Her courage and determination flourished, holding like a rock. She was determined to set about building a new life for herself. Mell's reputation was spotless, she was banking on this. He could help and she was now asking for this help. There would be no distractions by romantic notions. And yet her heart pounded as she placed her trembling hand on his arm. Perhaps it was simply her own uneasiness but the quietness was almost unbearable!

"Zola, the rest of your life starts now! Pick up on your self worth. You can be all you want to be with God's help. Do you believe that?"

Mell pulled the car to the side of the road and placed his broad hand against Zola's shimmering soft hair. She had not known this special tenderness and appreciated this dark figure of a man, big and powerful, now sitting by her side.

"I will believe whatever you want me to believe. I can't give more than that!"

"But I have something special to give to you, the sharing of our time together for a few minutes. Not exactly a one night stand, but nevertheless memorable moments privately shared by two discrete adults fully aware of our time."

The enchanted moment burst upon Zola as a vein of surprise, had she lost her reasoning, or was he the crank, Don Quixote! In either case she cared not. Life at the moment was bliss, cloaked in a moment of fascination! She felt a warmth in her face yet frozen by paralysis being unable to move. She wondered how Mell felt, but quickly dismissed the thought, knowing she would never know.

"Zola, I'm going to pull up to the old Hutchinson lane, get off this highway. They'll all be passing by soon. We can talk there."

As the car moved along then turned down the narrow trail, both were quiet. Only the light from the full moon shone on their faces. Mell stopped the car and got out, then going to the other side he opened the door for Zola and taking her hand, he helped her from the car. A breeze fluttered the leaves and carried the fragrance of wild roses which grew in profusion along the lane. For Zola it was a night regained from lost paradise, regardless of duration in time. For Mell, his thoughts as Zola expected, were still unrevealed.

Somewhere in the distance a whippoorwill called again and again finally to be answered by another across the prairie fields. A cow called for her calf and the swishing of the breeze made a gentle sound rushing through the pines. The couple made no sounds. Zola waited for Mell to speak his mind though unsure he would. Mell waited because it was difficult to speak to her directly. Without speaking Mell reached out and taking her by the hands, pulled Zola to his side. Her fingers were strong, slim and warm against his rough and calloused hands. His stance with her emphasized the force in his body. With her heart beating faster, Zola wondered if his broad shoulders ever tired of the burdens she knew he carried. She dared to hope his masculine arms would press around her waist. She wanted him to mention her name, just once in a personal way. She knew time was passing but she would have this moment forever!

Mell squeezed her hands and looked her straight in the eye. He set his chin like blue steel and veins in his neck became visible in the pale light. He tried to speak through dry lips only to feel the embarrassment of a cracking voice. This, with the sweaty palms told Zola of the difficulty he was having in trying to communicate. But he was trying!

She gave him time and room to move. She wanted him to know this was his choosing and that he was in charge.

Mell was never heard using profanity, that was a well-known fact. One could only surmise that given the circumstances he could, under his breath, utter such feelings. The course of events had now brought him to this situation. "Zola, I've got to have a smoke!"

As he reached into the car for his pipe, Zola kept her position against the car thinking that this was not one of his virtues. She hated tobacco smoke! The smell and obnoxious odor drifted through the night air like river fog, filling her nostrils and coating her clothing with a staining smoke!

She had strength for this, too, and said nothing. Toying with the pipe until the fire had gone out and the smoke had all but disappeared, Mell laid aside the briar. Although he was unwilling to face her in this manner, he was unable to turn away. Still wavering, trying to comprehend just what it was he wanted out of this maze of love. It was not his inexperience or awkwardness that tormented him. The situation was just simply beyond what he could absolutely know for certain as the only way to go. So he stood before her absolutely befuddled! It was his eyes that caressed her first. Her beauty took on a special glow in the silvery light. He saw her long straight hair as silver threads among her strands of pearls. Neither did he fail to notice her softness and reluctance to be free. He moved closer to her side. She was no longer evasive, but responded with her arms about his neck as he held her fully in his arms. She felt a quiver as he gave his body a twist and pressed hard against her. She had never experienced such emotion and the ecstasy of the moment lingered for the long blissful hold.

Entwined in this passion they held each other close and felt the heart beats that separated them. The blossom of young love bloomed again in the season of summer. When Mell loosened his hold, Zola raised her head from his throbbing chest and softly kissed his cheek.

In a low tone, scarcely audible to Zola, Mell remarked. "If things were only different!"

"But they aren't, Mell!"

"I wish you knew how things really were Zola. I mean there are a lot of problems we must face. Just being together here tonight adds to the long list of woes."

"Tell me about it! Do you think I don't know? I hear it from all angles! I hear lies, half lies and innuendoes. Your kids talk to mine, and in turn they tell what they have heard from yours. It's a viscous circle. At least you are somewhat sheltered from a lot of the gossip. I'm sure of that."

"Well, I'm not. They, whoever 'they' are, pull out all the stops! I'm spared nothing. Would you like a list of just how I'm expected to run my life and who thinks what of me?"

"Pardon me, but aren't you exaggerating a bit?"

"Exaggerate, my foot! Obie expects me to play with him, then complains that I work him too hard. Then when he's unhappy he reminds me, 'People say, poor boy, he needs a mother.' He's beginning to believe it."

"And . . ."

Mell looked away, then continued with his list of expectations. "Clem's at the age where he thinks he knows it all. Seems to me, he can't begin to phantom life's problems, least mine."

"He's a teenager, Mell," then tenderly she pressed her hand against his. "Give him time, don't hurt him or drive the wedge deeper between you."

"Yeah, he'll grow out of it, won't he? Then there's Martha, she's sure I'm bent for hell and that I'll take you with me."

"Don't you have that backwards? I'm going to hell and will probably be responsible for your going there as well."

"Scandalous talk! But even I can't keep her mouth shut! I'm not blaming her for wrongs that I've made, but isn't it interesting how everyone is so willing to tell you how to run your life. Some going so far as telling you where to go with it and how to get there! Cheap advice is often worthless, remember that, Zola."

"The truth is, it does hurt and there's enough truth to make it painful. Sometimes I think I'd like to go away and hear no more of all this hellish talk that scatters like fine seeds in the wind!"

"You'd probably have to take a long trip, and by yourself. And that's not always best. No, I think what one has to do is face the music, choose a prudent course, and aim for the target. Let the chips fall where they may."

"I think the chips are falling, right around my feet. I imagine folks saying, 'Climb out if you can.' Mell, I intend to do just that! Like the great Phoenix bird, I'll rise again. Do you believe me, Mell?"

He was quiet for a moment. She thought perhaps she had misread him. Then he spoke the assurance she needed, "Yes, I believe you, but I'd bet your rise won't be swift and graceful!"

"That's all right; I've got time. We'll watch it together. Mell, you know I wouldn't be here with you now if I knew you would get hurt. I have more respect for you than that.

Mell, I do care for you. Yet, I must tell you in all candor, thanks for the moment, it's precious to me!" Casting all restraints aside, she placed her head on the powerful chest of the man she secretly idolized. Feeling his forceful arms around her, tears filled her closed eyes and she was lost in love for the moment!

Again there was silence except for the harmonious sounds of nature. The constant cadence of the katydid sounded from high up in the trees. From around their feet came the familiar cricket sound while frogs croaked away at a distant pond.

"Zola, they're brightening up our night," said Mell, pointing out to where a myriad of lightening bugs flashed their lights on and off.

"Glow, little glow worm, glitter, glitter," Zola softly sang. "Can you imagine a pleasant summer night without their dancing lights?"

VIII

White unto Harvest

SOUNDS of the late night crept away while those of the predawn moved into play, heralding a season of sound gone mostly unheard. There were, however, those in the hills who arose very early, and to them, these sounds helped welcome the new day. In fact the folks at Briarcliff Cottage made an assortment of noises themselves. Some of them penetrated into the guest room and awakened the sleeping evangelist.

Briarcliff Cottage was merely an extension of the great forest. Shrubs and small bushes blended with the wilderness always close at hand. The proliferation of these accent plants and the natural deep foliage of the vast wildwood, was said to be like living in Sherwood Forest. To the extent of their being covered by the canopy of green, one would not wonder but what this was so.

Jeremy lay awake for a few moments, listening to the outside noises. Especially he listened to the rooster which seemed to be crowing from twenty feet up in the sycamore tree just outside his window. Arising, he dressed and stood looking out into the early dawn to see a small sliver of light far down in the lower valley. Then, not far from his window, the rooster crowed again. Looking more closely he saw there was a small flock roosting in the tree. They were the Hamburg variety, and could gracefully fly like birds, from tree to tree. And that is just what they did.

Then his eyes caught the distressed frame that hung by the window. He was captivated again by the originality of the collared frame. For a few moments he reflected upon its harshness. Having a mind to clearly see the face of Christ as his now famous friend intended it to be seen, he lit the lamp. Only a few years ago the young artist was unknown, but to a few of the church, now he had found fame, all because of the face of Christ! Jeremy knelt by the side of his bed and prayed in the name of Jesus for blessings to carpet Mell's life.

Then proceeding to an old cane bottom rocker, he ruffled the pillow, sat down and began a study in the Word. Page after page of the old Bible was turned with reverence. The old message came alive every time he read its promises. New physical and spiritual strength uplifted and filled him with encouragement for the day.

A soft knock on his door brought a quick response. "Yes."

"Reverend Hallenbeck, I wonder might you care for a hot cup of coffee?"

Immediately Jeremy rose and opened the door. "Good morning, Martha, and yes indeed I would like a cup of Java, thank you."

Martha moved a step closer to the pastor and held the wooden serving tray within his easy reach. "I know you're going to like it; it's a special blend Granny calls Ozark Chinquipin. She takes a bulk coffee, adds a pinch of wild roasted chicory root and a good amount of powdered chinquipin. I've let it steep just the right time to bring out the best flavor."

Before she had completely finished giving her famous formula, Jeremy had already tried the aromatic concoction. To his amazement, he knew they had truly reached the zenith of coffee blending. Before he realized how much he had drunk, the small cup was empty.

"Then you do like it?"

"Indeed I do, may I have a second cup. I promise not to gulp it down this time."

Giggling, faintly enough to be heard, she proudly poured him the second cup, then smiling she returned to the kitchen.

He returned to his study by the window but then the picture again caught his eye. His thoughts were no longer on the Word, but rather on the Lord. He could not dismiss this quaint wedding of the two expressions of art. On the one hand the painting had been brought to life from a vision and the reality was that it brought fame and fortune. On the other hand the frame signified the harshness of reality, little known and of little value. The godly lives of both the artist and the keen-eyed beholder were blessed. The devoted servant stood quietly, reflecting upon the twenty third Psalm, "Thou preparest a table before me . . ." The one table had been filled to overflowing, while the second table was being prepared.

"Everybody, get around the table," called Martha.

Mell took his place at the head of the table and Rev. Hallenbeck was seated at the opposite end. Clem was seated to the right of his father while Obie and Martha were on his left.

As was the custom, Mell asked the visitor to say grace. Prayer at mealtime was only given when company came. For that reason Martha was especially thankful for company and remarked, "Your prayer, pastor, is special. It's like Sunday fried chicken, just doesn't come around every day. Like I always say, if you eat you should pray, and if you pray, you will have eats."

The table, properly set on white linen had the look of a well-to-do city home. Yet, it was laden with the more typical country breakfast. There was no pretense of gourmet cooking, Martha didn't know the meaning of the word, but that's what set before them nevertheless. Home cured elder smoked bacon filled a platter while the aroma filled the room. Sourdough biscuits, cooked to a deep golden brown, were Mell's request. There was a variety for everyone's taste, none of which were jaded around this table!

"My trouble is that I never know when I've had enough," remarked Jeremy.

"My trouble is," said Clem, "I just never get enough. Pass the muscadine preserves please; I do love that musky flavor! Try some pastor, they're Martha's specialty."

Reaching for a biscuit, Mell voiced his fondness for the fresh wild honey, "Now you take this mountain produced honey, it's an accumulation of all the best. The color is deep and the flavor is uncommonly hearty. We use all we want and I sell the rest for a dollar a gallon. Most folks like it better than a store bought variety."

The pastor quickly glanced over the table which had been filled to overflowing then remarked. "You're certainly blessed, Mell, all this food. Why there are many across our land who aren't that fortunate. We're living in troubled times. There are hobos, transients, folks going here and there, just being driven by the hot winds of summer and the sharp swirling sand. Yes, we do have much to be thankful for."

"Oh, I know that's the truth."

Then as to change the subject, the pastor looked to Clem, set down his coffee cup and spoke. "Tell me Clem, what are you doing now. I hear you've been away."

"I've been on that big job you've been hearing about over at Ponca City, working on a derrick, dirty but pays good. I'm on what they call compensation, you know, drawing money because I was hurt on the job."

"Nothing serious I trust, you seem healthily enough."

Pausing, Clem continued, "A pipe hit me in the back, about the kidneys. When the doctor gives me a release I'll be going back." He looked at Martha, and smiled, "I'm wearing what the doctor calls a girdle, it helps me some."

Looking toward Mell the pastor spoke again. "Don't I recall you worked for a time in the oil fields, Mell?"

"That's been a good spell back, but yes, I did. I worked during the big boom of El Dorado and then later Ponca City. Then Thalia's illness forced me to come home. Fortunately, I had saved some and got started here at Briarcliff. Speaking of a start, when we're finished with breakfast, I'd like to take you to the high orchard. That was my start in paws and they're usually ahead of the others in coming into production. I want to see if that's holding true."

With mealtime being finished, the two older men left for the pawpaw orchard. As he had planned earlier, Mell then would take Jeremy down to the project for a first hand look.

As the morning sun rose higher and the warmth made its presence felt, the men were walking about the trees looking over the fruit. As he expected, Mell soon found ripened paws. Hanging on a low branch alone, a large paw with excellent color dangled in full view. To Mell it was like a medallion being worn by a lovely lady, truly a thing of beauty. Carefully Mell gave a twist and the fruit was off the tree. "Here Jeremy, you have the first fruit of the year." Then taking out his knife, the pawpaw was cut in half and each man quickly sampled the savoring tidbit. What joy both men felt, for both knew what they were expecting and it was all there.

"We've got it, Jeremy! Color, size, and taste blend, it's all here."

"The taste is a perfect blend of desert melons, with the texture of custard pudding. They're impeccable, Mell."

"Yes, Jeremy, we've got a winner! The skin is as smooth as a baby's bottom, no blemishes, just super thin." Then spitting out some seeds he continued, "You know, Jeremy, if I could just produce a seedless paw, I'd have it made. I'm working on it with the experimental department of horticulture at the University of Arkansas."

"Are they giving you any encouragement?"

"Oh yes, they're making improvements. They'll have a much improved paw on the market soon, still have the seeds, although fewer ones. Yes, we're in this market to stay; it's just getting started. When you consider that only a few years back the public had never purchased a paw in the store, you can see where we're going. I'd like to check farther out in the middle of the orchard, if we find several good ones we'll take them to the foreman down on the project." Anxiously the men walked to where Mell started another search. Here, too, pawpaws were plentiful, good sized and nearly ready for harvest. "We'll put them in my hat until we get back to the truck, I don't want them to get bruised."

"Speaking of proper packing, how in the world do you ship them to distant cities and have them arrive in marketable condition?"

"That's just one of the many headaches associated with production and distribution. Our shipping cases, as you have seen, hold two dozen. These are only packed two tiers high, we've found that's the best way. Each paw is hand packed into an 'egg case' divider which has been bedded with extra soft shredded paper. When this is done, they arrive in excellent condition. While we're loading a car, we keep the temperature at about forty degrees, at that setting they have a long shelf life. But you got it right, there are always headaches and frustrations but we have to keep working to stay ahead."

"Man, I give you all the credit in the world, an entrepreneur if I ever saw one. You could take thorns and fashion them into a crown, turn a poor clay farm field into a pottery factory. If you can sell sassafras bark you could get acceptance for peddling anything!"

Returning to the truck, the men carefully placed the hat full of paws upon the cushioned seat between them and started down the winding bumpy road. "This is another reason for change in Arkansas. If we are ever to see progress, we must improve our transit system. At last we have a governor pushing for these things. The past several were asleep at the helm. Now I'm not a politician but I see good things blowing in the wind."

Then the pastor broke in, "What about the church, Mell? What do you see there?"

For several moments neither spoke, each giving thought to the passing orchards, just ready for harvest. Then the godly man of the cloth spoke again. "As bountiful as the orchards may prove to be, I'm reminded that all those great trees came from a seemingly insignificant seed. Each had the life germ of a new pawpaw. Once this infant germ finds the proper stimuli, such as moisture, warmth, and light, it germinates. A seedling comes forth, grows into a sapling, then in time a producing tree such as we see here. Such it is with the horticultural world. But you see, Mell, we are far from the likes of a tree! We are from God the Father, and it is His will that we become like Him in spirit. That is, the Spirit of God must occupy and control us, the stimulus if you will. I like to put it this way, if we are to find productive maturity we must believe in and rely upon Him! Well, I didn't mean to preach but there it is. I guess the bottom line is that the Spirit gives life.

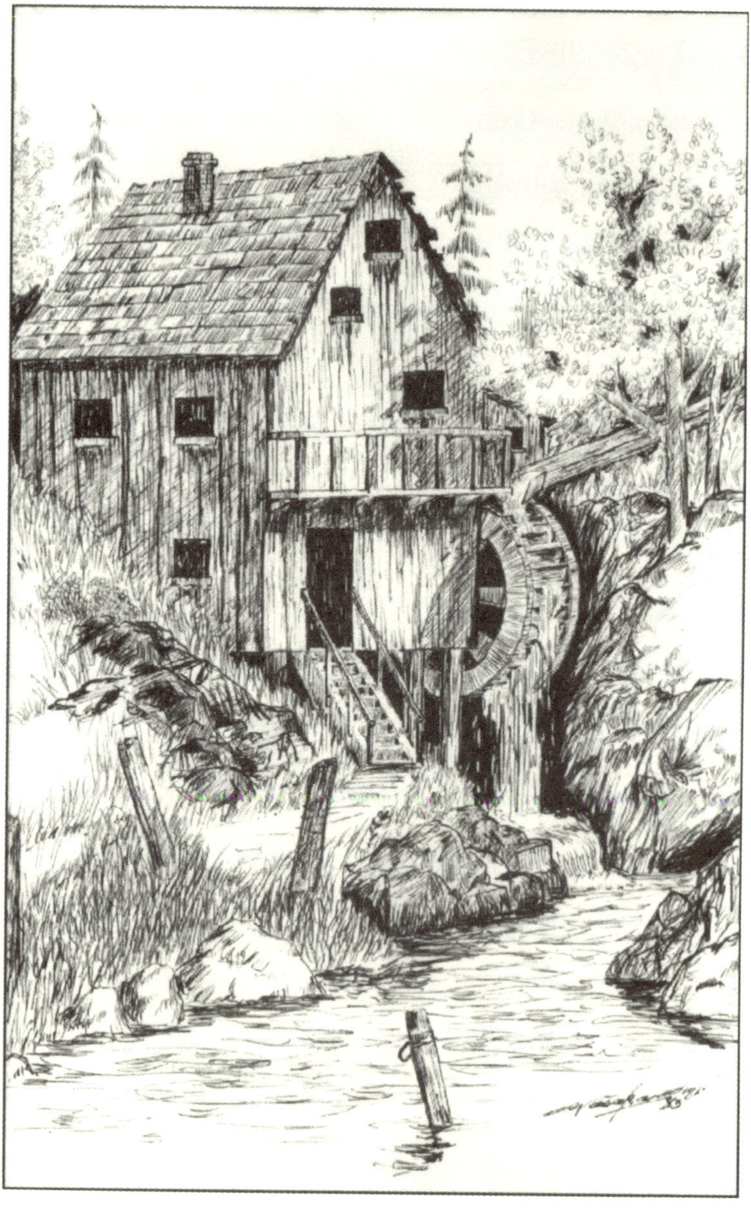

"The vital question should be, do I have this life? That's what I was asking, Mell, what condition is the church in?"

They were now leaving the orchards and Mell kept his eyes on the narrow lane winding along the side of the hill. "Pastor, I think you'll find the answer to that during the revival. The word says, 'The Lord added to the church daily . . .' I'm sure it was He who timed the revival. We'll just have to wait and see who's added, and how the church might be motivated."

Approaching a clearing, Mell pointed out part of the valley below. "That's it, that's the old grist mill, abandoned and now to be lost in the government project."

"Yes, I can see some equipment and a lot of dust. They're transforming that beautiful little valley right before our eyes. My, my, that's on a larger scale than I realized. I read about it in the paper but this defies one's imagination."

"As we get closer you'll be able to see the devastation brought on by the recent flooding. Of course without the flood these folks down here were just living on starvation. They had to plow rocks to lay the corn by and this just didn't keep the mill going. They'll be better off. But you can't hurl defiance in their face, so you're charitable and say nothing."

Jeremy strained his eyes in disbelieve at the happenings in the valley just below them. He now recognized this was to be no ordinary dam. "Look, Mell, in the midst of that machinery to the right." Then a cloud of dust covered the scene. "What do you make of that, Mell, isn't that a lady moving about at that old shanty?"

As the dust lifted, Mell replied. "I see men working around the cabin, but I can't make out anyone else. They must be getting Zola's things out. It's a pitiful situation. That woman wouldn't have any luck at all if it wasn't for bad luck." Then Mell raised his voice, "That is Zola, what in tarnation!"

"Is this the lady I met last night? You mean to tell me she lived in that hovel?"

"One and the same, but I wouldn't call it livin', and most folks around here don't call her a lady."

"Really?"

"Really, but I'll talk about that going back. Let's move on down and get in the middle of everything."

Mell drove on down to the construction site where they met Buck Jones, the foreman. His welcome was, "Good morning men, come in." Then he led them into the small mobile office filled with blueprints and layouts. A table and much of the wall exhibited the extensive project. Pointing to a chart he tapped it with his pencil, "Here is where we are today, this cut will go down another thirty feet. On the opposite hill there, the men are drilling and that will be blasted and cut down, perhaps next week." Then he moved toward the window and pointed to the old cabin. "All that will be razed in a couple of days and dressed down to bedrock. You can see a couple of our men moving Miss Porter's belongings. Those are the last worldly goods, such as they are, to leave the valley."

Jeremy looked impressed, fingering the blueprints on the table, he remarked, "Then this is the dam?"

"Yes, where we're standing will be under a hundred feet of water." As the man who called the shots smiled, he removed another design, and placed it over the first. "This is the artist conception of the lake and spillway."

The artist had laboriously detailed the drawing, and Jeremy marveled at the concept. "What a thing of beauty," he remarked. "What name will the lake go by?" Then shaking his head, he remarked again, "Beautiful."

"Indeed it will be an asset! But as for the name, I hear that is the political question of the day and the dam as well. Talk is that it could be named after an early senator who held much influence in the area at the time of statehood."

"That's politics," said Mell, "Could wind up being named Roosevelt, now wouldn't that be the berries."

Buck just smiled, "We're just builders, I guess the name will finally come from Washington. Regardless of that I'm sure the impact of the project will overshadow what it might be called. In fact, I doubt we can imagine at this time, just what the ramifications will be."

"Well, Buck, we don't want to take any more of your time. I just wanted Jeremy to see first hand what was happening down here." Then as Mell was about to get into the truck, Buck spoke again.

"Before you leave, Mell, I'd like to show Jeremy this hidden mountain spring." Then he led the way from the office to a spot just above the old house. Willows lined the pathway along the creek formed by the clear bubbling water. Islands of watercress formed tufts along the stream sharing a foothold with the stronger anchored bosk along the waterway.

As they walked the well-worn path that was old before the arrival of the white man, Jeremy paused, then with emotion verbalized. "What a pity this marvelous valley, cut in its jagged swath, has been virtually hidden in these backwoods and now to be lost to the world in a new lake."

"All is not lost, entirely, I'm happy to say. A scenic segment of this great Ozark country will remain."

"What will happen to this pristine footage?" asked Jeremy. "Will it not be lost to the murky water at the bottom of the lake?"

"No, through an engineering feat, it will miraculously be saved. Mell, you're familiar with the lower spring, aren't you? The perpetual flow of this spring will be encased and piped to a location near the other spring. So you see, we're not losing anything at all. Both springs will become part of a planned spa, including a lodge and a small amphitheater. All this will be landscaped to the hilt, big time stuff. Eventually, if the bill before the house passes, this will all become a national forest. I'm convinced more folks will see it then, in just one season, than have ever seen the springs as they now are."

As they moved along, Jeremy stooped down and cupping his hand, drank his fill of the pure clean water.

Perplexed by Zola's absence, Mell inconspicuously studied the commotion down at the cabin again. Then he, too, drank from the running water.

"Thanks for coming down, Mell, and bringing the Reverend. I'll see you under the brush arbor tonight, pastor."

As the men drove away, a cloud of dust billowed up behind them and drifted across the valley. Shortly Mell pointed out the lower spring and stopped. "Many years ago there used to be an old still hidden just up the hollow from the spring. All these parts became known as the old Still Place. People 'bout forgot DeBolingjer's name, they just call him old Mr. Still."

"Whiskey, you say?"

"Yes, lots of it. I expect the old man and his boys run off many a gallon of bootleg whiskey, none of which the Feds ever found. Oh, they looked! Two Feds slipped into the valley one day looking for stills. The old man and his boys had been tipped off and the government men were never seen again. Before the locals knew what was happening the whole place was teeming with revenuers. Virtually all stills were shut down and all whiskey making came to an abrupt end. Legend has it that the hoodlums shot the two in cold blood. At certain times of the year people still hear moans coming from the area where the revenuers were allegedly slain. Thalia used to say it's a wailing sound, like a damsel in distress."

Standing by the monument, Jeremy read the plaque in memory of Ivo and Joe Burns. "Mell, this plaque was only put here eight or so years ago."

"Yes, I remember when that took place, but their disappearance was way back at the height of bootlegging in Arkansas."

"What's the theory, Mell? Were there no conclusions as to what happened?"

"The theory most often heard, tells of weights being tied to the bodies which were then thrown into the depths of the whirling waters of the spring. Some say the putrid smell will never go away."

"It's a sulphur spring, isn't it Mell? Strange, the upper spring so pure and clean, while less than a mile away this spring is so strong of sulphur. Another riddle I suppose, no bodies, no crime! What happened to the DeBolingjers? Are they part of the legend?"

"Sure as shootin. Pardon the pun. If you believe in those old wives' tales, take your pick. You can have them saddled up with the Jesse James boys who were all killed in the Lincoln County war. Or, you can have them taking their illicit gains and going back to the old country from which they came. No one will ever know for sure. And who knows, if these hills could talk, we might hear them say, 'You're standing on a grave!'"

"My, my! What a sad commentary! The sins of man cover a sad spectrum of life so long as he walks in the shadow of death. And lives without God are never more than a fading shadow. There is no light in them. And now like a fleeting cloud, their shadows are gone, the good with the bad. I pray the government men knew the Lord! And Mell, there's just as much need in today's world as there was back when this dastardly deed was perpetrated."

"We have one clear voice right here in our backyard, speaking to that very need. Some say he's an Ozark version of Billy Sunday. The other end of the spectrum is that he is only a 'country hick.'" Then Mell was silent for a few moments, seeing Jeremy holding his hat as he stood beside the monument.

"We both know the godliness of Brother Wright, if that is who you speak of. Too bad he had to be away for the revival. I understand his retired father is not expected to live, is that correct?"

"Yes," replied Mell, "I'm afraid so. Both saints have done much for the church. In due time they shall receive their rewards."

Jeremy turned, donned his hat and started down the rocky hillside. Carefully he made his way along the path of flowing water, Mell closely following. Loose rocks rolled down before them kicking up dust and sending echoing noises of their downward trek. The men stopped, having arrived back on the flat valley. There Jeremy turned, taking in one more view of all that moved and all that was still. "Mell, I feel we're in the presence of the Lord! He's here now and I believe He'll be here blessing this project to the end. Could we ask for more than that?" Slowly they moved on to the truck.

Inside, Jeremy spoke again of the pressing need for godly men to take their stand in the seemingly godless world! "Mell, you mentioned a voice in the Ozarks. Beyond our own church there's another great evangelist, John Brown. I met him in a citywide evangelistic meeting in California. He spends a lot of time out there you know, doing radio broadcast and making appearances on behalf of the Ozark schools. He calls it building an endowment to guarantee the future of the institutions. I hope it works, I've heard they already have some pressing needs."

"I think that's mainly with their school in Sulphur Springs, you know he bought the old Kihlberg Hotel which was associated with the so called miracle waters. But you know, I don't put much stock in the powers of these springs, just because they have a foul smell. They didn't do much for Ponce de Leon. Now you take Clem's girl friend, Nellie, they took her up there. And day after day, for I don't know how long, she drank the stuff, bathed in, and sat in the mud. Wasn't worth a hill of beans. They finally ran out of patience and tried other cures."

"What is the nature of her illness?"

"One doctor diagnosed her with dyspepsia, but then others say she has a bad liver. Now there's talk that she's a lunger. One thing I know is that she's very sick. I've talked to Clem about it but it doesn't seem to make any difference. I think it would be better if he stayed over in Ponca City awhile longer, maybe take his mind off Nellie."

"Has anyone been praying for divine healing? God's still in the business you know! Miracles are not new to Him. He's healed the sick, and raised the dead and he's still working with the faithful. Yes, I must speak to her about that. Yes indeed, I seem to have a lot to speak about tonight, I trust His Holy Spirit will allow me to do so. Mell, you know I have found that over the years my whole spirit, emotions and will, become more mature the longer I walk with Him! I am transformed, by some small degree, from what I was yesterday and by His grace I shall be still more like Him tomorrow. My Armenian persuasion tells me I must believe in and rely upon Him for stability and the serenity I need for my life, all of it! My appetites, drives, desires, and instincts can be governed by God. How sweet the truth of our teaching that it's possible to live a godly life of moderation and temperance in testing times, and these are! 'I beseech you therefore, brethren, by the mercies of God, that ye present your bodies a living sacrifice, holy, acceptable unto God, which is your reasonable service.' Mell I appreciate so very much the banner you folks have above the arbor, HOLINESS UNTO THE LORD, that should be our motto going into every meeting."

At this juncture of the road, Mell drove onto the detour leading to the newly completed road. It was much higher up the hill, wide and level. "This road had been talked about for years. The old one flooded out every spring. Jeremy, the state's finally on the move. And we can thank the Lord for that, too!"

"And I do, Mell. Indeed I do."

Approaching the river they drove across the newly constructed steel girded bridge, high above the water. Acres of rich river bottom farms were covered in maturing corn. As the road gradually rose to the prairie, herds of cattle dotted the fields.

Soon they would be back at Briarcliff and Mell still had not spoken what was on his mind concerning Zola. With difficulty he abridged his thoughts and spoke of them to the pastor. "I have a confession to make, Jeremy, you can keep this under your hat." Then he began in a manner he could only be comfortable with knowing the confidentiality of the subject. "Like I said, Zola is not well thought of around here. She's, well, been on the wild side. I guess the two kids each have a different father. But she was telling me last night that she really desires to change. I've gotten to know her better lately, she seems quite nice."

There was a silence for a moment, then one word, "Well." Then looking straight ahead Jeremy continued. "But then don't most folks, when you get to know them? Does she attend church often?"

"Oh no, I've never seen her darken the church door before, but she does have intentions of reform, so she says. Our meeting last night after church took place quietly, away from peering eyes. We parked on a side road and talked, just talked, then I took her home. She fully understands what folks would say if they saw us together, even in church."

"Will she be back tonight? Is she under conviction? Have you talked of spiritual things?"

"Yes, to all the above."

"Well, I didn't intend for it to sound so mechanical, so rigid. Nevertheless, I'm glad for the positive answer. That's in her favor. We'll see about it tonight; I'll talk to her, firmly."

"I held her last night, Jeremy. She brought out a feeling that's been dead. I enjoyed her touch. It was that of a refined lady! Very reserved. I put my arms around her and held her tight. She merely allowed it to happen, but then later she did say that she, too, enjoyed the evening. I'm aware that I could become the laughing stock of the community."

"And why do you say that?"

"Well, as I said, Zola isn't appreciated by many. And she knows that."

"I can understand what you're saying. What she needs to do is become accepted. Now the best way for her to do that is for her to start at the beginning. Looks like to me that our job is cut out for us."

"But Jeremy, I'm just no good at such as the likes. I just don't have that much talk in me."

"The next time you feel a 'touch' coming on, think of its worth, don't tell me you have no gift of gab! Use it!"

"Maybe this is a feeling of pity rather than say, passion," explained Mell.

"Well, let's do say, for the moment. But still I suspect you are rightfully being attracted to her. Whether or not it's a Christian charity or merely a little rendezvous, time will tell."

"But Jeremy, it's not a habitual thing if that's what you mean."

"No, no, I didn't mean to imply that, not yet. But again, we're keeping in mind the cost versus the worth, if you get my drift."

"I do, but the poor woman is destitute, materially, financially and physically."

"Physically I doubt, even my eyes are better than that. But from what you say, I think it's safe to substitute the word spiritually poor. And on that note we all have room for improvement."

Quietly the men turned each to his own meditations. The pastor's reflections on the day naturally stimulated his thinking towards the evening service. Mell's thoughts turned to speculations centered around Zola.

As he rounded the curve to Briarcliff Cottage Mell's fears deepened. Parked under the low arching branches of the weeping willow tree, he saw the gaunt, long-faced figure of George Fetterly. Rarely seen away from his little country store and his three-legged stool, young Fetterly sat fidgeting behind the steering wheel of his Model-T. Dangling his feet against the running board, he seemed to be anxiously awaiting Mell's arrival.

Mell stopped the car with a lurch and hurried over to question George's presence. "What is it, George?"

"I was just about ready to leave, Mell, when I heard you coming down the lane. It's good you came in, Mrs. Moss needs your help. Martha came running all the way to the store taking the short cut across the old field. She was exhausted and very emotional in trying to relate the facts. She was scratched and bleeding, but I patched her up and sent her back." Then he paused, looking over the preacher man he had heard so much about from his father.

"Go on, George, go on," exclaimed Mell.

"Well, the best I can come up with is that Zola came up and after a while a lot of crying went on and I guess she had a spasm."

"She had what?"

"Martha's words were, I believe, 'Crying up a storm.' Being poorly, old lady Moss had some kind of an attack and Martha just went to pieces, a real shame!" Speaking in a lower voice young Fetterly continued, "Probably too much religion, Dad's the same way. My guess is the old lady just worked herself into a frenzy, know what I mean?"

Jeremy only heard enough of the conversation to know something was wrong. Mell heard it all and wondered if anything was right!

"Well, I know you're in a hurry so I'll be off." With that George tightened his skull cap about his head, then driving the Model-T around the curve, he went bouncing out of sight.

Only a short conversation followed between the two men before they too were closing their car doors and heading for Norwood Prairie.

They could not hear the slamming of the door at Hurst Manor, nor could they see who was being driven away.

IX

The Missing Moss

AS with the previous evening, there was much ado concerning various members. Non-members who weren't in the accompaniment of the faithful were also remembered. Delicately, some asked why the pillars were not in place. Pointedly, some had a ready answer. In contrast to the agitation sensed by the Reverend Hallenbeck, he appeared unperturbed calm, cool, and collected.

Again tonight the song service had been prolonged, well harmonized, yet for some, it seemed rather drawn-out. Perhaps it was more of a regional sound than some had expected. The prayer time, too, had been undeniably lengthy as Old Brother Fetterly led, remembering the prayer requests. Everyone knew this was the one time his rheumatism allowed him to humbly kneel. Tonight he knelt for a very extended time!

Inevitably these times allowed for unnecessary clamor and the pastor was now dealing with its effect. Properly restraining from over reaction, he moved on to the sermon.

The space under the arbor was at high premium again tonight, with many being from other movements or denominations. As always, the Baptists made up a good number of the visitors. Reverend Hallenbeck went out of his way to make them welcome. The revival had not been undertaken with any kind of ecumenical planning, yet many folks did, as always, move from church to church for such revivals.

From the beginning, his delivery and the power of His Word held the people as though in a spell. There was melody in his words, more noticeably than last night. His effective voice was a lullaby one minute and a balm in Gilead the next. His message was filled with good cheer, hope and above all, promise. When his voice rolled, the people's faces reflected his changing mood with an 'Amen' here and there.

Obie, sitting under the watchful eyes of Martha, poked his finger in her ribs and pointed out and up into the dark sky. Without so much as turning her head, Martha whispered in his ear, "Settle down, Obie, and act your age." He sat, gasping at the passing meteorite, a phenomenon she never knew passed in front of her very eyes!

Quietly he continued to watch the sky as the streaking body with a long bright tail moved quickly away. Then he studied the countless stars in the band of the Milky Way as it stretched across the heavens. As so many nights before, he thought of the verse, "Twinkle, twinkle, little star, how I wonder what you are." He did not hear the message, he was just being a little boy, and for the moment Martha could not interfere.

There were other folks beyond her complete domination as well. This was, no doubt a factor in her less than amiable disposition which seemed to surface tonight. She would not, however, let such matters interfere with the spirit of the message or serve as a distraction from the Word. So she and Obie, so it seemed, soaked in every word.

Pastor Hallenbeck's theme on salvation moved spiritedly along, holding the congregation with the "good news," the gospel. His stern message for mankind still groping in the darkness of sin, was the promised deliverance. Terms of the sinners pardon were graphically given, being born again by regeneration or conversion. He used the old "boot strap" example, saying lost man could never pull himself up in such a way. Folks listened.

"Most of us here, have, not so long ago, made the change from horse and buggy to the automobile. We converted. And I might add, glad to. Do you see how we recognized the better way? We are no longer burdened and enslaved by the old horse and broken wagon. And we are sensitive about this. Well, so it is with His way. The Scripture tells us, 'The Spirit itself beareth witness with our spirit, that we are the children of God.' We saw the need, recognized His conditions and accepted Christ as our Saviour!"

Perspiration ran down his temples as he mopped his brow with a fresh white handkerchief. Still pausing, he reached for the glass of water before him and drank heartily. As with most men of the cloth, preaching under a hot and humid arbor, Reverend Hallenbeck refrained from wearing his suit jacket. Now it had become time to loosen his tie, then he held up the old Bible and commenced again.

"I am here tonight, dear friends, but for one cause, to show you the need of salvation, and help you find the way to the Father. Jesus said, 'I am the way, the truth, and the life.' The mind of man is a marvelous thing! Reaching the age of accountability, we intuitively know that sometime, we will be required to give account of ourselves."

The pastor, through continuous use of the Bible, could turn the pages with artistic beauty. When he wished to read a passage it was always at his fingertips. It no less accurately rolled off the tip of his tongue when being quoted verbatim.

So it was as he looked over the congregation. He moved gracefully about, holding high the Bible as he again quoted from the Word. Once again it conveniently opened at the chosen page, Romans 3:23. He tapped the printed Word with his long slender finger and in the stillness, that gentle rap was heard along with the challenge for repentance. "All have sinned, and come short of the glory of God." There was a long pause, time for anyone to reflect upon the past and see his sins pass before him. It was evident from the expressions he saw on their faces that it was working. "Beloved, we are so constituted that we can enjoy the pleasures of the world or endure its pain. Likewise we are destined for an eternal glory or to everlasting punishment! You see, we are free to choose and it's imperative that we choose redemption."

Another moment was taken for their consideration while he again took time to combat the falling perspiration. Those in the congregation were also fighting the heat by constantly fanning themselves with the little fans from Wasson funeral home. This brought precious little relief yet, like the sermon, it went on.

Reverend Hallenbeck knew the message was getting through. As pastors do, he had a good perception. The moving of the Holy Spirit was present, and the congregation sensed it as well. In his conclusion he brought forth a couple of very strong points, appealing to their sober reasoning. Then looking out at the dark sky filled with its sparkling stars, he spoke with a awe-struck voice. "It's a beautiful world! You are a lovely congregation, but folks, more is required than that."

On cue, the pianist began softly playing "Amazing Grace," a standard hymn with which all could easily identify. While they were standing as he had asked, he spoke again of the urgency of the hour. Then he quoted the all important question from Hebrews, "How shall we escape, if we neglect so great salvation?"

The hushed silence held, then melodious voices flowed through the arbor like the breeze. He raised his hand as they finished the first verse and spoke again. "It's not enough to have quit some of your grosser sins, or even joined the church. Those acts never saved anyone. How about you who attend regularly and support this church? Again, that lacks the same effect. Ye must be born again! It's not merely my suggestion, it's a commandment from God. 'Except a man be born again, he cannot see the kingdom of God.'"

The second and third verses were sung, then, as the last verse neared its finish, the pastor raised his arms and called for sinners to come and gather around the altar for prayer. His manner had been from the practical approach rather than from the deathbed scare tactic. It was working! From the back and along both sides of the aisles, parishioners made their way to what he called the old-fashioned mourners bench. Abe, who only recently turned to politics, walked silently to the front. Being hefty and head and shoulders above everyone else, young Abe stood out like a sore thumb. Immediately following him and kneeling by his side was Brother Fetterly. With his long white beard and looking for the world like a real Amish gentleman, he prayed — not as a Mennonite or a Baptist but simply as a man of God, a man who knew how to touch the heart of God!

Others came forward, among them was Fay Eidson, a friend of Clem's. Tennessee Snodgrass, another teen-age girl, joined her around the long altar. Then up jumped Obie and he, too, made his way to the front. Sarcastically speaking, the boy who sat behind Obie remarked, "That's the third trip that boy's made up there this week, wonder what his problem is?"

Then from the friend seated next to him came the soft reply, "I don't know what in the Sam Hill is going on, do you?"

"No, but it gives me the jitters, know what I mean?"

"I do exactly, Jed. I'd up and leave but I'm afraid I'd just get jittery and join them. Start singing and act like we're happy, unless you want one of the saints to tap you on the shoulder and take you up front!"

"I can hear my heartbeat!"

Charlie leaned closer, audibly whispering above the appealing refrain, "They can't. Sing and remember to smile once in a while."

There were a few near the back who did make their way from the arbor. Jed and Charlie were not among them, they stood there like gentlemen and sang like canaries.

After the final stanza had been sung through twice the music stopped. Hankies clutched in the hands of the saints now dried eyes as folks moved about for hugs and handshakes. Pastor Hallenbeck gestured the congregation to be seated.

"I'm sure many of you recognize the fact that Sister Moss is absent tonight. I just got word a few moments ago that she's in the Siloam Springs hospital. Apparently she had a mild stroke. I assume Mell and the other members of the family are with her. Let us remember her in prayer." Then looking across the congregation, he added, "And there are others away from us tonight, perhaps tomorrow night we can all be back and bring someone with us. Thank you for coming tonight. Let us stand for the benediction."

As the service came to a close, saints across the arbor offered their quiet prayers as the pastor led them in this special request for the aging lady who had been taken to the city hospital. His prayer of thanksgiving recognized the hourly need and their dependence upon God. Carnie Moss had made such a commitment long ago, and when the Amen was pronounced, little groups gathered to learn more of the disturbing announcement.

Buck Jones, having been with the Reverend and Mell during the day, was troubled. Much of what he knew was a good sermon, had been lost on him. Quickly the engineer made his way to the front and began to inquire as to what had happened. A sun darkened and callused hand touched the broad shoulders of the man of God. Anxiously, Mr. Jones fired the question. "Do you know anything of Zola? She brought up the fact that she wanted to visit Mrs. Moss."

"Yes, I can tell you that she did indeed visit Sister Moss. She had gone there for spiritual help. Mell spoke with young George Fetterly on the phone and he just brought me the message. It seems that the ladies spent some time in matters concerning Zola's spiritual condition, finally culminating in a glorious conversion! Suddenly Zola is said to have noticed that Aunt Carnie appeared to be ill and sent Martha for help."

"Then Zola is with her now?"

"Yes, and Mell is there also. Clem had been with his grandmother prior to Zola's arrival and they had gone over a business matter. Apparently they both were weighed heavily upon by a letter from an attorney in Little Rock. Clem had packed a few things and left before Zola arrived."

"Is there anything I can do, Pastor? Do you know of any need?"

"No, I reckon not, the note said Mell intended to be back home later tonight, we'll know more about it at that time. I aim to go by Hurst Manor on the way to Briarcliff. By morning we should know more and if Mell doesn't call you, I will."

Jeremy, mindful of others who wished to confer with the pastor, shook hands and filed out into the disappearing crowd. As the lights from under the arbor dimmed, another rewarding night for the Lord was concluded. Those seeking, found salvation and went away, "Being made free . . ." A few didn't have an inkling as to what took place and only found a facade in the arbor. To them it was nothing more than a social, a promenade home, in the dark. For these few, Jeremy would pray again, hopefully for them there would be another night.

The majority went away understanding the severity of the hour. Personal needs became bared and the physical need for Sister Moss became paramount.

Alone at the Briarcliff, Jeremy bided his time for Mell's return, again kneeling under the collar framed likeness of Christ. His prayer time with Martha had been a physical drain! Her exasperations had been taken out on Zola and she was unwilling to treat the spiritual side in a holy manner, leaving such things to the Lord. He felt it amiss to believe morning would bring a change. Truth taught him it would take much more. He wondered, even after their extensive season of prayer, whether or not she was mature enough to let go and let God have his way. She was another he added to his late hour prayer time, then suddenly he spoke to the Father. "Lord, I feel weary and tired, give me an extra portion of strength!"

X

The Money Tree

FROM the seventeenth floor of the National Bank Building, Clem stood against the office window of Spradley, Coker and Lowe. From here the capital city lay sprawling beneath him in a dusty haze. It was just short of eleven o'clock, the appointed time he was to meet with an attorney of the prestigious law firm. As he stood nervously before the receptionist, he spoke to himself, "What am I doing here?"

His anxiety and waiting were of short order. Rising from her desk, the smiling secretary led him into the plush office of Mr. Glover A. Lowe. As she placed an envelope on the attorney's desk, she turned, smiled again, and made the introduction. As the large man rose, the warmth of his smile echoed in his deep yet gentle voice. He stood for a moment, straight and tall like a towering pine. Then reaching out his hand Clem noticed the long white fingers and clasped them into his.

"It's good to meet you, Mr. Marshall. May I call you Clem?"

"Sure, and excuse me if I seem uneasy, I'm as nervous as a long tail cat under a rocking chair. It's the first time I've ever been in a lawyer's office and I don't have any idea of just what's going on!"

"I understand completely, let me explain a few things that should shed some light on the subject, then we'll take an early lunch. So just relax and if you have any questions just speak up. In all these files I should have the answers."

On the large walnut desk, polished to a shine, lay stacks of papers, manila envelopes, clippings and some old photographs.

"Clem, you are a very lucky young man! I've asked you to come down to fulfill a promise I made to the late Mr. Lloyd Sterling Churchill. You'll find that and all the information you need in these many papers. Mr. Churchill's wishes have been carried out and you are to have all the time you need with me. I have realized a financial gain, too. Mr. Churchill was a most generous gentleman!"

Although Clem could not relax, he was now prepared to listen and speak, "Why me?"

"Yes, indeed, why me? Since you know virtually nothing concerning the story which I now unravel, let me start at the beginning. I knew Mr. Churchill for a good many years, and developed a wonderful rapport with him. He came to thoroughly trust me, and I hope you will." Then he paused, and from a table the secretary had placed near by, he took a cup of coffee and gave one to Clem. Leaning back, he glanced up over his glasses and spoke again. "When I contacted the attorney in Siloam Springs and he verified the legality of the account, you were shocked, naturally. Has reality set in yet? Are you prepared for, 'Why me?'"

Clem rubbed his sweaty palms and popped a knuckle, "I think so, yes, I'm anxious to hear the details, Mr. Lowe."

"When your mother was a very young lady she met this Lloyd Sterling Churchill, and they fell in love. Thalia's maternal grandparents, Doctor and Mrs. Hurst, were influential with matters concerning their daughter, Carnie. Eventually, Thalia felt betrayed. Wedding plans were canceled, and the couple were driven further apart until Thalia's health began to fail. She never fully recovered from Lloyd walking out of her life. They never saw each other again, although Lloyd never gave her up in his heart. He believed in time they would get together again, but that was not to be."

"You say he walked out, did Lloyd live in the Norwood community?"

"Yes, up until that time, then as far as the community knew, he just dropped out of sight! Actually he went to England, spending a considerable amount of time there. Although he tried to make a new life for himself, Thalia was always on his mind! I suspect she always held a place in her heart for him, too. However, she and your father saw each other often through social activities and the like. Thalia now had another problem, the Marshalls did not take lightly to this arrangement any better than the Mosses had with their episode. Nevertheless love found a way and they were, in time, married. Then you came along and filled their lives with joy. Thalia's health improved, for a time there was a change and Thalia sought a closer relationship with the Lord. As the years went by, this never wavered. At that time Mell was unchurched, secretly she prayed daily for his salvation but it was long in coming. The hardships of life followed them as they moved from town to town trying to find work. Mell took anything he could get. For a time he worked in a smelter; when that played out he worked in a meat processing plant, and so on."

"As Thalia's health began to fail again, they moved back in with her folks and Mell found local farm work. The Marshalls and the Mosses had forgotten their differences by now and Hampton showed his appreciation for Mell in every conceivable way."

Clem smiled, recalling those early years, "I remember Grandfather as if it was yesterday. He would hold me on his knee and I would pull his long white beard. Then I remember we lost Grandfather!"

His face held a saddened expression, and conversation between the men stopped. As the minutes passed, Glover sensed the feeling and realized it was time to continue with what young Clem came to hear. "I have a clipping here that was taken from a letter written by your aunt. It came into the hands of those who were collecting such things. In part this is what it says, you can read its entirety later. 'Through these tragic losses, Mell now carried the painful responsibility of not only caring for his family and Mrs. Moss, but the work of the farm as well. Year followed year, for Mell the seasons seemed unchanged. They were long and terribly cold and lonely, or they were torturously hot and endless.' You must have a wonderful father, Clem."

"I do, have you ever met him?"

"No, I have not, but I should like to. Someday I shall drive up and spend a few days in the Ozarks. How does that sound to you?"

"That sounds great." Rising, Clem ambled toward the window again looking down at the busy street. Turning quickly to face Mr. Lowe, he spoke with a broad smile. "It's mind boggling, that's what it is. Do you have any idea what I mean?"

"Yes, I do."

"Here I am, a country bumpkin from the hills, live from pay day to pay day, eat out of a tin can and paper bag. I've stood in long unemployment lines, always living in the shadow of want. How am I to deal with this, Mr. Lowe? Man, do I need help!"

"As administrator of the estate and with the power of attorney which I have, I am helping you. I would like to be retained as your attorney and help you through the momentous times of change. As far as your capability I have no qualms. You can do it, Clem. Just remember to keep cool, talk little and for now, trust no one!"

"I wish Dad was here. Do you suppose you could come up and meet him? Maybe you could help with some things from that end."

"I meant it, certainly I'd be happy to go up soon, but some things have already been put in place. For example, I have opened a bank account for you in Siloam Springs, all you have to do is sign the papers. Of course you're free to change banks or do as you wish. As they say, 'It's your money.'"

"I can hardly believe it's true, dang if I can! It goes beyond any wild dreams I ever had!"

"A word of caution if I may. No doubt, you will be hounded for money, and those seeking your 'friendship' will keep calling. Stay alert! They surely will descend like vultures, be ready for them! I would advise professional help on all business matters, either myself or an attorney perhaps in Siloam Springs. Actually no one should be without this service, especially you at this vulnerable time. You see, Clem, along with having plenty of money comes the burden of proper management. I am not concerned that you will spend like there is no tomorrow, just do not let it all go to your head!"

"When the questions are fired at me, what do I say?"

"Say nothing. I have prepared some remarks you may want to follow. Go over them and decide how you want to handle it. Basically, for now you may simply have 'no comment.' You might consider leaving town for a few days, going incognito if you please. Keep a low profile, thus being unavailable for comment."

"I can sure do that! In fact I could leave on the next plane out of Tulsa and take Nellie with me. I love that girl, and I'm going to marry her! Yes, I'll propose to her when I get back home. She's in the hospital now. The doctor said she needs the desert sun to clear up her lungs. Well, I guess that can be arranged."

Mr. Lowe raised his arms and stretched, pushing himself away from his desk and stood up. "You know, Clem, I envy you." The large and slightly overweight businessman was just one of many in his field. He was, however, the one constantly sought after by those who were in the know. Not that Clem understood this, he was just lucky. Again it was the astute manner of the late Churchill that afforded their coming together at all! But deep within the recesses of his heart, Clem now knew what the folks back home did not. Here in the big city he had found someone he could trust!

Glancing across the broad desk, Clem had noticed the photographs laying near other articles associated with Churchill. He assumed them to be pictures of the benefactor and was curious. Lifting his face to meet Glover's, Clem spoke, "If those are pictures of Lloyd, may I see them?"

Glover, now standing by the table, reached down and handed Clem the requested pictures. "There are many such photographs, in fact among his personal things are albums, and news reports which you'll find very interesting, I'm sure. This was his last portrait." Glover commented, "It was taken at a local studio."

Clem held the likeness, studying the features carefully. "No, I never saw him. If he was ever around our area I didn't know it. He looks pretty healthy to me, what was the nature of his illness?"

"He was never ill nor had he ever been. He was a very active fellow, traveled a lot on planes. He flew one time too many!"

"Are you saying Lloyd was killed in a plane crash?"

"Yes, it's all there." Again Glover pointed to the stacks of papers on his desk. "In many ways the entangled legality of his final flight has been representative of his entire life. Always the pro and con, plunging low or rising with the wind to the zenith. Whether he was at the top or in between, it mattered not — he was loved. And speaking of love," he then reached across the table and picked up a small scuffed box.

Excitement shone in Clem's big bright eyes and his curiosity was written across his face.

"This may prove to be most intriguing." With a faint smile he lifted a gold watch from the red crushed velvet box. Clem's hands reached out and held it by the beautiful chain. His examination was absolute, and instantly he recognized its worth! Bold dimensions outlined both sides of the watch. The motif was of a fisherman standing by a stream, fly fishing. Details were so remarkable, Clem held the timepiece for some time, studying each facet. Finally he pressed the clasp atop the winding stem and the cover popped open revealing the decorative work on the face. Time had been stopped at the eleventh hour. Never, for him, had he held such a special watch! Then the light of the room gave a sparkle on an engraving on the cover. Now it became more than one of a kind, it suddenly held notability!

Softly he spoke the words, "Agape, Thalia."

"It was to be his wedding gift. Then he told me one day, 'It constantly reminds me of the fragile roots of a young transplant whose roots are broken, so was our young love!'"

Quietly reminiscing, Clem sat holding the unique railroad watch. "From Mother to lover, now to me. I shall cherish it forever." Then he snapped it closed and secured the chain to his belt. "I'll only use it occasionally, today being one of those special days."

"Love weaves an interesting web, my boy, and I think you should know the other side of the gift exchange. For example, Lloyd's gift to your mother, that is Thalia."

Looking surprised, Clem anxiously waited to learn more of the unfolding episode. "Do you know what it was?"

"A broach, a very exquisite one!"

"Could it be a locket, about the size of the watch?"

"Locket, broach, pin, yes, I suppose it could be called any of those."

"Then I've seen it. I'm sure it's in Granny's trunk. When I asked about it one day she would only say, 'It was your mother's.'"

"The item in question was imported from Italy. The front is delicately hand carved from ivory, depicting the Mona Lisa. The reverse side is a gold inlaid mother of pearl! A real gem. It seems they knew how to appreciate the finer things of life, yet they were both stilled and silent in an untimely way."

Silence prevailed again, it was a sobering experience for Clem in particular, where age and experience was on Glover's side.

"Clem, all that had been so invulnerable and dear a short time ago, has faded like reflections on the water. One stone then the other was tossed into the pool by Father Time and caused it all to ripple and vanish forever."

"I sure wish Nellie was here, dang if I don't. Things are sure going to be different now. I see it with my own eyes and find it hard to believe, how will I be able to explain it to others?"

"With excitement I would imagine, but have no fear you'll find a way. When your generosity becomes a fact, the fictitious notion of just make-believe will suddenly disappear! Take my word for it."

"It's like having a money tree and in this case it's dollars from Heaven!"

"Only as long as you remember, these trees are definitely not everbearing. Nothing lasts forever! Clem, I'm sure you understand the unquestioning generosity of this pious man who has given so much. I've known from the outset just what it would mean to you and yours. My sincere hope is that you shall indeed be blessed with the results you make of it. It's all in your hands, and the way your head reacts will tell it all. A lesser man might become stingy and a recluse, or waste away and want. Take the higher ground, follow your teachings and walk in His steps. Having done this, you will achieve enduring success yourself."

Both men wore smiles, obviously pleased with their discussions. Clem was at the verge of uncontrollable joy. Yet unsure of himself, he could only give a silly grin. There were, however, wheels turning in the back of his mind. Only a fool would fail to see what was just beyond the horizon. Clem was not an imbecile, nor for that matter, a country bumpkin as he had jokingly stated. His limited education, and his time out in the world had at least taught him a valuable lesson. Sitting in the attorney's luxurious office, being afforded time with dignity, he saw another virtue in human worth. For the first time in his life, he knew he could and at this very moment would, take control of his own destiny!

"I've thought about it for only a brief moment so to speak, but Mr. Lowe, I can tell you one thing now, I'm not going back to work. Someone else can have my job in the oil field. I'm going to finish my education. But before I do that I'm going to marry Nellie and take her to the Arizona desert and there I'll enter the university. I'm going to make something of myself. Do you think I could take business and become a financier?"

"First of all let me say, whatever your future holds, at any point or any place, you will be able to look back and say, there's where it started! How it started will be forever meaningful as well. And, yes, you can be a successful tycoon!"

"Had it not been for Mr. Churchill's generosity I should never have been able to even suggest a future. I shall be obliged to his name and his honor." Shifting his long lanky frame, Clem glanced about the room, seemingly for the first time paying attention to the lavish furnishings. Then to himself, he spoke in an nearly inaudible voice, "Someday I'll have something like this."

The man from the hills of Northwest Arkansas felt a new force; he possessed a new drive! Where he had dealt with the realism of poverty, he now quickly recognized the coming of power. His self respect had never been lacking but he could see in others that "Old Clem" was just not taken for full face value. This he knew had changed and it created an awesome feeling within him. His strong will had never allowed him to be just a yes man. More often than not he had a strong opinion and had little reservations in making them known. He had never been led like sheep and wouldn't now. Clem like all members of his clan had great respect for the family. He knew the lack of money had not been their downfall nor would being rich take them lower than they had been. Unlike his sister

Martha, when it came to religion he didn't have much to say, but he was a believer. Basically his teachings of right and wrong guided him in a positive way and he bore not the burdens of hidden shames as many young men he knew.

The storms that blew his way had bent but never broken him. He would forever be thankful his mother's final wishes were fulfilled. When he looked to her old and faded picture on the wall, he always remembered her gratefulness to God for answering her prayer. Young Marshall bore so many likenesses of his mother that he became weary of hearing them repeated over and over. He always wanted to be like his dad! Yet with all due respect he knew no one had loftier ideals or higher goals than did his mother. All these virtues would forever be his goals, too.

The attorney saw but did not understand why a tear welled in Clem's eyes. He could not know the longing the young man felt nor the wish that Clem had that somehow his mother could know that all was well! Finally the silence was broken as Clem rose and spoke with a strong firm voice. "I've got to have some fresh air what do you say we go to dinner?"

Glover responded quickly by rising, then reaching down he picked up the envelope that had been in front of him. "Here, Clem, this will hold you over till you get squared away at the bank." Then he placed the manila envelope in Clem's hand. A broad grin came across Clem's face as he immediately opened the container which he knew held a good sum of money. "I ain't laid eyes on such a bulk of cash in a coon's age! Dang, if I can believe it's mine!"

Glover slapped him on the shoulders and gave a hearty laugh. "I'm happy for you, Clem. Now let's take these boxes to your car and we're off to dinner. I know a little place where they serve the best chicken and dumplings this side of London.

And scones, well, they melt in your mouth. Their selection of English tea is renowned. How does all that sound?"

"I bet it cost an arm and a leg!" Then he added, "If she can cook scones as good as Grandma's they're something else."

After placing the packed boxes in Clem's car, the men got into Glover's roadster. Driving to the quaint little restaurant, neither man had a lot to say. Clem was curiously looking the big city over as they drove along Latham Avenue.

Before the hill man had time to suspect they were there, Glover pulled up in front of a large building and pointed, "There it is, Number Ten Downing Street, there in the basement." They left the car parked at the curb and walked down a short flight of stairs that seemed to take them into a gingerbread house. The Tudor designed structure was missing its thatched roof, but the interior was lacking in nothing. Large copper kettles hung near a fireplace where the men waited to be shown to a table. An old gentleman who appeared to have stepped from a Shakespearean stage seated them at a dimly lit table. A pale, burned out candle welcomed them to their booth scented heavily with heather.

Glover could well understand Clem's curiosity of the place and tried to put him at ease. Light talk was soon interrupted when a pretty young maiden placed a scrolled menu in front of them, along with a large pot of tea. Glover helped Clem choose from the foreign-like menu, both men ordering much the same. "I come here often," said Glover, "And I have yet to be disappointed."

The clientele obviously spread over the city with attire to each his own. Clem felt comfortable and his appearance reflected his easy going style.

A piping hot bowl of soup with curls of steam sent an aroma all about the table where the men sat. This was the beginning of a most pleasant meal which progressed with light conversation.

Clem began by asking the attorney where he was from, what he did as a young man, and how did he like being a lawyer.

This brought a jovial grin from the man, who up to now had not been asked anything at all. "Well, I guess it's hardly called a place, but I was born in Wabash and picked cotton there. It's just a little farming community, not far from Helena."

"Helena, I've heard of that, but not that other place."

"Don't let that bother you, generally speaking, I just say Little Rock and let it go. But you see that has to do with what I did. Now let me tell you, I picked cotton! Everybody picked cotton! I recollect grabbing those cursed cotton balls until my fingers bled! And I hope to God I never have to pick another! Now, to my chosen profession, by no stretch of the imagination is it a gravy train. But yes, I like it, and I'm doing quite well."

Clem pushed aside the finished bowl of soup and touched the large white napkin against his thin mustache. "Sounds like your experiences in the cotton fields were about as unpleasant as my episodes plowing among the flint rocks. I can tell you I've had my belly full of that!"

As the meal progressed, both men ate with gusto and conversation drifted from fine food to a round of appreciations. Clem had thoroughly enjoyed the meal and the small talk they had exchanged. He had gotten to know the attorney as a friend and thought to himself, it's good to have a friend in high places.

Leaving the table Mr. Lowe placed a generous tip under the edge of his plate, an act carefully noticed by Clem. At the cashier's desk Clem stood smartly behind Mr. Lowe who paid the check. As the cashier rang up the sale and handed him the change, she thanked him by name. Then smiling she said, "You men have a nice day."

Soon they were back on the city's boulevard returning to the law offices of Spradley, Coker and Lowe. Clem felt it had been a good day, he had achieved his aim and a good deal more. He was unsure of just what this trip to Little Rock would really mean. But he was sure of one thing, life would never be the same!

Suddenly Clem noticed they were leaving the avenue behind. The gradual climb up a hillside revealed a speckling of trees and interesting shrubs. He turned and looked back for a final glimpse of the Arkansas Valley and the broad expanse of the mighty river.

Smoke and steam rose into the bright blue sky as a double engine train coughed and belched its way across the silver bars, taking it away from the city. River boats and barges passed as would strangers in the night. Trucks, cars and passengers were on the move, the city was alive.

For a moment Clem took his eyes from the work of a busy afternoon and smiled at the driver, "This must be the heart of Arkansas, certainly unlike the sleepy little towns of the north." Then he paused, "But I wouldn't want to live here. I love the simple little valleys and pine studded hills which seem to amble off in every direction, going nowhere. I thrill at the hills when they seem to disappear into the clouds on a foggy morning, only to reappear with little pockets tucked here and there as shimmering lakes." Then speaking to himself as much as to Mr. Lowe, he quoted from the naturalist, John Muir, "The place seemed holy, where one might hope to see God." He was filled with the blessings of life and it was welling over.

Glover let him talk, then arriving at a quiet spot at the top of the hill, he pulled over to the side of the road and stopped.

At first Clem took it to be a fashionable city park but then in the distance he saw headstones and realized where he had been brought.

"It's only a few blocks out of our way and I thought you would like to see Lloyd's resting place." Then he continued driving for some distance. "There, near the tall poplar," pointed Mr. Lowe.

Close to the tree and quite alone stood a rather large stone. Neither of the men spoke for several moments. Then Clem said, "Let's be going, I have the place fixed in my mind. I'll stop back by on my way home. I'd like to place a spray of roses on the new turned earth. Thanks for bringing me by."

The rest of the drive back to the high office building passed quickly. Farewells from new friends were spoken and each went on his way. Glover returned to his office desk and Clem was soon to start his winding way to the high hill country.

Recalling a large flashing neon sign only a few blocks away, Clem drove out of the parking lot and down the busy street to the florist shop.

Horticulturally speaking, the place was filled with interesting assortments from which to choose. Clem had, however, already chosen what he wanted. Standing against a frosted glass case, he spotted an unusual arrangement of roses. "I'll take those," said Clem to the approaching clerk.

As the young lady came from the cooler, she smiled, "Would you like a card to go with them?"

"No," replied Clem, "That won't be necessary."

Minutes later Clem paused, then placed the bright red flowers against the newly set stone of Lloyd Sterling Churchill. Kneeling, he said a simple silent prayer, then looking north, he thought of the winding road which would take him back to the Ozarks. Thoughts too, were of the winding future, beyond the road.

Sounds of the city were soon heard no more and traffic became lighter with each passing mile. Clem's anxiety caused him to wish he could fly. He could, however, channel his thoughts and he had plenty of time on the road for that. To begin with he speculated around the future of his life with Nellie. The aspects of that alone seemed endless. His hopes and aspirations had been dashed before. Would wealth cause a drift again or enfold them forever in eternal love? Where would the paths of education take him? Would he be willing to follow that broad road? Then there was the reflection on the church, whose church? Bells rang so clearly he could imagine his passing one now. He could envision the steeple and fine stained windows. Then he recalled actually seeing the drawings some time back of the new church someone had concocted. He wondered if they were still just dreams of the future. Perhaps they were never meant to be anything more.

Clem's conviction on tithing had been firmly established, pounded into him some might say. It was there, however, thanks to the Christian influence of his saintly grandmother. Giving, in the past, had been a joy. A few dollars here and there had never seemed a problem, would it become so now? Thinking about it was easy enough, but what about tapping the wallet like an oil well! That could be a horse of another color! Then the words of Paul flashed before him, "I am debtor." I, too, am a debtor; I owe much to many, thought Clem.

Then again the thoughts of Paul's words, "So, as much as in me is, I am ready," in Paul's case, ready to preach. Clem's admission was ready to tithe. The apostle had been accused of turning the world upside-down, now Clem wondered in what way would he be accused! Clem well knew the stinginess of mankind, the "it's mine" attitude.

He had heard it said that if tithing was against the law, many wouldn't have enough evidence against them to be found guilty. He did not want to be among those!

Shadowed valleys and sunlit ridges created changing patterns among the hills as Clem looked out over a crystal clear setting of the day. As far as he could see in any direction, there was nothing else to see. The constantly changing of the blue shadows deepened and finally, one by one disappeared.

The sounds of night took over the forest and from tree to tree the serenade was the same. So was the picture before him as he drove through the swarms of fireflies that lit up their part of the world. It was as if he were trying to find his seat in a large darkened hall while the orchestra played around him. That was always the Ozarks, ever changing with the hour and the seasons.

Now he realized in all of this, changes were inevitable. A chapter of his life had closed. In fact a whole new era of life was about to unfold. He was to set sail upon an adventure for which he knew nothing about.

Headlights from his car lit up the trees along the roadway and mile after mile of narrow winding road led upward. Occasionally the monotonous night drive revealed a clever message from Burma Shave, and Clem would smile. He had passed the little hamlet of Mountainburg, and soon would reach a tourist court and campground at the top of the Boston Mountains. This was Mount Gaylor, a true plateau before the road started its downward plunge toward the university city of Fayetteville. Often, as tonight, tourists filled every available cabin. Bright neon lights told the story, "No Vacancy."

Without lights, a crude sign pointed to the side, "Camping — $1.00." Quickly he chose a place on the hard dry ground and unrolled his bedding under the whispering pines. He would settle up in the morning. For now his mind was open to the avenues of speculative thought which only this morning would have been preposterous! As he lay looking up at the stars, he knew the mathematical probability of such a dream that now ran through his sleepless mind. But this was not just wishing on a star, it was reality! He knew this truth whether anyone else would believe or not. His mind was spinning around like patterns in a kaleidoscope! In time and with expense he realized all would come around to reality.

As he lay sleepless, peering into the night, he closed his eyes and again gave thanks for what was seemingly his miracle! He was a simple man and gave a simple prayer of thanks. The gratitude from his heart however was nothing less than explosive. Long after his sleepy eyes closed he had again gone over and over the fantastic happenings of the day. Tomorrow he would think of the plan for building the church. Without further ado the thankful and proud people of Norwood would see its spire rise high into the sky. The night seemed to darken, and the stars lost their luster. Reality suddenly became nothing but dreams on the quiet plateau called the Ozarks.

A thousand voices broke the quietness before dawn, and echoed across the hills. Clem added one more, his. "Good morning, world," and he was ready to see the part of it that led him homeward. Rays of the rising sun filtered through the thick forest, occasionally broken by drifting smoke from nearby campfires. As Clem stood watching the sun peek above the horizon, the soft tones of salmon lit up the massive blocks of stone columns that flanked the canyon. The mammoth stones appeared to be what might have been an old quarry and gave reason for the name Quarry State Park. Inch by inch the sun rose higher and the hues faded like ashes of roses. In a short time natural chalky ecru bluff would accent the various colors of green shrubs and trees that grew along the craggy cliffs.

The clear clarion call from a church steeple again sounded in Clem's ears. He could hear "Rock of Ages, Cleft for me." This is what he wanted his people in Norwood to see and hear. This would be their challenge.

As the miles clipped by one by one, Clem anxiously anticipated his return home. There he would gather the family around him and tell of his findings down in the big city. He could not dismiss from his mind just why he was the one to receive such a gift. He was hopeful that someone had known far more than they were telling. He was sure there was more to this riddle that he had been able to find out. Why had no one spoken of the matter? How could such a truth be kept secret all these years? He must know the answer to such questions, yet with dread and trepidation he would hesitate to press too far. If it came down to that, he could dismiss it from his mind and go on with life.

Clem reached back and felt his wallet, it had never been bulged to such a degree! He had never felt the comfort of so many bills of such large denomination. Surely his time had come and he knew not what it would bring.

The beautiful summer morning quickly gave way to afternoon and while Clem drove through his grand forest, his thoughts were elsewhere. He thought of the vast western desert and what he had heard of the inhospitable climate. But it was the life-prolonging healing effect that moved him to believe there was hope for his Nellie. His knowledge of a lunger told him Nellie would certainly be no better today than yesterday. There was little hope that she would be any better in the several tomorrows. She needed that dry desert air; it had helped several who had gone out there. They would go. He was acquainted with a couple who had sold everything and gone to Tucson. They would go there. He identified the old university there with quality education. Then taking courses in business management, he would try to help run the family affairs from the wasteland of hope, if his help was needed. He speculated that it would be. In fact he wanted to be able to assert some of his new power — not just for himself; he wanted to see to the betterment and happiness of his family. What a strange feeling, planning with certainty and having the ability to deliver. There was no thought of bearing the burden of cost. There would be no need to keep tabs on who got what. No sooner had the thought escaped than a chill ran up Clem's spine, causing him to speak, "Can it really work?" Then he answered himself in the affirmative, "Of course it can! God be my witness!"

With the early afternoon sun bearing down hot and in his anxiousness to reach home, Clem looked flushed and feverish. He was neither, it was a state of mind that he had never experienced. "I think I'm in a state of shock, without medical disadvantage. Could one ask for more than that?"

Driving the downward side of the mountain was slow and required caution. He was reminded that many folks across the years had ended up here as statistics. The highway was named "unsafe" by some. Weary travelers often went away saying, "Go around the Ozarks, roads there are dangerous." Then he recalled that the governor of some state warned his people not to travel across Arizona. It seemed that a couple of campers had been killed at a roadside park. Then the "sufficiency fund" law came to mind. It had caused his Uncle Joe and Aunt Minnie Moss to be turned back at the California border, being sent back across the Colorado River into Arizona.

This, he hoped was the dark side of travel. Surely the apple knockers to the prune pickers could, in reality, enjoy the real beauty of travel. He knew the answer would be found when he and Nellie started traveling to Tucson. He would soon see for himself just what "66" was like. Clem kept a journal of almost everything. He expected the one to the Old Pueblo to be filled with such as he had heard from wayworn travelers.

Approaching another crest in the hills, Clem saw "The Old Man in Stone," verging on the edge of the precipitous bluff. Then dead ahead are the notorious signs that send chills up the spine of travelers, "Test your Breaks, Dangerous Curve, 20 miles per hour." Clem responded as directed and safely continued down the steep grade. Nestled on lower hills, the city of Fayetteville came partially into view.

A few more miles and Clem would be home. His anxiety tightened muscles, giving him extra tension and fear the closer he came to his Norwood Prairie and the family. He wanted so much to be able to present this in a proper manner and he knew there was no one to help. He was home. Again the question came to mind, why me?

Several days of busy summer filled Clem's life while he waited to get all the family together. Every day he asked himself the same question, and every day waited for the answer.

His grandmother had been released from the hospital and was able to join the other family members tonight out on the lawn. With Martha's help she had made a crock full of thirst quenching Kool-Aid for the still hot evening. Like the others, she waited to see what Clem had found out in Little Rock. She was apprehensive about the matter, thinking the subject closed long ago.

Nellie, too, had been allowed to leave the hospital for a few days, and anxiously linked herself with Clem's family. She knew Clem well enough to know he was holding an ace up his sleeve, but what did it mean? So was the question on everyone's mind.

Mell seemed a bit baffled by it all and called out, "I haven't the faintest inkling what's going on. Bring me some Kool-Aid, Obie, and let's get on with it." The two men had been spending long hours in the pawpaw orchards together. Mell knew Clem had been acting strange but had not pressed for information.

Tonight the family sat out on the lawn enjoying the late summer evening. While small talk continued, Obie captured the fireflies that came too close, placing them in his fruit jar for observation.

Clem finished his drink and placed the empty glass on the well casing. Taking a moment he looked over at his grandmother lounging in a recliner. She returned his smile. "You look wonderful, Grandmother, and it's good to have you home again."

"Thank you, my boy, and I'm so glad to be home." Then the young man looked to Nellie; he could not smile. She did not look well and he knew her sadness.

Martha watched all that went on. She, too, knew Clem had been hiding something, but knew not what. Then bursting out she asked, "Why all this silly mystery?"

Clem then looked to Obie, "All right, are you ready for this, Obie?"

Shrugging his shoulders he replied, "I guess so."

"Well then, let's not procrastinate any further. I'll begin with my trip to Little Rock and why I had to go. Martha, you remember several days ago of bringing a strange looking letter from the box, backed to me? Well it was from an attorney in the capital city. The gist of which was, could I come down to discuss and partially receive an inheritance!

"That's M-O-N-E-Y, lots of it! Besides that, there's stocks and bonds, books and personal items. Dad, can you believe, I don't even know yet just how much I have received?"

All were speechless and dumb founded! "It seems that the late Mr. Lloyd Churchill left me much of his fortune!"

Confusion reigned for a moment, everyone wanted to say something. The question they wanted to know now was, who was this Mr. Churchill!

Only Carnie knew the answer. Only she spoke, "I knew him; I remember him quite well. I've often wondered what happened to that boy." She paused, taking a long drink then raising her slender bony arm she spoke again. "Here is what I know, and I don't want you to add or take away from the facts. Let's see, you know his parents came into these hills when the young lad, Lloyd, was about seventeen, the age of Thalia. They were originally from England, from well-to-do stock I understand. They brought lots of money and lived lavishly, but they didn't fit in here. They were too eccentric, extravagant, too worldly. Well, as fate would have it the young man fell in love with Thalia. I raised my foot from the start but to no good. Hampton said little about it leaving it all to me. I could do nothing but watch, day by day as they carried on. One day Thalia told me that they were planning on getting married. I was outraged, terribly hurt! Then I heard by the grapevine that old Mrs. Churchill was sensitive about the matter and apprehensive! Well, I reckon so! She didn't want her young lad marrying the sick child! Thalia had never been strong. Then Mr. Churchill returned from one of his many escapades and the fat really got in the fire. When some of the neighbors called him a gigolo, which he was not, well, that did it. So the lovebirds, claiming to be heart broken, were separated and the Churchills moved away, back to England I heard tell. I never heard anymore about them. Mell, is any of this revealing to you?"

The son-in-law had sat quietly, never saying a word and now only answered her question.

"Yes, all of it. Thalia never spoke a word about it to me."

The ailing grandmother leaned over against Nellie who sat on a cot near by. "He does know what happened next," then she patted Nellie on the arm. "You see, the Marshalls moved into the community before the door could slam on the behinds of those leaving. Mell, now it's your part of the saga, I've said all I'm going to say, and probably more than I ought to have."

"I don't know any thing about any of this and I'd still like to know why, as you say Clem, you received an inheritance!"

"Dad, I know little more than what I've said. Lloyd Churchill has left me a substantial amount of money."

"Wealth?"

"Yes!"

Mell was obviously a bit wrangled and still confused over whether or not to believe his son's claim. As he walked toward the well he said, "I'm not from Missouri, but you'll have to prove it to me." Then he filled his glass from the large crock, and leaned against the well casing.

Clem walked over and sat down by Nellie, kissed her on the cheek then stood by her side. "Dad, and all of you, I want to tell you something else you don't know. A couple of days ago I pleaded with Nellie, reasoned with her and begged her to marry me. She knew nothing of my financial status, only that all of us together had little. The Marshall name stands for respect; the Hurst family is aristocratic; and Grandma, the Moss' likewise have always been held in high esteem. Now we come to Nellie Black, sister to Zola Porter and who are they?"

Carnie shifted her weight and took Nellie's hand, smiling she spoke, "Nellie, my dear, if you accepted his offer of marriage, I welcome you into the family."

Like a bride to be, Nellie's face was aglow, some of the whiteness had gone and her smile gave evidence of joy. "Yes, I will marry him, and for love; I know nothing of this money thing! Clem, please tell me what this is all about. Mell, I know you have reservations, but I hope you, all of you will be as kind as Grandma here." Nellie then put her arms around the old woman and kissed her brow.

Mell, without hesitation, was ready to accept the inevitable, walking over to Nellie he put his arm around her and softly spoke, "Welcome into the family, Nellie. You're one of us!"

Nellie bent over and cried as Clem rushed to her side. Nothing could be heard but her sobs and their embrace could be seen by all as true love. In a few minutes she regained her composure, "I'm all right, I love you all. How much did you tell them Clem? What do I need to say?"

"I've said nothing, Nellie, you may tell them what you want."

"We're going to be married in a few days."

"In the middle of the pawpaw harvest!" shouted Martha.

Nellie looked up into Clem's face, then to Martha, "Yes, I guess so. We'll be married in the old church. Then Clem will ceremoniously break ground for a new church, won't that be grand?"

"You mean, won't that be impossible!" shouted Martha.

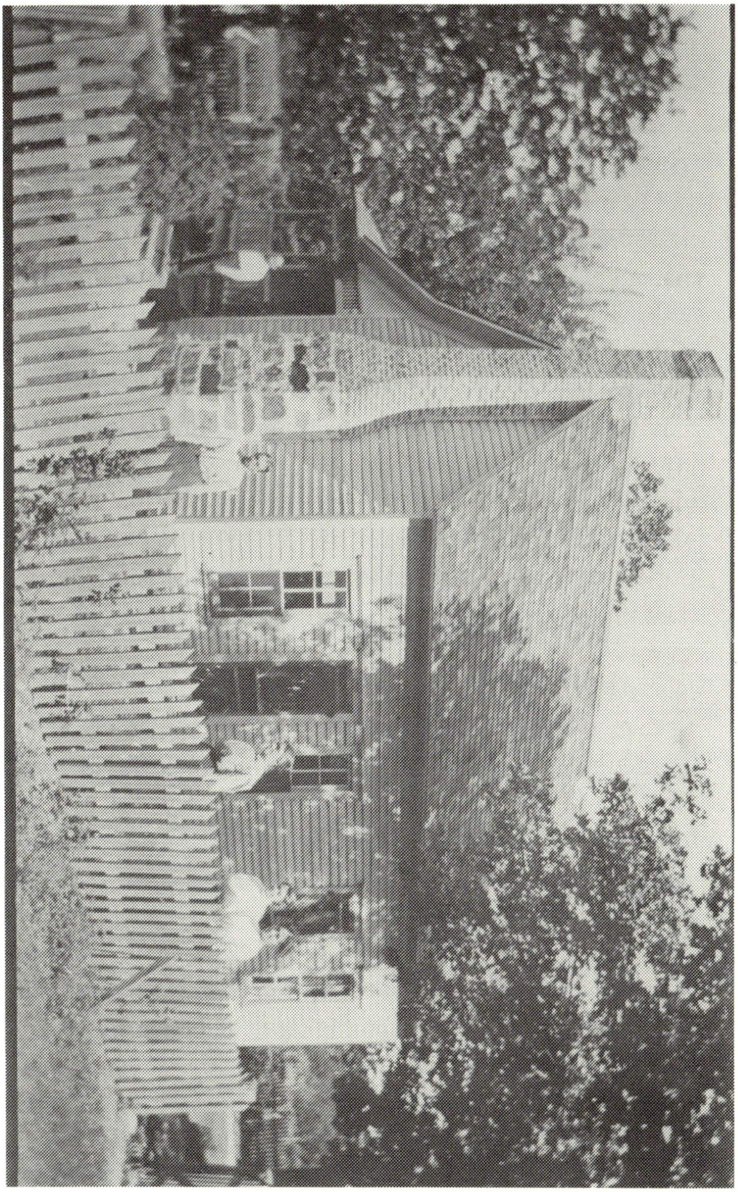

"It's not impossible, I have the means, and the church is doing what it can. The long hoped for new church will be a reality! A fitting memorial to Lloyd Churchill!"

"Shaw," said the grand old lady of reality. "You can do that? That money won't last till it's gone. Get out of here!"

"Son, are you sure of what you speak, how can we believe this? What will happen when word gets out that you have inherited such a sum of money? We could all be the laughing stock of the state of Arkansas! Hillbillies who got a few bucks and thought they were rich; do you get my drift?"

"Yes, Father, I do."

"I think we should say nothing more until we talk with an attorney up town, do you hear?"

"I have one, and I have a large account at the bank. My wallet is filled, here look at these." Clem opened his wallet and pulled out several hundred dollar bills. "Take one, Dad, they're real!" Then he walked in front of his grandmother and said, "You can have anything you want, Grandmother, just name it."

"Go away, you sound foolish," then she pushed him aside. "Are you really going to get married or are you just joshing me?"

"We are, Grandma, really. Tomorrow Clem is taking me to Fayetteville and I'm getting a lovely wedding gown! Oh, it will be a lovely wedding!"

Clem waited for Nellie to finish, "Dad, I know there are many things you should know, and in time we'll discuss them, but perhaps since you feel as you do — the uncertainty I mean, well, I guess later will be better. There is one thing though that I want to tell you now, and that's about our new home. Soon after the wedding, Nellie and I will be leaving for Arizona. I'm taking her to the dry desert near Tucson. The doctors say that's the thing to do. They think she can be cured. Others have gone there and were!"

"You're going to Arizona!" shouted Martha. "Isn't that where Uncle Joe and Aunt Minnie went? Don't they live on a desert?"

"They did," replied Clem. "But it's a good piece away from Tucson. They lived in Yuma until their government money caught up with them. I bet they never counted their chickens before they hatched again! We're going where the doctor recommended, that's why Tucson."

"Well, I'll declare," said Carnie, "Can you believe these goings on, Mell?"

"I can," said Martha, "If Clem said it's so, he don't lie. Then I bet we don't ever see the pretty roses on Mama's grave again, if you say the good man's dead."

"Then we'll do it, Martha, just the same."

"Oh, can I? Will you let me do that, even if it makes me cry?"

"Yes, Martha, you may do that and it will make us all proud. Dad, we've talked about how much Lloyd loved Mother for that brief season, how about telling of the years you two were in love?"

"Thalia had interference in that, too," said Mell.

"I reckon that's so," said Carnie, "I can't say I had any ill feelings toward the Marshalls, but the men folk were a bit crude I thought, including Mell. He didn't have a steady job, had quit school, and was something of a godless man and like Clara Churchill, I expected more for my little girl. But I couldn't do a thing about it. It was out of my hands. As Thalia's health improved I was so happy. Then too, Hampton would say, 'He's a nice boy, she could do worse.' Then as time passed we began to accept him and before you knew it they wanted to get married."

"Did Mother have a big church wedding? Were you married in the old church, Father?" asked Martha.

"Your mother and I rode horseback to the community of Logan, we were married in the home of the pastor there. Your mother was beautiful, wearing a long white dress she stood in front of a podium giving her vow. We kept those vows; we were in love. Sometimes I called her 'Angel' and she'd blush."

Martha's many walks and talks with her mother had taught her many things. She knew her mother had wanted a church wedding. She thought this was her chance to find out why it wasn't so. "Daddy, why weren't you and Mother married in the church?"

"I can't say I recall, something about — do you remember Grandma?"

"No, I don't believe I recollect a'tall."

"By gum, I'm going to have a big church wedding," replied Martha.

Obie had managed to keep quiet but a thousand things ran through his mind. "I still miss Mommy, why did she have to die?"

The youngest child sat on the ground by his grandmother and she reached down and patted his head, "Well, my little man, she . . ."

Martha interrupted. "I know why. I remember the night old Doctor Burganstall came out from town and, after talking with Mother, he took Daddy out on the long porch and stood against the banister. I heard them talking through the open doorway in the kitchen. Doc said, 'Mell, I've done all I can. I can ease her pain but she only has a short time left. The leukemia is taking her away.' It did, exactly four weeks to the day."

All were crying except Grandmother who was now being comforted by Nellie. Mell stood silent and emotionless as a stone. So much had been brought back that had once been put aside. Each sensed their pain to be the deepest, but it was perhaps Mell who really hurt the most. Certainly his thoughts ran deeper and for these years his life had been in shreds. Still he wondered, what was the proper way for change!

"Poor Mother," said Clem. "She had so little, if she was only here now!"

The grandmother leaned back on the cot, "But they're gone, one by one! Just before Hampton died he said, Don't worry, Carnie; Mell will take good care of you. Mell, you are still the backbone of this family, I don't know what we would have done without you; we still need you."

Mell did not respond to such talk, he didn't know how. He had always felt inadequate talking to Carnie, and to Martha. He started to turn and leave when Clem spoke.

"Dad, we do need your advice, and listen, everyone. Dad said we should be quiet about this money situation. No bragging, do you hear that, Obie? In time this will smooth out. You are all a part of this, all of us will be blessed, do you hear?"

"My, my," said Carnie, "How late it must be, I expect we've missed the revival service tonight."

The quiet peaceful evening bowed to darkness. The little prairie of Norwood and Hurst Manor lay silent and at peace.

XI

The Pawpaw Harvest

PAWPAWS were being stacked in the sheds and pickers manned the trees like birds in cherry picking time. Help was still being sought for what now appeared to be a bumper harvest. Quality, too, was up from last year giving Mell the right to be thankful for his successful operation of Briarcliff Orchards.

Doubters still drove by to see the results for themselves but left with more questions than they had in the beginning. The paws were being sold, even the ardent skeptics could see the pay off.

Mell had asked Clem and Zola to help him oversee the day's operation, which to Clem at least, looked to be of longer duration. On the other hand Zola was glad to be in the pleasant company of the man she had dreamed might share her feelings.

Standing by the conveyor line, neither spoke. The pawpaws moved along slowly. Zola wanted to learn all that Mell would teach her. He was tickled that he could get Zola for the job, knowing she would be a very valuable worker. Women always performed better as shed workers and Mell was sure Zola would exceed beyond the others. Neither did he mind having her in a favorable position where she would be seen, and where in turn, he could see her.

Zola's keen eyes and quickness filled the first requirement for which Mell was looking. The second, touch, was essentially as valuable. The fact that she had beauty and charm added the third dimension. He would catch the vision of what others were seeing and feel their reaction toward her presence.

By midmorning Mell had managed to get the basic operation for beginning, underway. Clem had stacked boxes of paws fresh from the orchard, near the conveyor belt. Bud would carefully pour the fruit on the line and the dry run would begin. Touching her arm as they waited for the moving paws, Mell said, "Working in the shed is much like a mother's responsibility in the nursery, takes total consciousness. You'll do well."

As the large "fancy" paws moved down the line and within her reach, Zola quickly removed each one. These were placed on a parallel line for the packers. The second grade, "standard" moved along to be inspected and removed by Valetta Kvasinikof, hired from the local university. Lugs were stacked at the end of each line, each bearing the proper label, "Ozark Belle" for the fancy, and "Arkansas Pride" for the standard. The paws that did not qualify for either grade were sent to the "kitchen" and became pawpaw butter.

At noon all operations broke off for lunch. Mell hoped the afternoon hitch would bear out his belief that another successful season had begun. Zola had proved herself as indeed all the shed workers had. Now Mell must wait to see what would be on the afternoon docket.

Clem started by placing picking boxes strategically throughout the orchard. Ladders, too, had been placed among the trees. Mell joined his son there and together they drove through row after row of the yielding fruit. Both men were happy as a lark for the super quality of paws that hung on the trees ready for the taking.

"It's been years of hard work, Clem, years of concern. We've had our nose kept to the grindstone but it's finally payday. There are several smaller operations about, but we're the original one and alone at the top."

"And it all started with a dream," said Clem. Mell gave him a serious look, "It was more than a dream. It was a vision of what could be; one does with what he's got! I didn't have much else. My folks had always taught me to save, whatever it was. In the spring we saved the lambs-quarter, made fine eating. We always gathered poke, and there's no finer greens than poke. Come summer we would pick dewberries, blackberries, you name it."

"And you taught us," said Clem. "I'll never forget all the chiggers and ticks we took home along with berries! Itch and scratch, scratch and dig! I guess I always liked the autumn season for that alone. I was always glad to say goodby to the dog days of summer."

"That was another harvest."

"Yes, and how I loved it. Gallons and gallons of chinquapins, Lord knows how many black walnuts and hickory nuts."

Mell, still driving slowly down the rows of pawpaws, smiled. "Oddly enough we paid little attention to the pawpaws. Oh, we ate them out of hand but never put them up, same way with persimmons, just let them drop for opossum food. But then some folks did cook up paws. Old Hon Hutch, well, she knew how to make the best pawpaw butter in the world, the kind we try to make and get paid for. Nobody ever knew what she put in with them, they just knew it was good. Back then no one ever thought of selling it like apple butter. I reckon necessity is the mother of invention all right."

"Anyway, here we are," said Clem, "pawpaws up to our neck!"

"Yes, thank the Lord. It means money in the bank and that's music to my ears, and to my banker."

"It's sweeter music to me, when it's my money. I can't get it off my mind, my money I mean. That feller Lloyd must've been some kind of a man; I mean to give all that to me."

"Well, it's for sure he couldn't take it with him. He probably figured that out ahead of time."

"Strange how Mother never told you of him, and stranger yet that you never found out about him."

"Forget it, and go on with it."

"And Grandma, she . . . "

"Forget it, I said!"

"I am! I going on with it, to Tucson."

"And I can give you another piece of advice. If you don't watch it, you'll be pouring sand in a rat hole. Before you know it, you'll be asking yourself where it went to."

Mell had not been convinced of this money matter by any means and disliked talking about the subject. He understood the truth of Clem's hint, someone was not telling all they knew! "I have to go into town this evening, and I'll talk with the attorney. I want to get this thing settled in my mind. Then, too, there's that last minute meeting with the festival committee."

"It's going to be some weekend," Clem remarked, "Nellie has set the wedding for Saturday, noon I think, then we'll go to Tulsa to catch a plane for Tucson. I had planned on driving, but Nellie's doctor said it would be better if we avoided such an arduous undertaking."

Mell listened as he drove through the narrow rows of trees being harvested. He would miss Clem's help but said nothing about it. The decision had been made and there was nothing more to be said.

Preparation had obviously measured up to all of Mell's expectations for start up tomorrow. He and Clem now drove to one of the machine shops and again checked for extra motors, conveyor belts, and other items so often needed in the course of an average day's work. All was indeed ready.

By late afternoon both men joined the few pickers who were still learning how to properly handle the paws. That had to be learned. They would in turn supervise the orchard labor through the harvest. The day's work had been very efficient and Mell was pleased, ready to call it a day. He and Clem drove to the sheds, leaving the field men to bring in the last pickings of the day.

Having finished loading the day's shipment for market, Mell recognized Buck Jones's fancy vehicle driving up behind him. It was Sadie. They exchanged greetings as he drove away to the railhead.

Sadie had driven Nellie and Martha to Fayetteville on a shopping spree. The Jones' were accustomed to such quaint shops, but the others, well, they had never been in a bridal boutique. Zola and Valetta ran to meet the ladies so vibrant and full of joy! Zola hugged her sister, "Tell us what you found."

Nellie had never looked so radiant and full of life. Zola knew it had been a successful trip. She hoped it was just the beginning of things to come. She saw a bit of Mell in the tender emotions of his son. She also felt a bit of this in her heart and knew the enchantment Nellie held in hers.

"We did it!" said Sadie. "We had a ball!"

"Oh, wait till you see it, Zola, I got one of them pictured in the window. The train is a mile long and the veil comes down to here. It must've been appointed by the queen."

"Well, it had to be the king's money and he will kill you by appointment, too."

"He's got plenty, wait till you see what else I got."

"Honey, no man's got plenty."

"Clem does," remarked Martha, "You'll see."

"It's so exciting," said Nellie. "I feel as if I've died and gone to Heaven."

"You probably will before morning, and what's Mell going to say?" inquired Zola. "Tell me that?"

"Martha's right," said Nellie, "You'll see. Martha, I'd love to have a dress rehearsal tonight. Do you think we could all meet at your place?"

"I don't know why not," replied Martha. "Grandma will love it."

"Sadie, could you round them all up and be there around eight? Zola will you stop at Fetterly's store and pick up some goodies?" Then walking to Valetta's side, Nellie put her arm around her and smiled. "I hope you don't mind, Valetta, but I took the liberty of getting you a very special gown for the float Saturday. Would you mind wearing your National Czech costume tonight? I'd love Aunt Carnie to see it."

The student from Prague was stunned, "You purchased me a gown, just to ride in the parade? You natives are hard to understand, but I love you. Yes, I'll wear my native costume, that will make me happy! Thank you for the special frock!"

Nellie spoke again as she and the other ladies returned to the car. "We're going on up to Martha's. We'll see you there tonight." The new Mercury sedan moved quickly out of sight leaving a trail of dust to settle over the grading shed and the two ladies standing by.

Zola and Valetta returned to tidy up the shed, assuring everything would be in order for the start of tomorrow's work. "If we're finished Zola, I'll pick up my things and start for College Hill. Remember, I'll pick you up this evening for the little party. Are you sure you don't want a ride home?"

"No, thank you, Valetta, I'll wait and see if Mell has something else for me to do. I'll be ready when you come by." With that the young lady headed for her car and drove away.

Zola busied herself with what she could find to do, wondering when, or if, Mell would return to the shed. She wondered, too, at Mell's acceptance of Nellie as a daughter-in-law. That speculation only added another suspicion, why was Martha being so docile! As she patiently waited for Mell to return, Zola found plenty of time to reflect upon Nellie and Clem's wedding. She was glad to know that where Nellie was weak, Clem was strong. Where she lacked in self-esteem, Clem stood tall in confidence and believed in the future. He was sure of himself and more importantly, sure of their love for each other. She allowed a sparkle to fill her eyes when she let herself at least believe Mell might hold a mystery. Not so, her heart whispered back! But then had he not gone out of his way to be close to her today? Had not his casual touch been more than just a passing thing? If not, would there be a convincing touch?

She was certain now that she was in love with him! She was determined not to reveal her feelings and fought hard against the tears she refused to let fall. He would be coming soon, she must be about her work. Perhaps, she thought again, someone might have noticed his closeness with her today and speak to her about it. Her excitement concerning the turn of events was kept in low key, a nonchalant matter of fact, when inside her soul she was bursting with happiness and joy. "Tonight, I'll know a lot more of just what is happening." It was like all the great seasons rolled into one, the fiddlers were playing, and she felt like dancing!

Mell was alone when he pulled up and parked the empty truck near the grading shed. He was whistling softly to a tune she did not recognize, then he stopped and spoke. His voice, deep and sensual, sent a ripple of awareness through her. Then he bent his shoulders and whispered in her ear. She smiled and neither moved for a moment while Mell brushed his beard against her creamy soft face. "I have to go to a Festival meeting tonight in Siloam Springs, would you like to go with me? Perhaps we could go to dinner after that."

Hesitating for a moment, Zola thought of the plans she had made for the evening. What a dilemma. Mell had never asked her to go anywhere with him. Up to now she would have given her right arm to go for such an offer, but tonight was the prenuptial shindig! It only had to cross her mind and she read it like a book. There would be another day, another soiree. Tonight she would spend her time with Mell! "Well, yes, if you'd like, I don't have anything to do."

He placed his powerful hand upon her arm and drew her close to his side. "Fine, then I'll pick you up about six-thirty." Still holding her close, a radiant smile broke across his bearded face as he continued to speak. "Has anyone told you lately that you're beautiful?"

Her flushed face lowered for a moment, then her sparkling eyes met his. Again, she held his hands to her heart. "Not lately, but my mother told me that when I was a little girl, but then she was known to be partial to her children. She thought we were all pretty and above average." Then a rather coy grin broke up her otherwise somber face. "Did your mother tell you that you were a very handsome young man and that you might well be able to mesmerize young ladies some day?"

Mell gave a hearty laugh and placed his head against her long silky hair. Sheepishly he felt like a young man in love and realized it had been a long time since he acted in such a rash manner. He enjoyed the feeling, and ruffling her hair, he squeezed her close to his body.

"You're teasing me, Mell." Then she tolerantly pushed away.

"No, I'm not teasing and you don't have to push me away. We're not being two naughty children. I love you, Zola!" They buried themselves in the moment of time and the season of harvest.

Members and guests of the festival committee filed into the newly opened Community Building. The grand and impressive edifice was constructed by the Public Works Administration. Folks here knew it simply as P.W.A., or one of Roosevelt's Alphabet Soup Kettles. Nevertheless it was greatly appreciated and would fill a multipurpose need of the city.

Following its grand opening, this was the first official meeting. It would be filled to capacity. Mell seated Zola on the front row, then took his place upon the stage amongst the other committee members.

The local attorney, Sam Elroads opened things up by way of introductions. Next came the reports from various groups. Ethel Moses, in charge of publicity, spoke how, with the help of so many local women, the city was awash with bright-colored banners. It had been reported that folks were driving into town just to see the flamboyant banners furling in the breeze! Then she took time to read an article taken from the Fayetteville Times. "Banners Proclaim Pawpaw Festival. Siloam Springs. This little farming town on the Oklahoma border pays tribute to the odd and little known pawpaw fruit this weekend, with a grand parade and free pawpaws for all!

"Festival queen, Valetta Kvasinikof, a student at John Brown University, will reign over the first festival. Mell Marshall, grand marshal for the parade, produces the largest acreage among the growers and is the entrepreneur who originated the unique industry. The parade begins at two P.M. Saturday. An estimated crowd of ten thousand is expected to attend."

Mrs. Moses then mentioned the page dedicated to the Festival by the local "Herald-Democrat," and thanked them and their advertisers.

Next to speak was Bill Hillhouse, director of the Chamber of Commerce and strong supporter of the pawpaw industry. He stated that they were successful in introducing the fruit along the rail belt from Kansas City to New Orleans. Several of those users in the market area were invited and would attend the festival. A welcome booth at the depot was in place to welcome them as well as other travelers stopping off here.

The commercial shipping department fell to Ben Davis, general manager of Davis Shipping Co., and shipping manager for the pawpaw industry. "I have several commercial floats in the parade, one each from Tulsa, Oklahoma, and Noel, Missouri. Other entries come from Fort Smith, Springdale, Rogers, Fayetteville, Bentonville, and Siloam Springs. These floats, as well as all others must support the theme, "Mr. Pawpaw Reigns," and exhibit his trademark somewhere on the parade unit. The extent to which floral material must be utilized, is minimal and left to the discretion of the float committee. This year's "Queen's Float" is sponsored jointly by the city of Siloam Springs, and her community sister, west of Siloam Springs in Oklahoma.

"Don't be surprised if the United Pawpaw Industries snatch the Governor's Award. I understand their entry will be covered entirely by pawpaw wood, leaves and fruit! The Noel unit is one to be watched also. It's from a nursery who has kept close wraps and tight lips over their project. On that one, we'll just have to wait and see."

Mell was next to speak. "On behalf of the growers, and bankers, and believers, I want to say thanks for your supporting role in being here tonight. It's been a long hard row to hoe; many said it couldn't be done! But the way I see it, we have achieved more than a nominal success and we've just started. It is being done!" The audience interrupted his speech with a loud roar of applause. Someone, audible above the babble, was heard to ask, "Where is the doubting Thomas?" More laughter.

Mell continued, "Oh, there are some still about; others have changed their tune. It has not been easy, I won't deny that, but does anything worthwhile ever come easy? Look at the troubled chicken industry. Believe me, it's just a phase, they'll outlast it and go on to do great things.

"Our forefathers came here with little more than the shirt on their backs. Deliberately, came here, at a time when others were saying, 'Go around the Ozarks, it's too rough and rowdy and has nothing to offer.' Aren't you glad they came and stayed?" Again the audience gave a big round of applause.

"Folks, this country's depression will not last forever; it, too, will pass. Look to the future, it'll be here before you know it. Now take the government project out at the gap. How long have we waited for that flood control thing? Well the dam is going up and with it comes more and cheaper electricity. God only knows what else it will bring! Keep your chin up, if I can do it, so can you. And one more thing, come out and see for yourselves what the pawpaw industry is doing. You'll be given a free tour and a sample of fruit. Lugs of fruit will be reasonably priced. And now for the commercial, take some home with you. It's a nice time to be out in the Ozark hills. See you there."

For the next introduction, Mr. Elroads read from a prepared note. "On the social calendar, we all consider ourselves fortunate to have Miss Iva Eidson, keeper of the rules of etiquette. She brings grace and dignity to what otherwise might well have been overlooked. Herself a beautiful lady, Iva coordinates the plans for the queen and her court. Her talent in harmonizing floral colors with fashionable fabrics is well known. I present to you, Miss Iva Eidson."

Exquisitely she stood, dressed in a silken tiered gown of peach georgette. "Thank you, Mr. Chairman." Turning to the audience she smiled and softly spoke. "It has been my privilege to work toward this eventful day we have all waited for. It has taken a lot of thought and planning, talent and time. We have seen the best in coordination and congeniality. Beginning Friday the Pawpaw Festival will be ours! The beauty pageant, held here in the auditorium, will present to us, Miss Siloam Springs! Special menus are being offered by the Youree Hotel, the official headquarters for the festival."

Turning to whom she helped choose for Grand Marshall, she smiled and addressed her friend from Norwood Prairie. "Mell, I can assure you, pawpaws will be served in every imaginable way." Then she added, "and probably ways that aren't imaginable." The audience laughed heartily. "Just one more thing, thanks to all of you who have worked so long and so hard. God bless you all!"

The audience again gave their expression of gratitude. Again they cheered and were now ready for the musical performance. The chairman quickly strolled across the stage to the podium. Looking back at the participants leaving the platform, he thanked them and spoke again to the audience. "I hope you will all stay for the big show we have lined up for you which will get underway immediately."

No sooner had the stage cleared when the curtains opened and the program got under way with "The Arkansas Traveler." The old timer, a native, made the fiddle "talk." It brought down the house!

Those leaving the auditorium early included Mell and Zola. They made their way to the Youree Hotel for dinner. Through the lobby and down the marbled corridor, the couple made their way to where a banner hung, "The Pawpaw Room." They were seated at a secluded table. Screened by palms and lush ferns, they enjoyed the privacy of the moment, a true season of the heart.

Leisurely looking over the menu, Mell was unaware Zola found it confusing until she spoke. "Mell, I've never been here before — I feel like a fish out of water. This menu, it's altogether intimidating."

"I'm sorry, let me help you." He put aside his menu and placed his hands over hers. Intimately he scooted closer and felt her long soft curls brush against his neck. "I had planned for a quiet relaxing time; don't be threatened." Then he pressed his leg against hers, "Do you like the flowers?" She glanced at the bouquet in the center of the table, "You had them put there, they're from you." Then what she had been tempted to do before became a reality; she kissed his cheek! It was an awakening experience that left her spinning inside. Reaching to the bouquet, she plucked out a budded rose and placed it across her plate.

"Here, let me help you order. I know what I want, squab. Would you like to try that?"

"Squab?"

"Yes, squab." Then he read from the menu, "Quail a La King, marinated in a buttery sauce of fresh herbs, garnished with a trace of cardamom." Smiling, he looked at her and said, "I can tell you're not impressed, would you rather order Frog Legs."

"Oh no, it's not that I rather have Frog Legs. No, I'll try the squab." Still reading the menu she glanced at the dessert, "Oh look, Mell, they have pawpaws for dessert, are you going to try them, too?"

He smiled, "Aren't you?"

As he spoke, the waitress took their order and returned quickly with the beginning of their scrumptious meal. Leisurely they lingered at the table, casually discussing events of the day and those coming up for the weekend.

Zola was basking in the glow of all that was happening. Here she sat and dined with the man she had secretly admired for months. This was his day, it had been his evening and he would claim tomorrow as well.

Desperately she had tried to act like a lady, unable to forget him and not yet willing to believe she should! She had refused to accept the fact that she was in love with him. Now there was no denial, he made that quiet clear. Life had taken on many new quirks since moving to Norwood. Finally she felt there were nice people around her, friends, not judges! Her relocation from the flooded valley and the old shack had been a Godsend! Bud's very life, spared from that torrent was a risk of life for Mell, a miracle in itself.

Her season of yearning for a better life had been long in coming. Seated here with Mell, her reminiscing ran the gauntlet of precious moments they had shared. None of them were more dear than the moment at hand.

"It's been such a perfect evening, Mell. Thank you for allowing me to share it with you. The meeting, the dinner, our time together." She held the large white linen gently to her flower-soft lips, and sweetly kissed him on the cheek. "You have made me feel like a lady, Mell, bold, longing for your desire. Please forgive me if I seem precocious, in blossom before my time."

"It has not been me, Zola; it is He who has made you a lady again. I have only helped you to see your worth to Him and to me. No, my dear, you are not being forward. You are in blossom, like the rose. Why don't you wrap them up while I go pay the check?"

She watched and admired him as he strolled across the fine carpet. His style was that of a man with character, dignity and pride. The modest sport suit, which she had never seen him wear before, fit him perfectly. Now she saw him pictured as a gentleman where before she had only seen his heart.

Picking up the soft green paper, she took the roses from the vase and rolled them carefully, held them across her arm and joined him in the lobby.

The night was quiet as if the sidewalks had been rolled up and put away. In this privacy they, too, kept the silence as they hurried to the car and drove away.

On the return trip to Norwood Prairie and Briarcliff, Mell pulled up at a roadside park as they approached the scenic Illinois river. From under the canopy of the great trees, shimmering shadows reflected down upon the water. Zola sat snuggled close to Mell and for a few minutes they watched the silvery water flow by in front of them. They also watched the shifting branches, breaking the darting moonbeams and the flight pattern of the flickering firefly.

"Zola, I've been wanting to find the time to talk to you about your salvation experience. I've heard some from talk but tell me about it."

"Do we plan on being here that long?"

"All night if it takes it."

"Well, I can spare you a few hours short of that. Well, first of all, I talked with Aunt Carnie and she helped me get the courage to start again. Then before I knew it, that night at the revival, something happened. When the Rev. Hallenbeck called for those needing help to come forward, I did. I was just there, at the altar. I didn't know what to do, how to pray, just flashing thoughts of my sins came to mind. Then someone knelt down beside me and asked me to pray the sinner's prayer. Then's when all hell broke loose. Pardon me, but that's the way it was. This awful hideous face of the devil came to view, even with my eyes closed!"

"I thought I heard you saw him on the wall or something, sort of a smirking, cynical devil, if you please."

"Horror-stricken is what it was, yes he kept challenging me, shaking his head, 'No. Pay them no attention.' The hideous evil of reading his lips, just as if he spoke, 'no'! Relentlessly he followed me, both in vision and mind! I'll never forget that awful, well, hideous face!"

"How in Heaven's name did you break away from him?"

"You mean at the time? Pastor Hallenbeck rebuked him! In the name of the Lord!"

Whether it was appropriate or not, Mell didn't feel sure, nevertheless he drew Zola closer to his side. They sat, neither speaking, embraced in the warmth of love they were reaping.

The river rolled on by and its silvery sheen lost its brightness. The moon became hidden by the trees and total darkness took over the night. Neither of the lovers was naive, neither were troubled. Zola had resolved to leave such matters to Mell's sensitivity and good judgment. She believed in him implicitly. She was his lady, and she would never forget that.

Freeing herself from his embrace and raising her head from his chest, Zola looked close into his face. "Mell, I have never breathed such joy as I have found with you, but there I go, being sentimental again."

Almost before she could finish, Mell placed his weathered hand across her lips and brushed her face with a gliding kiss. "I do not doubt the truth of your joy, Zola, and you must not mistrust my love for you. We are well along as adults, I love you for what you are. Tomorrow is future, yesterday is past. Tonight we love, rest against my chest and listen."

She closed her eyes and discreetly felt her finger tips delicately touch his manly chest.

When again she spoke she held a sweet contentment, "So this is love."

"So it is, and I have felt it, too! Zola I promised myself some years ago that I'd never love another woman. They would mean no more to me than a stone picked up on a gravel bar."

"And your stony heart, is it melting like wax?"

"Melted, yes, thawed by your tender warming love. You have opened my eyes as well as my heart. I am loving again. Time in its seasons changes things, you have changed me."

Their tender gentle romance blossomed at the rendezvous by the river. Their yearning for each other, a genuine relationship, brought a platonic love of adoration and respect. The force of silence kept them bound like stalks of wheat in a sheaf! Oblivious to time as in nowhere land, the lovers dreamed away on the clouds. Unaware of the morning birds serenading them with their trill, innocently in love, for a few precious moments they lived in another world.

Following a busy and tiring day in the packing shed, Zola watched Mell approach from his loaded truck which had been readied for the railroad cars. She noticed his pace had slowed too, like molasses in January. She felt better. Standing by her side he reached down and threw the switch, stopping the conveyor line. "I intended to mention it earlier, Zola, but it slipped my mind. Nellie is feeling so much better that she wanted to help fix supper for us all tonight. Clem is there with her and Obie, at Briarcliff. They have arranged everything, nothing was left to chance, will you dine with us?"

"Indeed I would love to, Mell, if you have planned it that way. But then I wouldn't want to be a botherment."

"It was none of my doings. Strictly Nellie's, I think it's a good idea, don't you? I'll take the shipment of paws to the train. Why don't you go on over? I'll hurry back and join you in time for dinner."

With that he was gone, as he had been all day. So she would hurry with the unfinished grading and throwing the switch, the paws again moved passed and were boxed. She was the last one to leave the work place and quickly walked the short distance to the house.

Nellie and Clem greeted her at the door, both full of excitement! Nellie lost little time in hugging her sister, still spellbound from last night's get-together with the other girls. "Zola, I missed you so. Hurry, see my gown!" There on the wall hung the regal Queen Anne wedding gown! As Nellie took the gown in her arms, Zola cautiously touched the soft satin skirt. Instantly it held a striking impression. "Good land, girl, it cost a fortune! What have you done?" Delicate lace trimmed the train with embroidered appliques which now lay on the hardwood floor. Nellie, fiddling with the clasp on her necklace, left Zola holding the gown. Then donning the matching earrings, she smiled. "How do you like them?"

"Are they . . . ?"

"Pearls, yes, real pearls. Stunning, aren't they. Oh, Zola, I missed you when you were not shopping with us, and again last night. Yet I know how important is was for you to go with Mell. I do hope you approve of the selections I've made. There's so little time left!"

"I did, ever so much, want to be with you, Nellie, but my want to be with Mell was greater! How can I explain? His talisman effect is an obsession with me!"

"We're sisters, Zola, do you think I have not felt this and yet not understood your happiness?"

"Happiness, I feel like Cinderella, but afraid of midnight."

"Come with me." As they walked into the adjoining room, Nellie whispered, "From what Clem tells me, you have nothing to worry about." There laying across the bed were the bridesmaid dresses and accessories. Gasping, and placing her hand across her mouth, Zola asked, "Is one of those for me?"

"Yes, one's for you."

Then holding up the dress, Zola realized that they both were deeply in love with a Marshall. In their moment of sharing the other's joy, tears from both faces touched the lustrous gown. Zola brushed the back of her hand across her eyes, then noticed a string of pearls laying on the bed. Placing then around her sister's neck, Nellie said, "There, Cinderella, how's that for beads."

Touching the pearls as they lay softly against her throat, Zola could scarcely believe what was happening before her eyes. "Where in the world is this money coming from? Is this from the inheritance Clem came into? Can any be left, should you spend it like this, so lavishly?" Still holding the bluish green gown she remarked, "What a beautiful soft shade of green, what is it called?"

"They call it sea mist. I label it pawpaw green."

"Bear it no mind, I've never seen such loveliness in a dress."

"Martha's is exactly like this, she said, 'It's awful highfalutin,' of course that's just Martha. You don't think so do you?"

"If one can forget about the cost, and I judge you have, I wouldn't say it's uppity or excessive. But mercy, I hope he's got lots of it!"

"I'm going in with him tomorrow when he takes a load of paws and he's gettin' me a set of rings. He says he's going to get me real diamonds, now ain't that something else!"

The ladies were still carrying on when they heard Mell drive up and park the big truck in the backyard. They also heard the back door slam as Clem went to join his father. As the two men reacted to the day's production, they brought out the optimism needed for beginning another season. Mell was never one to count his chickens before they were hatched, but all things being equal, he was excited with the start up results.

"Did we finish the car, Dad?"

"And a good deal more. They're on their way to the Missouri Wholesalers Distribution Center, in Kansas City. Tomorrow a car goes south to Cajun Cafeteria Food, in New Orleans. Yes sir, Ozark pawpaws will soon be on the table for those with discriminating taste. In fact Zola and I enjoyed a savory dessert last night. They fix those darn things in a unimaginable way!"

"Dad, speaking of Zola, she's here. Aren't you seeing a lot of her lately?"

"Meaning what?"

"Well, like you must like her a lot."

Mell never spoke of love, in fact he seldom used the word. Nor could he be accused of mystical phrases. Old Hughey taught his boys it was just unmanly. But now a new awareness of the world allowed him a bit of freedom. Gently walking to Clem's side, the father placed his muscular arm around his son, and smiled. "Son, I must confess, what you see is correct, we're in love. Are you taken aback, dismayed by this turn of events?"

"Of course not. God works in miraculous ways." Then he hugged his father as he had not done in years. "I'm happy for you, Dad, let your heart be your guide, not the busybodies. Who cares what they'll say? Who knows? Now that she's got religion, they, may accept her!" With a tap on the shoulder the conversation ended with, "Here, help me take in the groceries." The men each carried in a sack of provisions, placing them on the kitchen counter top then joining the ladies who were still speaking of last nights events while watching dinner.

The amorous feeling in the hearts of the ladies dulled their sensitivity toward the immediate needs of all four of them. When had they last eaten? Mell, as least, knew it had been too long. Sniffing the fine food about the stove, he quietly joined Zola as she hurried last minute preparations and finished setting the table. She could read his mind, besides hunger, she knew what was really there. Success! He had made it to the top! Not an unholy arrogant pride which comes before falling, but a glory in thanks be to God! She knew he had many reasons to be justly proud though he never used the word himself. Basically his ingredients were: hard work, more hard work, and still harder work. The rift between him and his son from the earlier fallout had, to a great extent, healed. Tonight they would all join around the table with Obie, Nellie, herself, and her children. She would say nothing of her concern that with Martha's presence, there would likely be yet deeper rifts to bridge. The festive mood of the evening would prevail and Mell's achievements with the orchard would be the center of conversation.

Nellie and Clem had set a pretty table and the bride-to-be had arranged a small bouquet of daisies from a wild clump just outside the door. Clem announced dinner and seated them around the table. Quietness followed, no one knew exactly what to do. Then Mell said, "Let us pray." It was short and sweet and followed by "dig in."

Zola felt less than comfortable, it was her first visit to Briarcliff Cottage and her uneasiness showed. Clem, understanding her situation, tried to put her at ease. "How do you like the gowns, Zola?"

"I declare, it's the prettiest thing a girl ever did see, but the cost must've been outlandish! Mell, these weddin'ers may be from here in the sticks but it sure ain't going to be no hillbilly weddin."

"You can say that again, yep, it will cause tongues to wag." Then looking to Clem he said, "We can handle it, son, let them wag, Saturday belongs to you and Nellie." Clem looked at Nellie and squeezed her hand, he could see her color was not good, he knew she had overdone it but made no remarks.

Mell also realized she was very tired but also kept still about it, then he said, "Nellie, you did a wonderful job on the cornbread, pass the black eyed peas."

Leaning her head toward Mell's shoulder, Zola took a daisy from the vase and twirled the stem between her fingers. "Just think Mell, of all the history in the making! You're the hub of excitement, do you think you can last another couple of days?"

"We'll make it, won't we Nellie? And Clem, I want you to know you will be missed." Seriously looking to Nellie, Mell had that brave look as he spoke. "I hope the desert and the best of doctors will soon bring you good health, Nellie. We'll be keeping up to the minute reports from the Arizona desert, then one day your lungs will be strong and clean and you can shout, 'I'm coming home.'"

"And we will," said Clem, "On the first plane. And with all the family blessings. Obie, you and Martha will go to college and amount to something, maybe a politician in Little Rock, perhaps own a big business in Siloam Springs, how does that sound?"

"I want to stay with Dad and be a farmer."

"Well, you can stay on the farm and Nellie and I will live in the city, it doesn't really matter, just get that education. Then you can live where you want and do as you want, that's taking hold of your destiny. We don't have to stay in the doldrums, as a family, thank God, we're moving on!"

"Do you like living on the desert, Nellie?"

"Don't know Obie, never was there, but if it heals my T.B. I'll like it. Even with the healing we'll miss the hills. We'll miss all of you, the seasons from apple blossom to autumn. I'll miss the Mayapple and the persimmons, and I'll miss wading in Clear Creek. How about you Clem, what will you miss most about the Ozarks?"

"I expect mostly I'll just miss being here."

Silence for a moment then Zola enthusiasticly spoke up, "Well, when you do return things will be different. There will be the new dam, the beautiful lake and the power station. The governor is promising new roads, better schools, more jobs. He says 'We're pioneering the way into the future.' I say Amen to that, for too long we haven't been able to see the forest for the trees. At least someone has finally been able to see our plight!"

Clem spoke up, "You're right, Zola. I, too, see a new face of the valley and the prairie. And there will be the difference, personified in the glory of the new church and her people. I understand contractors are moving in some equipment, backhoe and the like."

"Mell, do you know long the old church has stood there?" asked Zola.

"Well now, let me see, reckon I don't. It was there before my time. Rev. Norwood donated the land, it was just timber land then. The church raisin' was a bit later, Dad helped on it but, no I don't exactly know when."

Light conversation continued until all the dessert was finished. The table cleared and dishes put away, the ladies hastened to try on their soft satin gowns, accentuated with strings of pearls, and sequin trim. Lace-trimmed trains swirled across the hardwood floor while light feet tapped about the room.

On and on into the late hours the family talked about the upcoming events and the change they would bring. One uncertain variation discussed by the father and son was, Martha. They approached the possibility of 'what if' Mell and Zola continued to desire each others company — what if they earnestly considered marriage! If it had entered Martha's mind she had not shown any response, and both knew that wasn't likely! She had been nice toward Zola, but both men knew it would end there. Martha had said on many occasions, that she wouldn't call anyone 'Mother.' Mell understood the dilemma, it weighed heavily upon his mind!

The lovely August night drew its curtain around the little party. Another perfect day had slipped away.

Early morning found a dull orange glow seeping through the fogged valleys. Drifting with the morning's gentle breeze, the sweet fragrance of jasmine filled the air around the little bungalow where Zola lived. There too, Mell saw the bright colors of the morning glory climbing about the porch banisters as he waited for Zola.

"I'll be out in a minute," came a voice from inside. Clad in a fresh clean pair of khakis she approached Mell with a welcoming smile. He replied and headed the car up the road toward the orchards. Both knew the heavy work load ahead of them in preparation for close down until Monday. Clem would be missed, today, and throughout the remaining harvest. He and Nellie would be seeing to last minute details today. Tomorrow, the wedding and Sunday they would fly to Tucson.

In the back of her mind, Zola could not help but wonder what the new life for her sick sister would bring. Nellie had never known a time when she had two thin dimes to rub together, now she didn't have the vaguest idea of her wealth! Zola herself was in a quandary as just what was going on in her life. For the first time in a long time she felt the warmth of a man who lit up her life! Still unsure of the mosaic pattern unfolding around her, Zola sat close to Mell as he drove to the shed. "These are indeed changing times, Mell. We'll surely miss Clem and Nellie. Tell me, do you think Nellie can really be free of her disease? She seems so frail, sometimes I worry about their marriage, what if things don't improve? What if they are mistaken and they don't have the means Clem claims?"

"Well, first of all Clem does have the means which he claims. Secondly, I do believe Nellie will be cured and that their lives will be filled with love and joy. And why not? And yes, we'll miss them. While they are leisurely frolicking in the sun we'll be getting on with our own lives, working the hills and reaching for the American Dream. Hopefully we'll find that chicken in every pot and two cars in every garage."

From the start of operations this Friday morning, the work day moved toward a tidy shut down for the festivities now at hand. Picking fruit had ceased. Packing and shipping moved to a clipping speed. Finally by mid-afternoon the car door of the Kansas City Southern slammed shut and another rail car was ready to move out of the yard and down the silver rails toward New Orleans.

Briarcliff Cottage had become quiet and abandoned while Hurst Manor upon the prairie, flourished with excitement and anticipation.

Martha had feverishly worked with Aunt Carnie in getting everything whipped into shape and spotlessly clean. For the next two days the White House and the old matron would be hostess to the clan. Every room's windows sparkled in the sunlight and were softened in freshly hung lace curtains. In the cool shadows bouquets were reflected against the highly polished oak tables.

The dust storms to the west which had been plaguing western Oklahoma and Kansas brought another pink glow at sunset. Another unforgettable sky with its changing colors brought the ultimate finale which closed with the gentle softness of night.

The hills had seen many such chapters come to a close, yet this one was destined to be different. It was a season of the heart which would live as long as life itself, with memories lasting forever. Night deepened, and in the faint twinkling of the stars the hills about stood guard over the little prairie and her people eagerly waiting the dawn of a new day.

XII

White Lilies

AT the dam site, final chunks of massive rock were felled from the mountain. The progressive excavation of the ponderous side of the mountain excelled the work of a stone man splitting granite in a quarry. This precision in dam building was making the name of Buck Jones a household word. He and his men were now ready to shut down much of the operation until Monday. From their work-a-day world, they would take their place in the old church, where nearby construction, too, had ceased.

The stories of "Rags to Riches" were just now hitting the press. Out of town reporters were busy with the negative aspects of "BIG" news, unconcerned with the poverty of Northwest Arkansas. Those that did come for a story of a backward community striving to move into modern times, found one! Buck Jones gave them pictures to fill the papers, and stories that would bring them to life. He was proud to be a part of the community and the excitement of the day.

Many of the reporters were surprised to find the unrelated story of the dam, but grateful to be able to kill two birds with one stone. They were grateful, too, for finding lodging. Many tourists were still in town enjoying the healing springs and touring the Ozarks. Dateline, Siloam Springs, was more than just a wedding; it put the small border town on the map!

One reporter speaking to a bather in a fashionable spa asked if she knew of the upcoming wedding. "Indeed I do," she replied, "And there are many of us attending, do you think that quaint?"

"Perhaps not. Do you know the party?"

"No, no, dear boy, but I shan't miss the storybook affair."

Apparently only one person saw any reason to be concerned about the holy occasion becoming a circus. Buck had spoken to Clem about this matter and Clem had dismissed it as preposterous. Soon the gathering in would begin and Buck was secretly concerned.

Tucked away in a quiet valley of Clear Creek, the house of a well-to-do family, away on vacation, had guests. The modern stone dwelling, perched on a cliff, looked to be sitting perilously close to a misty waterfall. From their view, Nellie and Zola momentarily watched a pair of cardinals dart in and out of the wild hydrangea bushes that grew in the damp mossy ledge about the falls. Millions of violets, kept moist from the delicate spray, grew among the maidenhair ferns. The underbrush, mainly redbud and dogwood, though not in bloom, gave a pleasant soft green to the landscape all along the hillside.

It was to this quiet and serene hide-a-way that the sisters had been brought by Mrs. Jones. Privacy was theirs. And it would be here that the young Marshalls would spend the first night of their honeymoon before leaving for Tucson. The reporters with their cameras would be on the prairie, at the Briarcliff, and combing the city, to no avail.

At the church, final arrangements were under way for what appeared to be a Royal Wedding. The local florist was placing fresh bouquets of flowers about the platform and along the aisles of the old church. Bright satin ribbon attached to the age-old pews marked off the reserved section, surprisingly small for such a wedding.

Having stood on the spot for who knows how long, the old piano, scratched and flawed, was graced today by a crocheted doily, one of the last items taken from the old flooded shanty that had been Zola's home. Carefully placed maidenhair ferns were woven through the old ecru tinged lace. Near the center, an old family Bible lay open with white lilies across its pages.

Outside the church, one got a special look as well. For over the entry way and along the banisters were garlands of red cedar intertwined with baby breath and dainty ribbon. This did nothing for the chipped paint and weather-beaten wood. Still, the old church stood proudly against the prairie sky. A sign nearby did declare what was obvious to the eye, that a new church was in the making!

Every few minutes another team would be tethered to an old black jack or hickory tree. Then just as often a shiny black automobile would park some distance away so as not to frighten the animals.

People, some of whom were curiosity seekers, were milling about, coming and going from the church. While the ladies sat quietly in the pews, the men gathered in small groups around the wagons and discussed the weather, crops and fine spans of horses. Their eyes suddenly caught sight of a young couple tying up, and they were no longer focusing on their teams. Rather the lovely lady so fashionably dressed caught their attention as she was being gracefully lifted to the ground. She was escorted into the church and took her place at the piano. The long prelude of music began with soft whispers emanating from the pews. Neither the out-of-town elite nor local members of the Chautauqua club knew what to expect, but it was apparently clear this was to be a big show.

Cars, trucks and riders on horseback continued to fill the available space. Knowing space inside was limited, many folks had planned to remain out in the open. Reporters and photographers were frantically plying for a favorable spot, anxiously waiting any coverage that might be had. Many cameras flashed where the men were grouped; natives dressed in overalls, pictures of the teams and wagons were all fair game. So were the privies, as disgusting as it was to the hillfolk.

At Hurst Manor, Clem, dressed in his tuxedo, reminded Obie of a circus performer. In fact the entire family had never looked so funny. Even Carnie had changed from her usual drab colors and for this occasion at least, wore a bright flowery dress. As always, she wore her extremely long hair done up in a bun, but there was a bit of gaiety here as well. The new rhinestone comb sparkled in her soft gray hair and was coordinated with her handbag and gloves. She, like Obie, waited, trying to stay out of the way of the others until it was time to go to the church.

Martha, too, was ready, just primping the time away in front of the vanity table. She was somewhat skeptical about all of this and lacked the ardor in which the other ladies seemed to be caught up. Her shoulder length hair lay softly against her gown and sparkled like the pearls about her neck. Her unspoken thoughts now were, "If Mama could see me now, she'd be so proud."

Dressed in a business man's brown, pinstripe suit, Mell joined the other family members waiting in the parlor. "Let's get on with it," said he, waving his hand toward the car. "Obie, you sit in the back seat with Martha and Granny." The groom sat by his father. Soon the "push-mobile," as Obie sometimes called their vehicle, bounced along the bumpy flint stone lane that led to the state highway. Here they joined others who were on the way to the church. "According to plans we'll have a short wait, Buck will meet us here with Nellie and Zola, then we'll proceed."

While they momentarily waited, other motorist passed by, some craning their necks and staring at the waiting party.

"Shucks," said Granny, "I wonder if they recognized you at all, Mell, didn't seem to know you."

"Well, I'm not a bit surprised. I didn't recognize them either."

Looking toward her grandmother, Martha spoke in a low toned voice, "I bet Zola doesn't have any trouble recognizing him."

Carnie quickly gave Martha a frown and patted her on the arm, "You look sweet, Martha, a real southern belle." Further conversation was interrupted when a new fancy Oldsmobile pulled up and the driver, speaking through the open window, asked, "Do you need any help, my good man."

"No," replied Mell, "We're just waiting for another party, thank you."

The chauffeur gave a wave of the hand and slowly drove on. As they passed, they too had the look of curiosity written across their faces.

Finally Buck arrived and Mell slowly moved out into the lane of traffic again and on to the church. As he stopped the car in the proper place as planned, the sexton started pealing the bells. The clank and clatter continued for quite a spell.

As the party was organized for the grand wedding march, the bells were stilled. Quietly and with some pomp, the family was seated. On cue the organist started the familiar march, and all in the packed church rose and waited for the bride to enter and walk down the isle. Those on the outside stood, flanking both sides of the bride and her entourage.

The grand old church had never been so packed! Many were the common folk who made up the usual congregation, many others were merely visiting as invited friends. Then there were those whose curiosity led them to the "Rags to Riches" episode.

Those unable to enter the church, stood quietly and reverently on the large covered porch while others were at the windows, looking in.

Lohengrin's wedding march, softly playing, came to a quiet stillness. All was still. Pastor Wright looked out over the gathering, then smiled as he personally looked at the bride and groom.

"Marriage is as old as the family of man. It was instituted by Jehovah God in the Garden of Eden in the state of man's innocency. Moses, the great lawgiver of Israel, first gave legal sanction, and our Lord and Savior Jesus Christ, when He was upon this earth, gave it spiritual sanction. Rightly regarded, marriage is the highest and happiest of human relationships, the preserver of true love, the foundation of the home and the bulwark of society. The great Apostle Paul has said, 'Marriage is honorable among all men.'" Then looking out over his horn rimmed glasses, Pastor Wright again smiled at both of them standing before him. "If you have duly considered this relationship upon which you are about to enter, please manifest the same by joining your right hands."

"Clem Allen Marshall, do you take this woman to be your lawfully wedded wife, and do you promise before God and these witnesses that you will be to her a true and devoted husband; true to her in sickness and in health, in joy and in sorrow, in prosperity and in adversity; and that forsaking all others you will keep yourself to her, and to her only, until God shall separate you by death?"

With a strong voice, Clem answered, "I do."

Pastor Wright then repeated the charge for the bride. Again, a voice, though more sedated, solemnly whispered, "I do."

The rings, having been placed upon their fingers, Pastor Wright continued. "Therefore, by virtue of the authority vested in me as a minister of the gospel of Christ and in accordance with the laws of God and the sovereign State of Arkansas, I now pronounce you husband and wife. What God hath joined together let not men put asunder."

Then with a long pause, the pastor said, "Let us pray.

> "Almighty God, bestow upon these
> Thy servants, as it be Thy will,
> The gift and heritage of children;
> And grant that they may see their
> children brought up in Thy faith
> and fear, to the honor and glory of
> Thy name through Jesus Christ our
> Lord. Amen."

Pastor Wright, removing his glasses, smiled and looked over the packed congregation, gave the usual introduction. "Ladies and gentlemen, I present to you, Mr. and Mrs. Clem Marshall."

Down the aisle and out onto the porch the newlyweds made their way, shaking hands with those who chose to greet them. Among those were a number who had come to wish them well, and just to shake their hand. The remarkable occasion would, for them, too, be an everlasting memory. The wedding reception, to be held at the Youree Hotel in Siloam Springs would be for all these and others who might wish to attend. First, there would be the afternoon parade. Then the couple would join the Pawpaw Festival, followed by the big wedding party.

Little by little the gathering began to thin out, some going their own way. Most however were hurrying into the city to be on hand for the start of the Pawpaw parade and the festivities that would be continuing well into the evening.

Talk was in low key, subdued and polite. The wedding had however moved the hearts of the people. To be sure it was not all done according to Hoyle, but they all understood that around here, that didn't count for much. For those who had no knowledge of the hillfolk, they could say, "Wasn't that a quaint ceremony?" For the delayed reception, "Well, I never . . . I must attend the affair this evening and see how they do it." Many were heard speaking, "Remarkable," "A lovelier wedding I've never seen." Most of the talk was unheard and we shall never know of what they spoke.

Fruit stands were set up along the road to accommodate those who wanted to stop and buy available products such as pawpaw butter, jam, or fresh fruit. Growers calling cards were also available, offering free tours of the orchards. As the exodus from the church yard moved along, many tourists did stop and take advantage of the free samples and a chance to visit with the native hill folk. Conversation at these stops always turned to the wedding and the lovely bride. The visitors had never imagined such an occasion being shared with them and were astonished at the lavishness of the affair.

The road only went in one direction, so one by one the succession of cars wound its way back into the city. Some folks returned to their hotels, and courts while most joined those already on the parade route.

This was Sager Creek where Nellie had looked down from her hospital bed and found solace in its beauty. This was where she and Clem read together at the library. These were the springs where they sat together many times and drank the cool, pure, refreshing water. This was Sager Creek, flowing against the high bluffs that separated the town into two parts. Above the ageless limestone walls stood many stately Victorian homes where well-to-do families enjoyed a comfortable lifestyle. Below, on the flat low land was "Quaker Town," the other face of the hamlet.

This was the staging area for the parade and today was a beehive of activity. Floats were parked along the dusty streets where sponsors worked in a frenzy to put last minute touches to their works of art. Large amounts of greenery, such as cedar was used in abundance while much lesser amounts of potted and fresh flowers were used.

At the appointed hour the city high school band started the march and music filled the air. Following the bright new colors of the local marching band, Mell as the grand marshal rode in a new open car up Tahlequah Street as the parade moved along its route through downtown. Bright colored banners hung from the center of the streets all along Broadway and Main. Onlookers were lined three and four abreast along the sidewalks while many watched from windows and atop roofs. As units passed by, so did more marching bands and clowns throwing candy to the children.

The high stepping strutters of the equestrian team performed their bowing act and drill, receiving much applause. Riders of the roam, chestnut, sorrel and palomino were dressed in dashing rodeo outfits, splashed with silver. Saddles adorned with glittering gold sparkled in the bright afternoon sun.

Another round of applause went up for "Miss Pawpaw" as she came into view riding the Pawpaw Growers Association float. As recommended, most entries used pawpaws in some manner. This float had, as expected, utilized the greatest amount of the fruit. This lavishness won it the Governor's Award.

Next in line was the Church of God entry which won the city of Siloam Springs award for its theme, "Harvest is past, summer is ended." The horse drawn float, covered with the golden yellow foliage still tinged with green, truly expressed the harvest of autumn. Several members of the church were centered about a Thanksgiving table featuring a cornucopia.

The commercial division honored the local canning company for its entry with, "Eat all you can, can all you cain't." The company is experimenting with a pawpaw drink, the puree of the fruit with a rare blend of apple juice. The limited production of last year's fruit was an instant sellout. Output this year is expected to substantially increase, though still fall behind demand.

Proper respect was given to each float, but it was the same from end to end of the parade route, exuberant cheers for the newlyweds! They were vivacious and filled with the effervescence of life! It was as if they had been awakened by the excitement of the crowd, given new strength in life and were enjoying every moment! They responded to the public like seasoned politicians kissing a baby; they were just doing all the right things.

The float recognized for originality went to the McDonald County Nursery of Noel, Missouri. The theme, "We start your business," displayed experimentation with seed development and germination. Flats of young seedlings, older saplings and well-shaped pawpaw trees covered the company's float.

Distance, having been its achievement, the Hubbard Implement Company of Tulsa, Oklahoma took honors for their farm equipment and machinery float. Another float that drew much attention and had little folks hedging up close, was the apple wagon. The Bentonville float glittered in the afternoon sun with its bright red and highly polished apples. It was a stunning display of the area's main export. Also on exhibit were the many medals of honor and numerous ribbons the apple association of Northwest Arkansas had received from across the forty-eight states.

The parade, having run its course, passed the Isle of Patmas and headed up Saint John Street. The queen and the newlyweds were met by Brother and Sister Brown, who along with Storm Haley took them to the studios of KUOA.

The red light above the studio door began flashing, "ON THE AIR," Mr. Haley took the microphone. "From the campus of John Brown University, this is KUOA, the voice of the Ozarks, in Siloam Springs, Arkansas. With us this evening are a few distinguished guests who have just stepped from their respective floats of what was the first annual pawpaw parade."

"Nellie Black Marshall, may I start with you? Nellie you look so radiant and happy, and for the radio audience who may not know, may I say she is a lovely young bride, as of about noon today. Nellie, I must say, you had a lovely wedding, and we wish you both success and happiness."

Next, the announcer turned to Clem and introduced him. "These newlyweds postponed their wedding reception until seven o'clock this evening in order to be in the parade. What did you think of your reception along the parade route, Clem?"

"Well, I guess it was all right. It was exciting, I'll say that."

"I understand you're leaving tomorrow for your honeymoon in Tucson, Arizona."

Smiling and holding his bride's hand tightly, he looked at her then back to the announcer. "Yes, we're going to one of those Dude Ranches out on the desert."

"Clem, as a reporter, I must ask you about what perhaps is the best kept secret in the Ozarks. Is it true you have inherited a substantial amount of money?"

"Yes, and I shall ever be grateful!"

"Has that changed your life? It certainly doesn't appear to have done so."

"No, it hasn't, Storm, but it will. First of all Nellie and I can afford to seclude ourselves on the desert for her health, and secondly I will be able to enter the university there and finish my education."

"I can remember, Clem, and forgive me if I speak out of turn. I remember a few years back when you and your Dad neither had two dimes to rub together. Now he's doing well in the fruit business and you and Nellie are sharing the happiest days of your life! And not a financial care in the world! May God bless you both and I'll see you at your reception tonight."

Receiving a sign from the control room, Mr. Haley continued. "We must take a quick break for the local Pet Milk suppliers and when I return I'll be speaking with Valetta Kvasinikof. Don't go away." These few minutes of commercials gave the guests time to relax, and clear their throats. With the exception of President Brown, they were new to radio. Brother Brown was a featured speaker on the station, and spoke eloquently.

When again Mr. Haley continued the interviews he looked to the evangelist, "President Brown, would you please introduce our next guest?"

"Indeed I will. Today she reigns as Queen of the Pawpaw festival, Miss Valetta Kvasinikof. Valetta would you tell us where you're from, your major at the university on the hill, and your plans after graduation?"

"First of all may I say what a thrill it is to reign as the Pawpaw Queen! It has allowed me to meet many wonderful people both locally and across the state. In fact some time ago I made a trip to my hometown of Prague, Oklahoma in behalf of the Pawpaw Growers Association. As you may have noticed, our city sent the high school band as a marching unit in today's parade. I was happy about this."

"Is there any connection Valetta, in your surname and the Oklahoma town?"

"Not really, although Kvasinikof is a Slavic name. Our city, unlike the European city, is pronounced as if it was spelled 'Prag,' I don't really know why. But back to my major, I'm studying in business and will be looking for a job in that field after graduation."

The evangelist quickly spoke up, "I might add that she's certainly a blessing to our music department. Her sweet soft soprano voice is like that of an angel!"

Mr. Haley, in his remarkable radio voice, once again spoke into the microphone. "Ladies and gentlemen, this concludes our live interview with the newlyweds, Nellie and Clem Marshall and their incredible story of 'Rags to Riches.' Also, thanks to Brother Brown of John Brown University, and to Miss Pawpaw Queen, Valetta Kvasinikof."

As the studio lights went out on the campus, Clem and Nellie were driven to their suite at the Youree Hotel, although they secretly had no plans of spending the night there. This too had been well arranged. They would be in the suite for the convenience of the reception only. Quietly the plan was for them to be whisked away to the rendezvous. Clem did not want Nellie to be exposed to the likelihood of a charivari. He knew they were exhausting and exasperating; they could do without both.

Alone at last, Clem closed the door behind them and listened for the click of the lock. As some kind of a miracle, Nellie was doing well. He knew she must be tired, but it didn't show. Instead, what he saw was a lovely bride, waiting to be kissed. As he put his arms around her, she rested her head against his chest. He felt the beating of her heart and it grew faster. She stood before him in loving submission, his wife. For a moment she shivered, and holding her tighter he yearned for her to rest upon him and their meaningful relationship together in His agape love. He laid across the bed and gently drew her close to his side. Repeatedly he kissed her soft warm cheeks and whispered in her ear the things she wanted to hear. In their enchanting moments he pressed his lips to hers and felt the pleasure of his new bride. Lying there several minutes embraced in their new found love of matrimony, unspeakable joy filled their hearts. Clem, releasing his arms from around her, smiled, "Nellie, do you realize we have fasted all day! I'm starving and you must be weak from hunger as well. What do you say we have room service send us up some dinner?"

"That would be nice, yes, let's do it!" They discussed their choices and Clem called the order in. When it arrived Nellie was sitting at the vanity table combing her hair. Clem answered the door and let the bellboy in. The well tailored young man soon had the food arranged around the large bouquet of red roses that had been placed on the table. As he turned to leave, he spoke to Clem, "The bottle of champagne, sir, is on the house, I hope you enjoy it." Then he left, closing the door behind him.

As players in a great orchestra, each without a cue, moved to enhance their first meal together. Nellie lit the candles, Clem turned down the lights. As a lover of music, Nellie turned on the radio to the new sound in the city, that of FM classical music from KUOA. While the dinner music played low and softly, Clem again embraced his bride and properly seated her at the table. "Oh Clem, I do so much appreciate the roses, never in all my life has anyone given me flowers."

"My darling, tomorrow you shall have two white orchids in a silk corsage to wear on the plane."

Taking him lightly she said, "Don't be silly, Clem." Then she giggled and reached out and touched his hand.

"And the next day you shall have posies that grew on the barren desert, and I will pick them myself. What do you think of that?"

"I think you're being funny again. Flowers don't grow on the desert, do they?"

"Wild flowers do, you'll see." Then he placed a small piece of steak to her lips, and she obliged. Their ceremonious meal was both savory and charming and when finished, Clem rang for service, and the table was cleared away.

Unknown to the two up in the "Honeymoon Suite," the hotel below was beginning to fill with guests for the extraordinary reception. While the wedding in the old church was steeped in traditional ceremony, a merry, festive mood prevailed tonight among those waiting for the bride and groom.

The entire first floor had been reserved and catering service from Fayetteville had elaborately decorated and provided the luxurious cakes, punch and hors d'oeuvres.

The guests were a strange lot, and dress stranger still! While most of the out of town tourists refrained from overdressing, some of the farmers from the country dressed as well as they could. Each noticed and felt a bit uncomfortable. This had been anticipated and a couple of hostesses were endeavoring to alleviate any uneasiness. It was working. A wealthy Cherokee Indian was introduced to a well-to-do couple from Kansas City. The farmers of Norwood Prairie were made to feel at ease with their brothers of the city.

As the moment approached for the bride and groom to enter the hall, a hostess stood by the piano and announced, "May I have your attention please. Here come the bride and groom!" At that moment the gay recessional was played as the couple entered and received a spontaneous applause. The bride was dressed in stunning light peach colored silken georgette. The sheer tiers wrapped like petals, created a most delicate look. There could not have been a lovelier belle found in Georgia!

Clem, too, was smartly dressed and the epitome of young manhood. Both were jubilant, relaxed and at ease with the crowd. As they slowly walked to the center of the room, cameras from all sides were snapping their image on film. Professional photographers were taking pictures of the large three tier wedding cake and their sharing of it with each other.

That, out of the way, as well as the reception line, folks enjoyed light talk and more punch. Again the hostess got the attention of everyone and introduced the Pawpaw Queen, Miss Valetta Kvasinikof, who would now sing.

Again, as planned, the scheme was in action. With little notice the bride casually walked to her side and they spoke for a few moments. Then with the singing of a lovely wedding song all eyes were focused on Valetta.

With little attention, three young men entered the hall through a side door, and joining in with the applause. Though nervous, their mischievous intentions went undetected. They would watch and wait, and when the opportune moment came they would move quickly, and hope to be successful in nabbing Clem for the purpose of a real old time charivari! Only moments into their scheme all three saw the unexpected. Dressed in full uniform from night stick to weapon, it was obvious he was here on business.

"I hadn't counted on a cop being here," said the heavy bearded leader, "Now we have a whole new ball game."

"Well, Harry, I told you he was a slick city dude, but wait, this is only the first inning." Further whispers between them were interrupted as the hostess began speaking about the couple unwrapping the gifts. As crunching paper broke the silence, the apparent leader of the three whispered to another, "Jack, when this touching little scene's over, slip out and fake something outside that will get the cop's attention, make it look good."

The opened gifts lay about the table. The bright copper kettles, shiny chrome toaster, and a pewter lamp, caught Jacks' attention. "Look at that stuff, I bet they don't even have electricity."

"Harry, do you suppose they got a Sears and Roebuck catalog for their privy." With a big laugh, Harry replied, "Not knowing, I couldn't say." With startled emotions Harry spoke again. "Wait a minute, where is Clem!" No one knew his whereabouts. Nor did they know how long he had been gone.

What they would never know was the fact that he had slipped behind a screen and made his exit.

"Well dang my cats," said Jack, "couldn't one of you watch? You two go check the rest room, I'll wait here in case he comes back."

Nellie, ever so graciously thanked those for the gifts, and asked Valetta to sing another song. Then, as quickly as Clem had disappeared, Nellie, too was gone. After a time when neither had returned, Jack, too, stalked out of the auditorium, headed for the back door which opened out on the city park.

While the singing continued with much emotion, Nellie had been helped to weasel her way behind a screen and through a set of hidden doors to a waiting "Delivery Truck," parked near a side door of the hotel. Clem had successfully managed his escape by moving casually down a hall then climbing out a window and into the waiting truck. Without apparent suspicion the little old driver slowly drove away. After winding his way several blocks around town, he was sure they weren't being followed. Pulling into a garage, the darkness still hid the troupe. "We've done it," said the little old man, "Now best be on your way, and God bless you."

Nellie hugged her dear old friend and Clem gave him a hearty pat on the back. "Thanks old timer, thanks so very much." With that Clem climbed behind the wheel of a sedan, and they were off to their rendezvous!

Valetta received a thundering round of applause which gave her a good excuse to do it again, and she did. More applause, but by now some wanted to speak with Nellie. "Dear me," spoke a lady obviously from the big city, "I did so much wish to speak with the bride before she got lost in the crowd."

"Where is she, lost you say?"

There was no further need to look for them, although the temptation was too great to pass up, and a check was made on their room. It was the ninth inning; the ball game was over. There would be no charivari! Then the hostesses made another announcement. "Ladies and gentlemen, it appears the newlyweds have taken leave. They are not in the hotel. In their behalf may I thank you for coming and let the party continue."

"Well, my soul, what a quaint way to end a reception, I never." As the lady spoke, she adjusted her shawl, "Come, Bessie, I think we'll be going." Others, too, began to leave, some to find the lovers, while a few perhaps felt slighted. Many remained and Valetta sang again while folks helped themselves to another round of cake and punch.

Long after the hall darkened and the last guest had gone, the lovers had not been found nor would they.

A soft dim kerosene light flickered from the living room window, casting a soft glow on the faces of Clem and Nellie as they sat on the patio. Perhaps if it had been only the loving glow seen on the faces of the newlyweds and only the moonlight filtering in through the trees, the glow would still have been just as radiant. In this moment of ecstasy little else mattered except their togetherness. As His children, they knew His greater love had seen them through to this precious moment of their life!

Tonight He had prepared for them a special visual symphony as the sky about them blinked on and off with the gentle movement of the fireflies that seemed to fill the sky.

"Oh, look, one has landed on my hand," said Nellie. "Have you ever held them in your hand?" As she spoke Clem placed his hand over hers and enclosed the bug. Its flashing light shone between his fingers. "When I was young I caught them by the dozen, put them into a little glass jar and would turn them out the next morning." She opened his hands. "There, fly away little firefly, light your way through the dark of night. I'd rather watch you darting about." As it took off, another landed in her hair. Clem said nothing, just embraced her and leaned back in the lounge chair.

Another provision He had put together for them was the sounds of nature. The babbling brook, only a few hundred feet beyond the patio, gently flowed over the rounded rocks in the mountain stream and cascaded twenty feet below. It was as if they were in their secret place of nature. Time stopped, and they listened, closed their eyes and let time take them away. While the night birds sang and the whippoorwill called, they dallied the moments away until dawn.

In time Clem rose, gently placed Nellie in his arms and carried her through the open doorway. This night in the Ozarks would forever be endeared in their hearts as they lay down together for the first time!

Sounds of the new day broke the spell of night and awakened Clem. Quietly he dressed and slipped out of the room, leaving Nellie asleep. A trail led down along the waterfall and out into the massive forest still shrouded in a pattern of fog. Heavy dew bent the grasses along the shadowed pathway while rays of sunlight began to beam ahead of him.

The trail led precariously close to the brink of a fault. He paused. Leaning against the snarled tree with its tangled roots deeply embedded in the rock, he let himself slide down its trunk and sat, contemplating. Here he was, a rich man in a rich land, could he successfully make the change? Could he leave his beloved Ozarks? He could and he would return, that was one of the comforts in leaving. He had often heard his father say, "You can take the boy from the country, but you can never take the country from the boy."

"Father knew well of what he spoke," Clem muttered to himself. Minutes passed as he continued to sit under the old oak looking far out across the valley, across another ridge, and an acreage of apples not far out in front of him. He had stopped many times at such a place, often called an "overlook" by the tourists, and at them all he filled his heart, mind and eyes with a special unction they provided. Filled with this new zeal, and enthusiasm for life and land, he lingered a few more seconds. Then stepping back away from the precipice, he retraced his steps back to the cottage.

Nellie still slept soundly. He wanted to kiss her cheek but waited. Slipping off his boots, he eased out of his trousers, hanging them over the bed poster and laid down beside his love. Her gentle heartbeat pressed against his as he held her soft warm hand, and his chest pressed against her breast. When at last Nellie did awake, their lips met again, and they were entwined in their irresistible passion and affection, each sensitive to the other. Her long blond hair, shoulthe his collar caused him to blush as he awkwardly removed the shirt and drew up to her again. "Nellie, I have never loved you more." Nothing more was spoken. It was not a time for words, it was a season of the heart, a time for love.

Hurst Manor had seen both the good and the bad, it had been entwined between sorrow and happiness. If the walls could talk, they would tell of the vulnerability of those who passed this way. Some were insecure and unsure. Others torn and tossed even by dearest family members. Harsh words had been spoken; vigorous lives waned and faded. Eyes had filled with tears, and all had been left to memory.

In brilliant, blazing contrast to all this, there was the other side of the wall. The sweet, gracious, generous Spirit of the Lord lived here and dominated. Love lived here, not in happiness, but in the total realm of Godly joy! These walls had seen guilt, forgiveness, and redemption. No sign or motto was seen on the walls, yet this idea, "I am right with God and He with me," was lived out. Carnie's expression, regardless of the season, was "God is in the garden of my life."

It was now past noon at Hurst Manor, dinner had been finished and everyone's thoughts were on the arrival of Clem and Nellie. As she sat at the pump organ, Carnie would play the sweet melody of a hymn, then glance out the doorway and up the lane for any sign of their coming. Martha, who had chosen to do the dishes, did them alone. Obie, who still didn't quite understand it all, sat at the table nibbling on what Martha had not yet taken away.

Sitting in the swing on the back porch were Mell and Zola. Because of God's presence within him, Mell had triumphantly transcended all previous turmoil of his time. He too, had turned over a new page; indeed this was the beginning of a new season of the heart, for him as well.

As each waited to say goodby to Clem and Nellie, all of them were ready to wish them well and see them off. Carnie was the first to see them come up the meandering lane and park just outside the yard under the chinquapin tree which had become the "garage." Rotating herself on the organ stool, the grandmother rose and hurried through the living room, down the front porch and into the kitchen. "They're here." Then hurrying out onto the back porch she again repeated the message, "They're here; the kids are here."

As the family assembled in the front yard, there was much ado over the newlyweds, hugs and kisses, tears and laughter.

"Go on inside everybody," said Carnie, "No need standing out here in the yard."

Moving quickly to his grandmother's side, Clem embraced her in his arms with a faith-clad lock. "Grandmother, we don't have a lot of time. We must soon be on our way to Arizona."

Nellie, now standing by Clem, also gave the old lady a gentle hug. With the corner of her apron, Carnie dried her eyes, "Oh, but I hate to see you go so far away; I know I'll never see you again."

"Of course you will, Granny, we'll not be gone forever. Nellie will be well and strong again and we'll return."

Then the grandmother reached out and hugged Nellie. "Dear child, do get well soon. We'll all be praying for you, don't you know."

Martha watched. She, too, was emotional and hoped not to break down. The siblings embraced and tried to be brave, neither spoke. Martha then took Nellie's hand, "I hope you like it out there and I sure will be praying for you 'til you get back."

Obie too, wanted to tell them goodby. Clem reached down and picked up the lad and held him in his arms for a few moments. "You'll have to write me, Obie, and tell me all about things here: about the pawpaws, school, and about your rides on Lena. Then I'll write and tell you about the desert, how's that?"

"Ain't you afraid the plane might fall?" whispered Obie.

"No, they're quite safe. Actually I'm looking forward to the flight."

"Is she?" asked Obie as he looked at Nellie.

"No, no she's not, but that will be all right, you'll see."

Little Obie felt quite secure in his brother's arms and was glad for the attention. Clem said, "Now, Obie, you'll have extra work to do, dragging up firewood, helping Grandma draw water and attending to the stock. But you can do it, I know you can."

"Yeah, I can do it."

Looking out over the pasture fields, along the edges of the forest, the small peach orchard, Clem sat Obie down. He was staring out in space for a moment then turned to Carnie. "Granny, I love this place; it's home. Our heritage, we'll be back."

Reminiscing, Clem reverently remembered a few of his forefathers, most of whom had gone on many years ago. All contributed much to the family, the community, and society in general. Even now Clem could envision the tombstones bearing family names: Rev. Obadiah Washington Moss, Dr. Robert Hurst, Hughey Marshall, Buoy Marshall and Fannie Snodgrass, Tennessee's grandma. "Yes, Grandma, our roots run very deep in these hills and prairies. Rest assured, we'll be back. Geographically speaking the Ozarks are just hills, but to us Marshalls, they are more. They're part of our blood, our heritage."

Mell and Zola had seated themselves in the car, Mell behind the wheel and Zola beside him. Clem set Obie down and opened the door for Nellie, seating himself beside her. Carnie once again held Clem's hand, and smiled at Nellie. Mell softly spoke, "We must be going now, the plane won't wait."

As the car began to move, Carnie braced for a smile as they moved away. "God be with you 'til we meet again." They did not know what would bring them back to see her again!

From Tulsa, the plane flew west and by car Mell and Zola headed east.

XIII

Autumn Leaves

AS the autumn days of 1936 grew shorter, rain brought relief from the drought that had plagued the low lying lespedeza fields as well as tall timber on Pine Mountain.

Autumn around Briarcliff laid down a myriad of hues. Patches of bright yellow gold outlined the pawpaw orchards. A deep contrasting green bordered them now and throughout the long winter. Oaks which had performed for generations, again seemed to have been artistically painted on nature's palettes. They were not alone on the seasons stage of best dressed trees. The crimson maple stood proudly in view as did the sweet gum, sumac and the remaining few leaves of the sassafras.

For this spectacular display that nature staged each year, tourists waited, then, at the precise time flocked to the hills like lemmings migrating to the sea. Unlike the little creatures, the tourists did not jump but rather showed caution, that they might return another year.

Not only had the autumn leaves brightened sooner, they were blown from the trees earlier as well. A storm like gale twisted the branches and ripped away many leaves before their color indicated it was time for them to fall.

Tourists to the hills were not deterred by a few hours of unfavorable weather, many rather enjoyed the massive build-up of thunder and lightning associated with the passing front. Two of the natives, respecting their moments together, watched as they stood on the porch of Briarcliff.

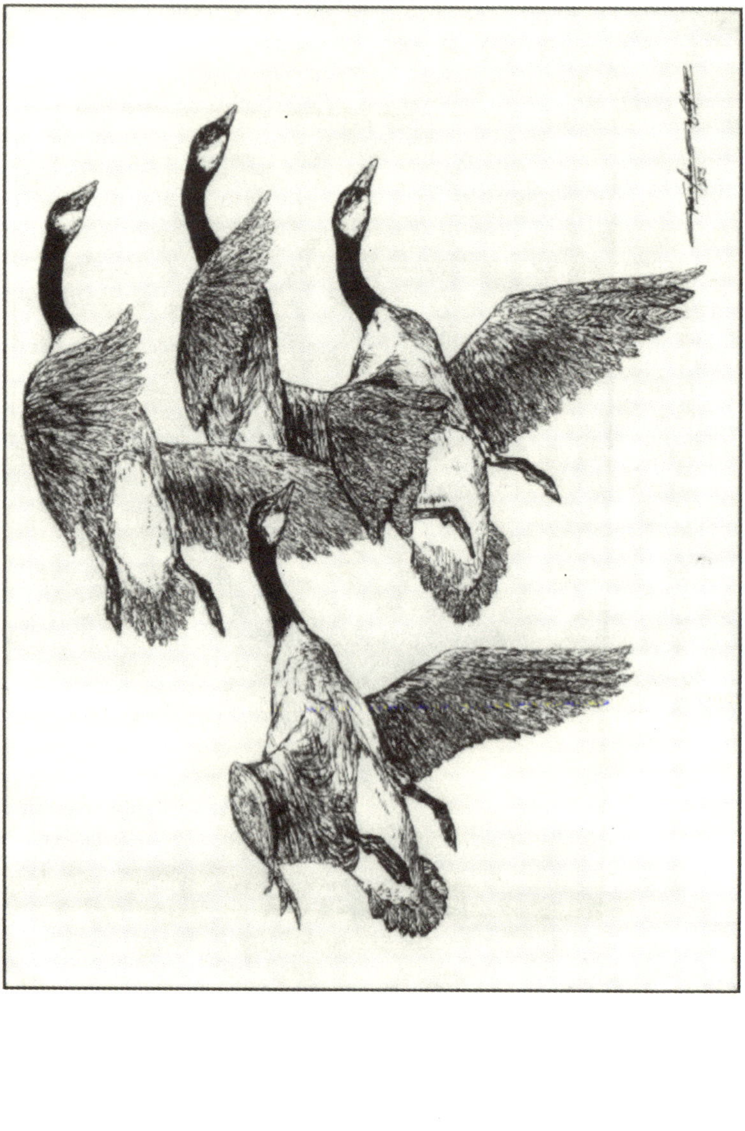

Also passing overhead was a flock of migratory geese returning south for the winter.

"Look, Mell, there in the twilight, see them flying across the moon? We could almost touch them."

Mell moved closer to the bannister. "They're going to settle on the lake."

They continued to watch and listen until all had passed. The cold wind had blown Zola's soft blond hair into a tangle, but she was very comfortable standing by Mell's side. She was where he wanted her to be. Mell fitted Zola's shawl more tightly around her shoulders and embraced her with tender love. Low moving clouds covered the moon and the sounds of geese were heard no more.

They stood looking out into that distant space entwined in each other's arms. "Let the night be night," said Mell. "We'll see it again another time, let's go inside."

As she held his callused hand and followed him through the doorway, she desired to kiss his cheek but she did not. "There," said Mell, "I'll drop a match to the little stack of cedar kindling and we'll have a beautiful flame of warmth and a pungent scent; won't that be nice?"

"It will indeed, I am a bit chilly. Will you excuse me while I fix my hair?"

While Mell poked about the fire Zola freshened herself and reappeared looking vibrant and full of life. Seeing she had returned, Mell turned from the starting tongues of fire and taking her hand, kissed her softly. "Zola, I want to show you some things I've kept all these years." As he walked over to an old trunk, Zola followed him and put her arm around him. As he opened the lid, neither spoke. It was a time of reflection for him, and an awkward time for Zola.

Lifting out the tray, he sat it across the open trunk and looked for a moment at the contents. "I have not opened this trunk in years," said Mell. "But I wonder if we should not look at this together?"

With mixed emotions, Zola, viewed the contents. A stack of letters tied with a ribbon lay near a knitted shawl. She moved her eyes about but could not move her feet. Reaching down, Mell picked up a satin covered box and once opened, paused for a moment before handing a string of pearls to Zola. She glanced at Mell, then took the pearls and held them in her hand.

"They were given to Thalia by her parents for her eighteenth birthday. She hardly ever wore them, afraid they would get ruined. They haven't been touched in years." Then taking the pearls he placed them around her neck and gently kissed her cheek.

"Do you want me to wear them?"

"I had hoped you could. I'm giving them to you. Will you take them?"

"Yes, I'll accept them and wear them with pride if that's what you wish." Slowly she embraced the man she loved. Finally releasing her hold, he took from the trunk, a family photo album. There were professional pictures of Carnie and Hampton, and Thalia as a child. Pictures of Lillie Hurst and her father, and Doctor Hurst, Carnie's father, were also a part of the collection. Mell carefully turned the pages. "This is the picture of Joe Moss, Hampton's nephew, remember the one we speak of who went to California?"

Another page was turned; there were pictures of Mell and Thalia that had been taken with an old box camera. The couple were well dressed and stood with pride in front of Hurst Manor. The next couple of pages were of Thalia and the children, the youngest in her arms. The silence was nearly unbearable for Zola, Mell too, turned the page with difficulty. The next page was unused, somewhat as a memorial. Then there were the grandparents again with the children, then only the children. Hampton had died and there were no more pictures of Carnie. As somberly as he opened the album, Mell closed it and returned it to the trunk. Other mementos were lying about, handkerchiefs, scarves, and news clippings yellow with age. Mell had little to do with such things that might wind up in a family trunk. Some of the items he had never seen, among them the cameo which Thalia never wore or spoke of.

Thalia, having been a seamstress, did many quilts. Some were laying unfinished in the bottom of the trunk. Kneeling down he lifted them out. The wedding ring, starburst, the wagon wheel, Zola knew them by name. She watched as Mell gently touched each one. To one side lay pieces of linen, many beautifully embroidered handkerchiefs, and items of tatting. Then Zola's eye caught a glimpse of a china doll. Mell, picked up the doll and handed it to Zola for her inspection.

"What a beautiful doll!" exclaimed Zola.

"Well, as you can see it's had no abuse as a toy. Martha has never had it out of the trunk."

While Zola held the doll in adoration, Mell reached for a small box and opened what he knew to be Hampton's gold watch. One turn of the winding stem and the second hand was in motion. Black Roman numerals were outlined on a white face for excellent vision. Then he closed the cover and pressed. Pop, the cover held in place.

Laying aside the watch, Mell picked up a pair of fashionable high button shoes. Still holding the doll, Zola smiled at seeing them for she had never owned such a lovely pair! Then quickly setting them aside, Mell reached for a box he knew contained Thalia's Bible. This he knew had been her most prized worldly possession. The gift from her parents was the King James version, beautifully bound in leather. It had been through her and this Bible that he had found Christ. As he bowed his head, Zola put her arms around him and kissed his forehead. "Memories are a precious thing, Mell, and they need not fade away." Suddenly he rose, drawing her to his side. She rested her head against his beating chest and for some time neither spoke.

"Zola, will you marry me?" Before she could respond Mell felt her go limp in his arms. "My land, she has fainted, Zola! Zola!" He patted her cheeks, and gently shifted her lackadaisical frame. "Do you hear me? Zola, Zola, Zola!" Having collapsed in his arms, she did not respond. He opened the door to the patio. Cold mist blew up against them bringing Zola to respond. "Zola, can you hear me?"

"Yes, I hear you, take me in and close the door!"

With the request, the door slammed shut. Zola stepped down to the floor. "I'm sorry Mell, what a time to pass out! But I haven't been feeling well lately, forgive me." As the words passed from her lips, her arms tightened around him still without answering his question.

"Let me start over, Zola, I proposed to you, did you understand?"

"Yes, I caught that, I fully heard." They stood entwined like a rose around a briar, each lost in that magical moment of first love. But it was not that for either. Somewhat less, it was indeed a very special moment. Folks in the Ozarks called times like this, "Seasons of the Heart." Zola and Mell knew they could not define their feelings sufficiently and bothered not with words. Mell touched his finger to a tear falling down his angel's cheek.

"Hey, what's the matter? You're crying and you haven't said yes. Will you give me the answer, will you marry me?"

Her pale color told him she was ill and her trembling body told him more, though he knew not what for sure. As with young love, to him nothing seemed to be relevant except the moment at hand. For Zola there was more than that, past and future passed before her. Years, all of them, flashed like little stars in the night. Suddenly the summer night, now months past, came into view. It had been a tender moment for her, alone with Mell out on the prairie trail. Tender and sweet, it was the summer season her heart began to live! She had forgotten much about the revival, but the starry sky and Mell's tenderness she felt, had been ingrained in her memory. Another tear rolled down her cheek. Then she looked into his expressive face. He was still waiting for the answer.

"Yes, yes, I'll marry you. I would marry you tomorrow!"

She fell into his deep embrace as shadows from the fireplace danced about them. As they sat in front of the glimmering fire she marveled that their love had come this far. Mell, now facing the facts, realized he had loved her for some time and silently asked himself why he had taken so long in proposing. Without further reflection he knew the answer was the mending of his shattered heart. Finally, what he had was the intuition that he had reached that span of time when he should and would move on with his life.

With a woman's intuition, Zola had mauled her images about, months ago, now only giving modifications as she found it to be necessary. She had known Mell since moving into the valley a couple years back but they seldom saw each other or spoke. That is until about a year ago. Neither took a shine for the other one for what was obvious reasons. As the pendulum began to swing the other way, slowly each saw values heretofore unnoticed.

For Zola, it was often fear and frustration, her self-esteem did not allow her to fancy such a man in her life. She had tried so hard not to drive him away now she still wondered about her new place in his life. Carnie had been so helpful, then through Christ, she recognized she had become a new and whole woman, free at last from the tarnished and tenebrous side of life.

Like a worn out poster left behind from an election campaign, they sat, watching figures in the fire. Zola heard wedding bells and watched the fire as asteroids, meteors and other flashing objects that normally flew through the night sky passed. Mell, too, realized they had sat there quite a spell and was distracted from their serenity. Like the poster, whose time finally came, they were ripped away. Through the rain pelted window Mell caught a glimpse of light bouncing over the hill and obvious coming their way. In a strong voice he spoke. "We have company coming, who in the world at this time of night!"

Zola quickly aligned herself for viewing the oncoming vehicle and held Mell's hand tightly. As the motor car drove up near the front door, she looked quizzically at Mell, "I don't recognize the car."

"I do."

The driver opened the car door and raised an umbrella against the rain. "It's George Fetterly, what in tarnation do you suppose he's doing here?"

Before either could speak the messenger had buttoned up his slicker, and holding the parasol tight against the wind, he bounced from the car. Mell met him at the door and ushered him in from the storm. "What is it George, what is the matter?"

Panting, George sat the umbrella down by the fireplace and hastily wiped his bared brow. Returning his handkerchief to his back pocket, he paused for a moment then faced Mell. "It's Mrs. Moss, you must go there at once. Martha came through the pasture asking me to 'fetch Daddy'. I only stopped a few minutes, but I'd say she had a heart attack, at any account she's in a great deal of pain." While the men talked further Zola removed the pearls from around her neck and carefully wrapped them in the white soft paper, returning them to the trunk. "We'll leave right a way, George, and if we find we need the doctor we'll come borrow your phone. Thanks for coming young man, and tell your father to pray."

"Oh, he's doing that all right. Yes, sir, he's praying." With those words he again covered himself with the umbrella as he made a mad scramble for his car. The tail lights disappeared as Mell closed the trunk unaware the pearls had been returned.

Checking their wraps which hung behind the door, Zola hastily put on her coat. "I had no idea Carnie was so sick, did you, Mell?"

"No, I didn't, perhaps she isn't. But then we'll hurry over and see what needs to be done." The bed of coals in the fireplace were covered with ashes as the couple made plans to exit Briarcliff for yet another emergency. Sheets of rain had slackened as the cold front passed the Ozarks, leaving behind a dampness that chilled to the bone. Clouds crossed the moon like slivers of cheese and seemed to billow around the couple as they made their way to Mell's car. Small branches, blown down by the gust preceding the storm, littered the vales along the lane. Carefully Mell drove the bumpy dark lane now becoming shrouded in patchy fog.

Hurst Manor was lit up like a hotel and it was obvious the fireplace produced a glowing warmth. It was around this hearth that the family now gathered. Carnie's pain had eased. Drowsiness left her quietly resting between the white sheets and the doubts. Between Martha, and Obie, exchanges passed to their father of what had happened. Both children presumed their grandmother was better, now that she rested quietly. Mell knew the truth and took Zola by the hand and walked to the edge of the bed. "We'll let her rest, when she awakens we'll judge what's to be done."

Mell led the way back to the fireplace where the children were waiting and watching. "Nothing can be gained by all of you staying up all night. Go on to bed, Zola and I will sit up and if there is any change we'll let you know." The rest of the night's vigil began as Martha went on willingly and little Obie was put on a pallet near the warmth of the fire.

With the coming of day Mell did the chores, and quietly ate breakfast with Zola and the children. "Grandma doesn't seem to have made any change; all I know to do is wait. In the meantime I'm paying a visit on Pastor Wright. If I'm needed Zola, you can drive the truck over and get me."

The morning was warm and dry. Mell and Pastor Wright sat in his office for some time discussing Carnie's illness and progress on the church but nothing concerning Zola. As the two men finished praying together, the sound of hammers came from across the way and a look at their work told of their headway. Ben Davis greeted Mell, "Looking good, ain't it, Mell? We'll have the rest of the trusses up today and before you know it we'll be framing in."

"Ahead of schedule. Well, that's good."

"I guess you're finished with the pawpaw harvest and glad of it," said the worker.

"All wound up for this year." Reserved in his speech, Mell paused, envisioning a finished church, and hearing the pealing of a lonely bell. "Mrs. Moss is poorly, remember her in prayer." As he slowly walked on he heard part of Ben's reply, then spoke to other workers along the way. "Good morning, men, nice day." Walking back to the car he turned and took another look at the new church rising higher day by day. He was proud of what he saw, and he was proud of Clem.

His gracious presence filled the room! Carnie felt it and was encircled in His radiance. Zola and the children were standing by the bedside for what loomed before her as the winter of Carnie's passing life! Where is Mell? Silently she prayed, "Lord, send him home!" Carnie's eyes looked down at her little Obie and she smiled.

"Are you happy, Granny?"

"Yes, Obie, I'm very fulfilled and grateful." Then she looked up into Zola's grim visage. "It's all right, Zola, I'm easy now, the pain has abated again, but I need to catch my breath." Carnie closed her eyes bringing Martha to tears as Zola hugged the granddaughter and patted Obie on the head.

"I'm sure your father will be back soon, let's let Granny rest for now. We'll talk to her again when he arrives."

Like the fragile roots of a young growing plant, the old matriarch lay undisturbed. The mellow melodies that whispered across the Ozarks went unheard. Likewise the tumbling streams and waterfalls stilled. The prairie grasslands were nothing more than a tangle sea of grass. Music, yes! It was the sound of Angels! They were singing the hymns of the early church, "Holy, Holy, Holy." Carnie had allowed the Master to walk with her in her garden. Now in her frailty, He still walked at her side and comforted her. The three figures still standing by the sickbed saw her sweet countenance, unable to conjecture the reasons for what they saw.

Fearful of standing there doing nothing, Zola bided her time still further, silently praying for divine intervention for Mell's arrival. "Dear Lord, he must come soon." He did.

For the next couple of days the beloved family devoted everything wholly to the care of the saint now hovering between life and death. Doctor Burgenstall, who came on such calls to Hurst Manor, still did. The finality of that was, "I've done all I can do." His visits were followed by Pastor Wright, who in turn with the local congregation sent up a constant appeal to the Father. Carnie was aware of their indomitable effort, never doubting their love or His power.

Above her, the picture of the Guardian Angel hung on the wall. The little boy and girl were walking on life's rickety bridge, safely in the outstretched arms of the Angel. Carnie sensed she now lay on her rickety bridge with nothing to fear. Unlike the children, she heard a voice conveying His final message, "Come home, my child, come home!" Sitting up against her pillows, she smiled and with her arms, motioned for them to gather around her bed. "Dear ones, don't be troubled. I'm ready and soon I'll be going Home!"

Telegrams had been sent of this possibility, yet such spoken words stabbed their hearts. Mell, able to cope with the ill tidings, put his arms around Obie.

"Where is it she's going to?"

"She's going to Heaven," said Martha.

"Now?" asked Obie.

The grandmother took Obie's hand, "It's all right my boy, if not now it would be later." Then the grandmother spoke to his sister. "Martha, promise me you will not be rebellious against your soon to be, stepmother."

Tears filled Martha's eyes and she found it difficult to swallow. "Oh, I won't, Grandmother. Somehow the Lord will make a way, I know that." Bending over she placed a kiss on the old lady's cheek and rested against her pillow.

"Now to you, Mell. You've been a wonderful son-in-law and I'm happy you and Zola are going to share in each other's lives. I'm sure it will be a blessed one, and I dare say it's time you both were getting on with it. God bless you is my prayer." Momentarily she closed her eyes, then taking a few deep breaths, she spoke again. "There is one last request, I'd like the ladies to gather around my bed and sing, can you arrange that for me, Zola?"

Startled, though realizing it could be done, even if she had never heard of such a thing, she replied. "Yes, Carnie, I'll do that, God willing."

Carnie heard but failed to respond, instead she had again closed out the world. Mell looked at Zola and shook his head. Then whispered in her ear the doubting words, "I wonder if it is His will!"

Darkness of the autumn night settled in and with it came folks to set up with the grand old lady of Hurst Manor. Elsewhere as the grim word was received, like preparations were being made. Clem and Nellie were now on their way from Arizona. Carnie hoped that Lillie, too, would be arriving soon. In the unlikely event she did not, Carnie had secretly given Zola a sealed envelope to be given to her niece on arrival.

Throughout the night neighbors kept a vigil around the bedside of their "Aunt Carnie." She had come to the Ozarks with her late husband, Hampton. Together they homesteaded on Norwood Prairie, started a family, and in more prosperous times, built Hurst Manor. For lo these many years, precious little had changed in her life. She, like Hampton, had always been held in great admiration. As a pillar of the church she stood staunch in her belief, sometimes to the point of being seen as dogmatic. She had given much of her life to the little indigenous church, now she was ready to give all.

Mell, with Buck Jones, met Clem and Nellie at the Tulsa airport and lost no time in returning to Hurst Manor. "She could go anytime," said Mell. "But who knows, she's a lady of steel!"

As they traveled the dark bumpy road back to the Ozarks, Clem tried to relate what it was like living on the desert, forgetting his father had been to those places.

"Nellie," said Mell, "I hardly recognized you, you're as brown as an Indian."

"That's where I spend my time, right out in the hot sun! And as you can see I've gained ten pounds from eating ice cream and drinking pop. I never felt better!"

"It doesn't seemed to have helped you any, Clem. Although I must say you do have a slight tan."

"Only that. I'm inside most of the time. The desert and I don't get along, we don't haf' to, I guess. What's happening out at the dam, Buck? Is she going up?"

"Every day. It's beginning to really take on the look of a first class dam. I tell you, Clem, it's going to draw folks like a moth is drawn to a flame."

"Reckon so, well it's about time for a change, we've had enough rhetoric. By the way, how's things coming with the new church — more than rhetoric, I hope." Then as they crossed onto the span of steel, Clem turned and looked down. "Isn't that Grand River down there, my, but it's a sight for sore eyes! Look at all that water!" It was quiet for a few minutes then Nellie asked, "How's sis? She hasn't been writing us much lately, surely there must be some news from Briarcliff or the Manor."

Mell hesitated, and Buck couldn't keep a straight face. "Well, yes there is, but I had intentions of leaving that to Zola."

"What is it, Dad? Don't tell us that Bud had to be rescued from some perilous adventure again!"

After a long stillness Mell answered what it was! "Clem, you're going to have a stepmother."

"I'm going to have what? Did you say stepmother?"

"That's precisely what I said, I've asked Zola to marry me."

"You are marrying my sister!" Nellie asked startled.

"Either that or she is marrying me."

"Are you serious, Mell?" replied Nellie. "Are you and Zola really getting married?"

"He's serious," said Clem, "I can tell."

"Well, anyway I'm happy for both of you," said Nellie. "And speaking of Zola, where is she?"

"In short," said Mell, "She's getting together the Norwood ladies's choir."

"At a time like this she's doing, what?"

"One might say, because of the time, that's just what she's doing. Carnie asked her if she would get the ladies together and have them sing around her sick bed. I know it might sound odd, but that's the way she wants it."

"Do you think that wise, I mean in her condition?" asked Clem.

"In her condition," replied Mell, "it's not unwise."

Buck, still driving in the rugged terrain approaching the hills, had said little. Following a hush he turned his face momentarily toward his peer. "Mell, you haven't mentioned the fact that Lillie Hurst is coming down, perhaps she's already arrived."

"That's right, and Joe and Minnie Moss are flying out from California. They should arrive tomorrow."

"Joe who?"

"Joe, your cousin, Uncle Joe and Aunt Minnie from out in Fresno."

"That's very interesting, I didn't remember them caring that much for anyone. All I knew was how hurt Grandma was when they ran out in the middle of the night not paying their bills."

"Well, there's more to it than that," said Mell. "But the gist of it is this. They got in with a tongues movement and got religion. I hear they've sent some consideration, trying to make recompense. Cousin Carl tells me they're doing very well in farming. I'm happy for them. Hampton used to say that Joe was his favorite nephew. It must have been a bitter pill for Grandpa to take back then."

Dim light in the eastern sky heralded a new day as the group arrived at Hurst Manor. Several vehicles were parked under the dewy deciduous trees adjacent to the yard. Mell stepped from the car, and greeted a few men who stood near by. Then leading the way, Clem and Nellie followed him inside.

"Aunt Lillie" met them at the door with her special greeting. Subsequently, Zola found the proper time to tap Mell on the shoulder, "I need to see you and Aunt Lillie, alone." As the three quietly walked the porch toward the kitchen, Zola took from her purse the envelope which Carnie had given her. "She wasn't sure she would make it till you arrived," said Zola, then she handed Lillie the sealed message.

Lillie refolded the paper, then looked at Mell, "I don't understand." Then she handed Mell the note. Unfolding the letter he read Carnie's words. "Lillie, will you do what you can to help, Martha? She'll need your help. Love, Carnie."

Mell returned the letter to the envelope and handed it back to Lillie. "I understand, I know what she means. Zola and I just told Carnie of our planned wedding and she knows Martha will strongly oppose. And now this grave illness, I don't know what Martha will do."

"I see."

"Mell, maybe we ought to wait," said Zola.

"She's always had confidence in me," said Lillie, "Let me handle it, and congratulations, Mell and Zola. I wish you nothing but happiness! Now let's go in and say nothing about this for the moment."

Reentering the kitchen some time later, Lillie joined Martha in preparing a breakfast. Martha took a cup of coffee to where her father was seated, "How is she, daddy?" He shook his head. Zola left the room, joining those around the sickbed.

By midday, Carnie seemed to have improved and was able to visit with Joe and Minnie when they arrived.

One by one, as the ladies gathered, they drew near and offered words of praise and encouragement. Others upheld her in silent prayer. Propped up by soft down pillows, Carnie was pleased to have their presence and to hear each voice. She took a moment to thank Sadie and Zola for helping with their arrival. From the adjoining room, Carnie gained a blessing as the family organ softly played "Sweetly Jesus Cares For Me." Someone read a Scripture from Psalms 30:4,

>"Sing unto the Lord, O ye saints
>of his, and give thanks at the
>remembrance of his holiness".

Other songs still filled the room with the melodious voices and their renditions of some of her favorite hymns. Music that had followed her through the years.

In the twinkling of an eye, the clock that had set on the mantel for forty years, stopped! Music hushed! The tired worn body of Carnie had eased away into God's presence before they knew she was gone!

Non-family members began to file out of the room, many going to the kitchen, others lingered on the porch or went to their cars. Of those remaining, Martha found it harder to let go. Lillie tried to comfort her and in time took her aside and talked at length of the situation. As darkness fell, the family stood bearing their sorrow together as they watched the black hearse being driven away with yet another fallen member of Hurst Manor.

It was Lillie who spoke first as the taillights of the hearse went out of sight. "Aunt Carnie would want us to act our faith as Paul wrote to the Thessalonians, 'That ye sorrow not, even as others which have no hope.'"

The Seasons
The Trillium of Spring emerge from the
earth, fragile and in splendor.

The summer flowers have faded
and insensibly fallen away.

The autumn trees now look
bleak, bare and cold.

The season of winter will be short
for I shall be with the Lord.

XIV

Bouquets

LILLIE, busy doing the housework with Martha, kept going over the distinct possibilities that would soon bear down on the young girl. Today there was time for meditation, tomorrow would direct more. As she kept one eye on the lane anticipating the hearse, Lillie knew she must act, it would not suffice to just keep these things and ponder them in her heart. Her thoughts were recessed as Martha bound into her presence and spoke. "Dear me, I don't know what I'll ever do! I wish I could get away from this place. I'd never come back to these sticks!"

"Oh child, you mustn't be so perplexed, time heals the heart." Placing her arm around Martha, Lillie went on with her conversation. "You know, my girl, our roots are here. Many of our forefathers are out there in the cemetery. Quite frankly you and I will join them there, someday. No, we can't run away, but we can make changes."

"What do you mean, Aunt Lillie?"

"Well, have you given any thought concerning your father and Zola's future marriage?"

"I've thought about it alright, but no, Zola will never be my mother!" Martha stiffened up.

"I know how you feel child, I really do."

"What's going to happen to us, Aunt Lillie, I mean Obie and me? I can't live with that bunch of urchins! I just can't! I don't understand what Daddy sees in them; can't he think about Obie and me?"

"He does care for you both, Martha, very much. Your mother, God rest her soul, has been gone several years. He's done what's right, but there comes a time when, well, he's got to go on with living. Give him a chance. I spoke of change, and we all have to adjust now and then. Now it's your turn. Let me help you."

"Oh, I do indeed want your help, I mustn't sound ungrateful, Auntie, but what must I do?"

"Now I haven't spoken to Mell about this you understand, but I'm sure he would be reasonable. Would you consider the idea of coming to live with me?"

"Live with you?"

"Yes, I get lonely, you would be a wonderful companion."

"But Aunt Lillie, I don't even know where you live."

"Kansas City, but that's no matter, you don't have to know."

"No, I expect you're right. Someone would throw a monkey wrench into that plan."

Lillie well understood Martha's reasoning,. It was not always easy dealing with the folks of the hills, and especially in trying times such as these. She had not forgotten her early childhood at Combs. Lovingly Lillie placed her arm around Martha and softly spoke. "I know just what you're going through my girl, I've gone through that myself. I left a part of my life back in our little home in Combs, but I moved on. Now we're both leaving another part of our lives here in Norwood, but again we must move on."

Martha sat on the edge of the bed and thought for a moment, "Later, were you glad, I mean did you know later that you had done the right thing."

"Yes, from the beginning I realized such a change was in my best interest. Was it easy, no, but I had the courage and took the opportunity. Martha, your chances for education and advancement in life seem to be little better than they were for me back in my generation, that's not good." Then she recalled her years of want as a child, she saw the likeness of a broken home, much like Martha's. She remembered the cemetery with its little graves, so many children, one a baby sister. Then she recalled later standing by the great granite stone that marked the resting place of her father, Dr. David Hurst. It had not been the hills that hurt or hindered, it had been the heart. She wanted this to be a new start for Martha. "Well, it's only an idea, let me discuss it with Mell, and Honey, say a prayer."

"Oh, I'll do that all right. I guess next to housework, I do best in talking to the Lord." Then going about her work she looked up into the heavens and verbally spoke, "Dear Lord, in these troubled times, help us."

The chilly afternoon overshadowed by a darker evening drew nigh, bringing in friends of the family to set up through the night. The casket had been placed in the back bedroom with a few chairs in a row across the way. These were for the family who would take turn sitting there for the night. Special pictures of Carnie were placed on the organ, where the ivory keys were ready to be played. A large spray lay atop the soft gray colored casket while another rested on an easel nearby.

One by one friends arrived, some bringing food which they took to the kitchen where Martha greeted them with tenderness and always a few words and tears. Hour by hour the long table's white linen was covered from end to end. These were not gourmet dishes of show but rather representative of fine southern cooking for this need.

By the time Pastor Wright arrived, a number of men were milling about outside while their wives were visiting in the living room. After speaking and shaking hands with them, he joined those inside and spoke to the family.

Never for him, had he felt closer to his people than at times like these. These were the seasons of their hearts which now brought them closer to God. Needs were greater, and they, like all men suffering great loss, had been brought low. Some could now look up unto the omnipotent God, and say, "Here am I." It was to these that he now spoke.

"My dear Brethren, let us begin our service this evening by going to His Word. 'For I am persuaded, that neither death, nor life, nor angels, nor principalities, nor powers, nor things present, nor things to come, nor height, nor depth, nor any other creature, shall be able to separate us from the love of God, which is in Christ Jesus our Lord.' Romans 8:38,39. Beloved, in her verse from 'The Holy Springtime,' Grace Dowling wrote:

>'God will be the Gardener,
>In that Great Garden of Flowers
>And all the time of eternity
>Will be filled with bright
>Springtime hours.'

"Let us remember Carnie as a great gardener. Both in the horticulture world and in the spiritual realm as well. The spray speaks well to this. Here we see white lilies, blades and leaves of flowering herbs, some collected from her cultivated garden. All were magnificently brought together as one day we all, shall be."

Following a short prayer he gave a nod to the song leader and again music filled the rooms. Song after song gave messages of hope, eternal life and a new spirit for the living. It was not a rigid service, folks came and went, and now and then one heard a whisper. Occasionally a smile could be seen, or a tear touching a face.

As the service began the kitchen door was opened from the covered porch, as was the door from the living room. Sounds emanating from the organ were followed by soft music of familiar hymns. Softly and sweetly came the refrain, "Sweet Hour of Prayer," then a stillness, and nothing could be heard. Undoubtedly the soft voice of Pastor Wright in prayer was inaudible. Singing continued again and folks began to file out of the kitchen to join those in the parlor.

Passing them was a young man in his mid-teens, who entered the kitchen and spoke. "Hi, Martha."

Looking over her shoulder, she recognized the man and crudely replied, "Howdy," and continued putting pies in the pie cupboard. While his presence was not welcome, she saw him standing there just the same. The tall, well built specimen of youth had spoken to her before. She knew he was not there to show his sympathy or to console her. Turning her back she hoped he would go away. Instead, he placed his hand on her waist and said, "I have something for you, come with me to the car and I'll get it for you."

"Never you mind, I don't want it."

"Don't be that way, Martha, I've done you no harm."

Martha stomped her foot, "Beat it, Buster." Her eyes grew fixed on him, big and glossy — the eyes that looked to kill!

Before she could stomp the other foot he turned and hastily made his exit. With her hand on the door knob, she quickly remarked, "Don't let the door hit your behind on the way out!" Then she slammed the door shut. Little did she know or would she have cared that she would never see him again.

Obie came along the porch as the disgruntled youth passed and heard the slamming of the door. Entering the kitchen he asked, "What was all that about?"

"It's nothing."

"I know it's not nothing," then snatching a chicken leg from the table, he hurried for the back door. Normally he would have drawn her wrath, but this time he got away with the comment and the chicken. Shaking her head, she turned down the oil lamp and left the room, slowly closing the door behind her.

> "Bringing in the sheaves,
> Bringing in the sheaves,
> We shall come rejoicing,
> Bringing in the sheaves."

Most everyone took part in the wake service. Mell, Clem, and Nellie, Joe and Minnie Moss were seated when Martha joined them. She picked up the refrain and sung with great gusto. Song after song, the reading from His Word, and prayer once again continued close to the midnight hour, when Pastor Wright called a recess.

At the close of the meal, apple pie, mincemeat, pumpkin, and other desserts still sat unfinished around the table. As was custom, some folks left at this juncture while those remaining took a long break.

When the service did take up again the melodious sound from the organ, again answered deaths silence and vibrant voices were singing the words to an age old hymn.

> "There's a land that is fairer than day,
> And by faith we can see it afar,
> For the Father waits over the way,
> To prepare us a dwelling place there."

A reverence for God and an earned respect, again brought stillness.

A life long lady of the church, Iva Eidson, took the floor, "We all know who Jesus was to Carnie, He was her constant companion. She found joy walking through her garden as it grew. Day by day she kept the faith and matured, ready for his harvest. Her Spirit has departed, terra firma can only claim the body.

"I would remind you God is not an august, austere, awesome judge. He is not standing aloof and apart from us in the agony of our human anguish. He is looking down on us calling us to Himself with love!

"Some of the world's 'Happiness,' passed her by, some of the common activities, she never knew. She never rode a train or a plane, never entered a movie house, never knew the luxuries of life and never complained. I remember a few years back when she and Hampton were working in the sweet potato field. She was laying aside the runners before the plow, when before they were finished a horde of grasshoppers swarmed from the sky and ate every leaf! Hampton had his shirt on a fence post and they ate all but the binding and the metal buttons! No, they did not loose their religion, instead, they asked for His help. And I want you to know there was a harvest! I can only state it this way, she believed in and relied upon Him!

"She had many other blessings as well, in fact she liked to quote Ezekiel 34:26, 'I will cause the shower to come down in his season; there shall be showers of blessing.' Her greatest blessings came from the family and her church! She worked tirelessly for both. Surely she knew the meaning, 'I must do what I can today, for I shall not pass this way again.'

"One of Carnie's commitments in which she believed strongly, was the temperance movement. Like the rock of Gibraltar, she stood solid. For the most part Carnie respected Carry Nation and met with her after the hatchet lady set up her home in Eureka Springs.

"In all her endeavors, Aunt Carnie impersonated the spirit of a virtuous woman. She was a pearl of great price, had charity for all and an unquenchable thirst for the love of God."

When she had finished, Lillie held up a paper-backed songbook familiar to all and said, "I'd like for us to sing the new song by the great gospel songwriter from the other side of the Ozarks, Albert E. Brumley's 'I'll meet you in the Morning.'"

Everyone was well acquainted with the song as it was constantly being played over the powerful clear channel radio station, XERF in Del Rio, Texas. Local singing conventions had also brought it into prominence. Teary eyes and deep emotions again filled the crowded room. To everyone, the chorus took on special meaning, "I'll Meet You In The Morning," was almost a promise!

With the conclusion of the song, Lillie sat down. Hankies dotted the dampened eyes and all the while the family sat painfully still and silent. In those early morning hours there was still no coming and going. The spell of His hallowed presence went unbroken. In the course of time Buck Jones, seated along the wall, rose and speaking a few words, offered a poem.

> She is gone but not forgotten
> Never shall her memory fade;
> Sweetest thoughts shall ever linger
> Round the grave where she is laid.

> The flowers laid upon her grave
> May wither and decay,
> But the love we bear for her
> Will never fade away.
>
> No one knows the silent heartaches
> Only those who have lost can tell,
> Of the grief that is born in silence
> For the one we loved so well.
>
> — Merrill A. Copperfield

The tall frame of Mr. Jones cast a silhouette against the wall even as the early predawn morning displayed a near imaginary ray of light. Carefully avoiding an embarrassing yawn, he opened a Bible and read, "Let not your heart be troubled: believe in God, believe also in me. In my Father's house are many mansions; If it were not so, I would have told you; for I go to prepare a place for you. And if I go and prepare a place for you, I come again, and will receive you unto myself; that where I am, there ye may be also. And whither I go, ye know, and the way ye know." Then closing the Book, he took his seat back against the wall.

Pastor Wright, perceiving the hour, chose to close the wake. "Is there anyone else who might have something on your heart before we close?" There was no response, and with prayer the watch night ended.

While the long tenebrous night had ended, the other side of the morning brought a beam of light and a spark of encouragement for the weary family.

The lowing of cattle sounded about the feeding pen, as Mell pitched fresh clover hay down from the haycock. He had stuck the pitchfork deep into the hay and slid down as Lillie approached carrying a large mug of hot coffee. Dressed appropriately for the shivery dawn, she handed Mell the cup then tightened the scarf about her sleek jeweled neck. "I would like to speak to you, Mell, away from the others. Would I not bother you too much at the moment?"

Lillie had been like an older sister to him and their respect had always been mutual. "What is it, Lill, and of course you know I have time for you." Lillie was never elusive as the leaves now being blown about in the autumn wind. In the true sense she was endowed with the indubitable quality of a school marm. Once again she was able to help the family, if given the chance.

"Mell, as you may be aware, Martha has been speaking to me of the uncertainty of her future. I'm speaking of your upcoming wedding." She made no secret of her feelings for she knew how strongly the child felt! "She has a point, you know. Mell, if I may, let me help."

"What would you do, Lill?"

"First of all, to her, as woman to woman I am offering to help her, myself. She needs love she'll never accept from Zola, and God knows how this must hurt you for I too anguish over the reality. Let her come and live with me, finish her schooling. Then I would add, make many new and exciting friends. Martha could do worse by trying to adjust, being a part of the puzzle that never fits, if you know what I mean."

"I do."

"Yes, well I was confident you did. That is, well Martha has a mind of her own, always has. She requires special attention, special consideration and above all needs a challenge. Would you agree?"

"Yes, those are all facts. Perhaps it would be best, as you say, that she spend some time with you. I can help you some financially, and still show my interest in her."

"Mell, I'm not thinking along that line, as you know I'm not exactly on bread and water! The child needs to expand her mind, to be occupied in the arts, stretch her horizons beyond the wash kettle, and the ironing board. Our world is changing, Mell, women must change; their lives, too, demand more."

Mell, looking out into space listened intently. After several swigs of hot coffee he faced Lillie and spoke. "Change seems to be the order of the day. It's found its way even to these hills. Look at the new lake, the church, better roads, if you can believe that. And look at our new W.P.A. school, no more a one room, one teacher. Who knows what will be coming up next. I have heard they're to build a big new post office in the city."

"It's good, Mell, so far as it goes. Nice and all that, but Martha needs and deserves a personal touch. Mell, I believe I can provide those entities she'll be needing so badly. Are you in harmony with my judgment?"

"I wouldn't mind her going with you, if both of you feel that's the thing to do. Yes, I trust your judgment on the matter, perhaps it would be best. And if Martha decides later to come back, she could."

The sleek jersey cattle feeding at Lillie's feet, caught her attention and she took a moment to pet one of them and run her hand over the animal's face. Lillie had been a farm girl and it felt good being able to enjoy the farm animals again. There is, however, only so much time for a lady to be silent. She wanted to be sure of their conversation. She wanted Mell to be sure — he would perhaps be loosing his daughter. Lifting her face toward him, she asked, "Then you approve of this course of action?"

"Yes, Lill, I do. I'll talk to her about it, and if that's what she really wants to do, we'll make plans accordingly." Mell stepped the couple of paces to Lillie's side and placed his arm about her waist. "Thanks, Lill, we love you."

The cattle were still feeding, a rooster again announced the newness of morning as the sun rose higher on a dismal day. Ready to face the ordeal before them, they silently walked toward Hurst Manor.

From the bell house the lonely bell tolled as it had for years at such a time. No one remembered when or from where it came. All remembered the pealing sound. Especially for the family, the muffled sound of today's toll, would not be forgotten. It had not been forgotten at the time of the departure of the many forefathers. The bell tolled for Thalia, and later hearts had been healed. It tolled for Hampton, and now the reverberations were heard again and no one had to inquire, "For whom does the bell toll?"

Within the shadow of the old clapboard church, the new house of prayer rose higher and higher each day. From the baptistery to the tower, workmen's tools forged ahead with the construction. Today, the workers put aside their tools and joined the many in the old church without stained glass windows or a belfry. They sat silently, some with prayerful hearts, listening to the sweetest music this side of Heaven.

Pastor Wright ended the service with the Scripture, "Lord, thou hast been our dwelling place in all generations. Before the mountains were brought forth, or even thou hadst formed the earth and the world, even from everlasting to everlasting, thou art God." Then looking over the gathering, he said,

"Having heard God speak to us in His Word, let us now take our sorrow to Him being assured that he will hear." Then reading again from the Book, "'Draw nigh to God, and he will draw nigh to you.' The services here are now concluded, and we will follow the trail to the cemetery where the internment will take place."

As the procession inched along, the pastor read and quoted scripture. "And I heard a voice from heaven saying, Write, Blessed are the dead who die in the Lord from henceforth: yea, saith the Spirit, that they may rest from their labors; for their works follow with them."

At the grave, the casket was surrounded by mounds of flowers and among them stood the hushed bereaved.

From a service book of poems, the pastor read:

Farther On

I hear it singing, singing sweetly,
Softly in an undertone,
Singing as if God had taught it,
 "It is better farther on!"

Sits upon the grave and sings it,
Sings it when the heart would groan,
Sings it when the shadows darken,
 "It is better farther on!"

Farther on? How much farther?
Count the milestones one by one?
No! no counting — only trusting,
 "It is better farther on! "

"Earth to earth, ashes to ashes, dust to dust. . . The peace of God, which passeth all understanding, shall guard your hearts and your thoughts in Christ Jesus. . . Now unto our God and Father be the glory for ever and ever. Amen." It was over.

Hurst Manor had never seemed so wanting. The big house was occupied only by Lillie and Martha. Tomorrow it would be empty and forlorn. While returning from the service, Mell had thoroughly discussed the situation with Martha, concerning her going to Kansas City. She would say her good-byes in the morning and with Lillie, take the train north.

The loneliness was all ready setting in. Martha would miss Obie, but he wished to be with his father, so she had to leave it at that. In some ways she would miss her father, too, but she told herself, "I have a purpose in going and I'll stick to it." As for Zola, she tried not to think of her at all — no, not a step-mother, she was glad to be going!

While Zola understood this, she had no ill feeling toward Martha. Zola knew she must bridge the gap between her and her father, paving the way for what hopefully would be better feelings between them. Martha had now promised to return for their wedding and wished them happiness. That within itself was a new beginning!

Immediately upon returning to Hurst Manor, Martha began packing her things, one by one, carefully placing then into a box. Lillie, entering the room was unsure just what Martha was doing, and asked, "Will you have many things to pack, Martha?"

"No, not even if I take everything," Then she went on with filling the cardboard box.

"Oh, child, don't you have a suitcase?"

"No, Aunt Lillie, I don't, I've never gone anywhere, none of us have, 'cept Clem. Going to Tulsa one don't need to pack. This strong box will do, don't you see?"

"Yes, but on a train," then she paused, "Yes, I suppose that will do, I have seen some folks do that."

Then looking about the room Martha reached for the Bible that lay on the dresser. "I'm taking this, Grandma would want that. It won't get lost will it?"

"To make sure, why don't you put it in my suitcase, it will be safe there."

"What will become of all her things, Aunt Lillie, who will live here? Who will see to everything?"

"Your father will be in charge, don't worry about it my dear, everything will be all right."

Then Martha brought a shoe box from a closet. Among other things it contained many family pictures, old and new. "May I take these?" she asked, holding up some of the old photographs.

"Of course, take them. They're yours." In the box Martha also found old broaches, Indian head coins, and the more rare, half dimes. One such coin had been placed in a small envelope and dated "1860." A note inside read, "This was my mothers, keep it for good luck." Along with it was a lock of someone's hair. Whose and from what time no one knew.

Bright morning sunlight reflecting through the window brought out the beautiful color in the plant Martha knew as "Roosters Gills," one of the few she really cared for. "I'm going to break off a stem and wrap it in a damp napkin, and carry it in my hand bag. Then when I get to your place I'll start it in water. It will work, I've seen her do it."

"Martha, it's not just 'my home' any more, it's our home."

"Well, whatever, any way when I get there, that's what I'll do. Do you have a big home?"

Lillie paused, she was modest but knew she must be truthful. "Yes, I guess you'd say it's large. And you'll find it very comfortable, I'm sure. It's in a quiet suburb, reminding me of the country. You'll have your own bedroom and bath with walk-in closets. And there's a lovely view out over a quiet park."

"My, it must be some place! It'll sure be a change, won't it?"

She had spoken the truth, it indeed would be a change! Confident of those alterations, Lillie sat on the edge of the bed where Martha had been packing her suitcase. "Changes can be good for you, Martha, they were for me. And they can be fun." Then she smiled and helped with the packing.

Throughout the day members of the family came and went. Clem and Nellie said good-by and returned to Arizona. Minnie and Joe Moss, after a short visit, returned to California. Claude and John Starr, who were going no where, stopped by to visit with Martha and Lillie and the visitors who came by. Finally, in the evening Mell and Obie came and having done the chores, stayed for supper. They would return in the morning and take the ladies to the station. Martha was closed-mouthed about leaving, saying little. Obie was excited and wanted to see the long shiny train pick up the passengers and hear the familiar, "All aboard." He thought not of the future, while Martha was unduly concerned.

Later that evening Lillie sat in her room, alone having devotions. It was difficult to keep her mind from drifting to the children. In her heart she knew Mell would provide for Obie and that the decisions had been made correctly. She was beginning to see the sweetness in Martha. Silently she thanked her for having placed a bouquet of autumn leaves on the dresser. "Surely they're sassafras," she murmured to herself. Their container, a quart jar, was the same type of vase she used years ago. Things at Hurst manor hadn't all changed, there were still pockets of precious memories and quirks of beauty.

Many thoughts ran through her mind, but then it became time to close her eyes and the final chapter on Hurst manor.

The Kansas City Southern line which wound through the edge of the Ozarks, had one of its steepest grades near Siloam Springs. As the passengers waited about the platform, the noise of the double engines became louder and more laborious each minute. The winding track and steepness of the grade made for slow movement on the north bound run and so the engineer wanted to keep the train on the track, the same of course could be said for travel south bound as well.

Finally the steaming diesels rounded a curve and came to a stop. Martha took notice of the finely dressed ladies disembarking. She wondered where they were all going and why so many were coming to Siloam Springs.

Well dressed men claimed fancy suitcases, and trunks, but she saw only one with boxes. "Oh, well," she thought, she could see hers on the loading cart being pulled away and then loaded into the baggage car. "It will be safe," she thought.

Most of the travelers had boarded when the call "All aboard," was given. Lillie gave Mell a hug and let the porter help her aboard. With tear filled eyes Martha, too, hugged her father and quickly stepped aboard. Like magic the train slowly moved away and Obie watched until the red light on the caboose went out of sight.

XV

From Trillium to Orchids

COLD blustery winds swept down from the northern plains for what seemed like days. Mell called this the Blue Northern. Great drifts of snow lay deep and troublesome to anything in motion. Only the sky was spared the color of white and it only had patches of blue. The thermometer read ten degrees below zero, but it was the tearing fingers of chill that cut to the bone! The Ozarks were locked in a deep-freeze, nonetheless Mell slowly and methodically mushed through the drifts of snow banked along the hedges and fence rows. Quietly he moved one foot at a time, partly due to the snow depth, but more to the fact he was hunting. This kind of hunting was not meant to be sporty, nor was it comfortable! It was however means of putting fresh rabbit meat on the table. Mell had perfected this hunt to an art, but it was more of a case of necessity that motivated him along this wintry morning.

Both he and Obie needed a change of diet. They had a hunger for rabbit, so he plodded along facing into the wind with determination. Keenly he watched for a vent of steam, it wasn't long in coming, for from under the red berried twigs of a hackberry bush came the tell-tale sign, a warm breath in the cold crisp air! Cautiously Mell raised the tightly held club and wham, for the hare it was all over. Another would be needed, then starting for home, that too, was quickly achieved.

With the gunnysack thrown over his shoulder, Mell moved slowly toward the house. The coldness had numbed his body, but he had accomplished his task.

Following supper, Mell stood by the window watching the reflected light from the fireplace reveal the deepening snow that drifted under the window. Winter would not quickly be going away and there would be many other such hunts. And for now he could only dream of sassafras tea, poke greens, wild berries and onions. Restlessly, he stood there for some time, just thinking of the past, and the miracle of spring, a time of fresh beginnings.

Other important issues far away from the Ozarks also caught Mell's attention. Daily the radio announcer was the bearer of bad news. A web was being dropped over Europe, like the jaws of an evil vise. Hunger was there too, along with rioting, wars and rumors of war. The dark clouds over Europe were moving, the question was, would they drift to our sunny shores?

Like many young men, Bud Porter lied about his age and joined the army and was stationed at Fort Chaffee. Zola heard occasionally and worried about him always. His winter, too, was long, cold, and lonely. Other young men across Arkansas turned to the C.C.C., W.P.A., or other alphabet projects. It was truly not the best of times, but it was not yet the worst. Day after day Mell would stand alone looking out onto the winter landscape and dream of better times. He prayed that peace would find a way to quiet the fears he and his neighbors held for tomorrow. As he finished the Lord's Prayer, thoughts seemed to retrieve the poem he learned from a Catholic friend and the appreciation he had for St. Francis of Assisi.

Lord, make me an instrument of Thy peace.
Where there is hatred, let me sow love;
> Where there is injury, pardon;
> Where there is doubt, faith;
> Where there is despair, hope;
> Where there is darkness, light;
> Where there is sadness, joy.

O Divine Master, grant that
> I may not so much seek
To be consoled, as to console;
Not so much to be understood as
To understand; not so much to be
Loved as to love:
For it is in giving that we receive;
It is in pardoning, that we are pardoned;
It is in dying, that we awaken to eternal life.

Finally the season of Mell's heart, like the season of the Ozark's spring, warmed, and a wonderful spirit sprang forth. All the folks in the hills knew it was spring! Mell knew it was the season of love!

Never had the red buds bloomed with such mass of color. Seldom had they retained their beauty for such a long time. Then one morning the rays of the early sun melted away a dusting of freshly fallen snow. That's the way of spring, untold beauty in a changing pattern that belongs to the hills. Across the ravine and clinging to overhanging rocks on the abyss, were the snarled and grotesque dogwood. Their petals still unfolding, told the story, so it is said, of the crucifixion of

Christ! Their thick white blossoms appeared to be great patches of snow long after the little flakes had melted away.

The forest floor was a nursery of carpeted leaves sending forth her variety of shapes and color. Of them, the bloodroot, with its crisp, white solitary flowers stood in contrast to the dull brown leaves through which they grew. The beauty of the delicate corydalis gave a touch of larkspur yellow. The rue anemone glittered pink in the morning sun. About them all stood the fruited May Apple. Seeping water, coming out of the rock, made beds of moss as green as the emerald isle! In this setting of grandeur came the playful squirrels, the birds and the first butterflies.

Following the old trail through the Spartan-looking forest came sounds heard only by these woodsy creatures. They were the sounds of two riders, passing in single file through the narrow trail by the century old oak that stood near the edge of the brink of Lover's Leap.

"We'll tether here," said the voice deep and solid. Then he tied up Lena to a sapling near the mighty monarch of the wildwood. Taking the reins of the other mare, he soon had her tethered close by. Ambling precariously close to the edge of the abrupt downward slope, Zola cautiously sat with her back against a near ageless snarled oak. The twisted roots held fast from down deep in the rock. The winds had blown the twisted limbs, forcing them to grow in one direction. Today however there was no strain at the great rock and all was secure. The bright afternoon sun warmed all within its rays. The snowy white petals of the bloodroot opened fully in repose. Bright red cardinals sang the song of spring while attending to nest building.

Mell and Zola, too, felt the love of spring and the joy of just being in love! Between God the Father, God the Son

Jesus Christ, and God the Holy Spirit there flowed Love in its most sublime form. Who would deny the purity of love between the two seated on the natural bench of His great making? Looking fully into Zola's face, Mell put his arm around her and looked off into the valley.

"It has been said that the cattle on a thousand hills belong to my Father. All that we see, Zola, belongs to our God, we are His caretakers, we will share our love with Him for what He has done for us. Am I speaking of a love that's too lofty?"

"No, my darling, you know the power of His love, and I will teach you daily of my love for you. Do we not share this irresistible force? Will it not endure; will it not last for eternity? God loves us, and in a lesser way, my dear, I love you and always will."

"And I love you. It will last, for it's strong as steel, enduring as a diamond."

"Mell, I think you know I've had my doubts about love, but that's all been left behind me, I love your power of steel, your lofty ideals, and your soft sweet touch of love."

As the orchestra continued to perform for the audience of two, Mell embraced his lover and held her more tightly than he ever had. He felt a flinch against his chest. "I'm sorry, did I hurt you?" Gently he let her go, and gave her a long kiss.

"No, my dear, I think our hearts just touched, and I felt that special moment I needed from my man of steel. Do it again!"

As they embraced, he again kissed her soft cheek and brushed her smooth silky hair with his callused hand. He was lost for words and felt inadequate to further express his feelings. She understood that side of a man, he did not need to speak further. Finally, reaching into his pocket he brought out something held tightly in his hand. "Besides my lasting love I have another lasting gift, will you take it, too?"

"A ring! Are you giving me a ring?" Then he opened his hand to reveal his answer.

"It is! I knew it was."

"I knew, you knew. And that's all right, you had to know it was coming. It was hardly a secret." He started to kiss her again when she spoke, "But I didn't know it would be today, and I didn't know it would be so beautiful!"

As if startled, Mell pointed toward the valley, "Listen, do you hear what I hear? Bells, off in the distance."

"I hear nothing, nothing but the birds."

"Neither do I, but soon we shall." He slipped the ring on her tiny finger, "There my dear, you're betrothed as surely as Mary was to Joseph."

"I hope the implication stops there but I see your humor."

She could not take her eyes off the sparkling diamond that now graced her finger. She had never seen such a gem except in the window of a jewelry store. "Mell, this is truly my day. I have never known a man with such love. Not only have you overlooked my faults and refused to see my flaws but you have made 'somebody' of me. I feel like a queen!"

"Now do you hear the bells?"

"Yes, oh yes, I do. And I can see them ringing from the new bell tower. They are ringing, my dear, for me and you!"

"And when you walk down that isle, my angel, her first bride, your face will glow in perfect love. Like the church, there are changes, we'll change with it and start a new life. Our faith will be renewed and see His lasting love in every stained glass window. We'll join the great family of God and all the congregation will be our family. And I can hear the music of the organ, the piano, the choir. Today they are playing, "Here comes the bride."

She had been resting in his arms and now felt his flexed arm as he squeezed her diamond hand. "Let's move down the trail to the valley." As they carefully made their way down the narrow path, neither spoke but let their hearts alone, harbor their feelings.

This was indeed nature's valley. Surging water flowed from the mighty boulder that bordered the pathway. Logs that bridged the stream were covered with moss. Treasures of morels grew along beside the blooming blue violets. Wild impatiens invited the darting butterfly for another round of nectar.

As the trail wound further into the woodland the density shut out much of the sun and they, too, were shut away from all but their tiny world where they stood. For several minutes they followed the little used trail along the stream to a spot called "The Narrows." White water splashing against the rocky sides of the creek, caught Mell's attention. Here he stopped. "If I were an artist this would be one of my pictures. I'd set up my canvas under yonder tree, then right where we're standing, I'd paint in an ageless oak, like the one up on top with its eerie roots at its snarled base."

"And what would you call your masterpiece?"

"Let me see, how about simply calling it, "On the Trail?" Against this background I'd paint in a couple of lovers, walking hand and hand. Seemingly two insignificant lovers. But they weren't, they were walking in a path of bright light, while all around them was in shadows. Shadows on the rough rock wall, shadows on the water." His fascination was so captivated by the view that he had it ready for canvas in moments.

Still caught up with natures magnificent splendor, Mell watched the running water for some time.

The Pawpaw

Then looking to Zola, he said. "Zola, do you realize that very soon this rushing water will be held back by a stronger force, the dam? Even now new fingers are being formed about the hills and lower valleys. Little gullies are disappearing, a giant lake is in the making."

The couple stood together for some time, watching, just looking at the scene. Then Mell turned and held Zola tight. They were in the sunlight. They were the two lovers, now unseen.

Some time later they slowly strolled on, still along the pristine trail. Mell spoke, "This is ours, Zola, we have a eye and a heart for it. It will always be in our blood!"

But it was in her heart that Zola was repeatedly saying to herself, "I love you, I love you, I love you. How can I hold any more love, my darling, I think my heart will burst! But it can't, there must be a tomorrow, and I will tell you again then of my love."

"Look, Mell, a thicket of pawpaws, all in their beauty of blossoms. I ask you, is that not another of God's little gardens? I wonder what it must of been like in the Garden of Eden."

"Well, I can tell you that there were two, a you and a me! And I think they were in love."

He reached above her head and plucked a small branch containing a couple of burgundy colored, orchid like blossoms and placed them in her hair. "There my love, you really are my angel."

Dry warm leaves lay under the pawpaw trees and Mell threw himself down upon them and reaching for Zola, drew her to him. Together they basked in the warm sun until it was no longer in sight. The glow of their love kept them warm, as it always would, and they would know love was eternal.

"Tomorrow, my Darling, tomorrow is our day!"

Neither ever knew, nor should they have been concerned, but God saw that they passed only inches away from the colony of the illusive spotted trillium. According to an old legend of the hills, He planted the first lilies under the pawpaw trees and whosoever passes by will be blessed and prosper. They shall find happiness and good fortune! God's love was still in the plan though again unseen, but only for a moment.

"Look, Mell, what a beautiful patch of trillium, could those be the ones we're looking for?" She recognized them for they grew abundantly along Clear Creek, near her old house. Here they grew in a fusion of tangled roots and a bending mass of bowing stems, arranged by the Master Florist, Himself.

"Yes, that's them, see the special spotted ones, there by the stake. It's too late to take them this spring, we'll come back for them in the fall."

"I'll fix a special bed for them, in the shade of the trees just above the spring. They will be a part of our annual remembrance of Carnie, and I'll tend them with love!"

"Speaking of love, come to me again my angel." Again they lay together on the bed of pawpaw leaves, so much in love. Yes, there would be many tomorrows, all filled in the splendor of love! "Yes, my angel, tomorrow will be our day and the enchantment will be lasting, but for today, we have this moment forever!"

"Mell, sometime ago I thought I had lost everything. There seemed to be little else to lose; happiness, peace, joy, they were all just an elusive dream. But that has all changed!"

"Then you found what you had been missing, what you wanted?"

"I found far more than I could have ever lost, thanks to Aunt Carnie, God rest her soul! Do you remember a while back when she asked me over? We had a long talk. 'Zola,' she said, 'I've asked you here for two reasons.' First of all she showed me my worth. She said, 'You can be anything you want to be.' Some how I believed her!"

"Yes, I knew that, what was the second thing she wanted to tell you?"

"About you."

"Me?"

With a girlish grin, she put her hand to his face. "She said, 'Don't let him get away.'"

They remained under the pawpaw trees for some time living the lesson of love they had learned, growing together. To Him they were thankful that each passing day would find them still stronger and further entwined together in love.

"Mell, if I live to be a hundred, I'll fly away on the morning loving you."

"And I'll go with you, thanking you for what shall have been a beautiful life together!"

The End.